First World War
and Army of Occupation
War Diary
France, Belgium and Germany

18 DIVISION
Divisional Troops
Divisional Signal Company
25 July 1915 - 1 January 1919

WO95/2028/1

The Naval & Military Press Ltd
www.nmarchive.com
Published in association with The National Archives

Published by

The Naval & Military Press Ltd

Unit 10 Ridgewood Industrial Park,

Uckfield, East Sussex,

TN22 5QE England

Tel: +44 (0) 1825 749494

www.naval-military-press.com

www.nmarchive.com

This diary has been reprinted in facsimile from the original. Any imperfections are inevitably reproduced and the quality may fall short of modern type and cartographic standards.

© **Crown Copyright**
Images reproduced by permission of The National Archives, London, England, 2015.

Contents

Document type	Place/Title	Date From	Date To
Heading	WO95/2028 1		
Heading	10th Division 16th Signal Coy R.E. Jly 1915-Jan 1919 Dec 17-Jan 17		
Heading	18th Special Coy Vol I		
War Diary	Havre	25/07/1915	26/07/1915
War Diary	Flesselles	27/07/1915	10/08/1915
War Diary	Heilly	19/08/1915	31/12/1915
Heading	18th Div Sq		
War Diary	Heilly	01/01/1916	24/01/1916
War Diary	Heilly	23/01/1916	31/01/1916
War Diary	Heilly	29/01/1916	31/01/1916
Heading	18 Div Signal Coy Vol 7		
War Diary	Heilly	01/02/1916	04/02/1916
War Diary	Ribemont	05/02/1916	06/03/1916
War Diary	Montigny	07/03/1916	20/03/1916
War Diary	Etinehem	21/03/1916	30/04/1916
War Diary	Officer i/c. A.G's Office. Base.	04/06/1916	04/06/1916
War Diary	Etinehem	01/05/1916	04/05/1916
War Diary	Corbie	05/05/1916	05/05/1916
War Diary	Cavillon	06/05/1916	05/06/1916
War Diary	Corbie	22/06/1916	22/06/1916
War Diary	Battle HQ. (L 16a. 8.2)	23/06/1916	24/06/1916
Heading	18th Divisional Signal Company		
War Diary	Battle HQ (Bray-sub-Somme)	01/07/1916	09/07/1916
War Diary	Grovetown	09/07/1916	12/07/1916
War Diary	Copse Ravine	13/07/1916	20/07/1916
War Diary	Hallencourt	21/07/1916	24/07/1916
War Diary	Renescure	25/07/1916	30/07/1916
Heading	18th Div Signal Coy R.E. Apl 1916 Vol 9		
Heading	Croix-Du-Bac	02/08/1916	19/08/1916
War Diary	Bailleul	24/08/1916	24/08/1916
Heading	Roellecourt	25/08/1916	27/08/1916
Heading	War Diary 18th Div Sig Coy.		
War Diary	Roellecourt	08/09/1916	08/09/1916
War Diary	Doullens	09/09/1916	09/09/1916
War Diary	Acheux	11/09/1916	24/09/1916
War Diary	Hedauville	25/09/1916	30/09/1916
Miscellaneous	A Form. Messages And Signals.		
War Diary	Hedauville	01/10/1916	05/10/1916
War Diary	Bernaville	06/10/1916	12/10/1916
War Diary	Albert	13/10/1916	23/10/1916
War Diary	Tara Hill	23/10/1916	31/10/1916
War Diary	Albert (Tara Hill)	01/11/1916	22/11/1916
War Diary	Contay	22/11/1916	22/11/1916
War Diary	Doullens	23/11/1916	23/11/1916
War Diary	Bernaville	24/11/1916	24/11/1916
War Diary	Yvrench	25/11/1916	25/11/1916
War Diary	Buigny-St Maclou	26/11/1916	05/01/1917
War Diary	Yvrench	11/01/1917	11/01/1917
War Diary	Bernaville	12/01/1917	12/01/1917

Type	Description	Start	End
War Diary	Marieux	14/01/1917	14/01/1917
War Diary	Bouzincourt W.7. B.3.7	15/01/1917	15/02/1917
War Diary	Third Street (X.2.a. 3.2)	16/02/1917	17/02/1917
War Diary	Bouzincourt (W.7.b. 3.7)	18/02/1917	28/02/1917
Miscellaneous	D. Signal Communications Issued With 18th Div. Instructions Of February 11th. 1917.	14/02/1917	14/02/1917
Miscellaneous	Arrangements Made By 18th Divisional Signal Company R.E Operations On The 17th February 1917.	13/02/1917	13/02/1917
Map	Telephonic Communications Atn Division Signals.		
War Diary	Bouzincourt (W.7.b. 7.1)	01/03/1917	03/03/1917
War Diary	Warwick Huts. (X.1.c.9.2)	04/03/1917	22/03/1917
War Diary	Dury (Amiens)	23/03/1917	24/03/1917
War Diary	Steenbecque	25/03/1917	31/03/1917
Miscellaneous	Scheme Of Power Buzzers And "IT's"		
Heading	Communications 18th Division.		
Miscellaneous			
War Diary	Steenbecque	01/04/1917	04/04/1917
War Diary	Pernes	26/04/1917	26/04/1917
War Diary	Habarcq	27/04/1917	27/04/1917
War Diary	Neuville Vitasse. (M.18.d.1.1) (Sheet 51 B)	28/04/1917	30/04/1917
Miscellaneous	18th Divisional Signal Company R.E.	08/04/1917	08/04/1917
Miscellaneous	Training Of Signal Personnel.	08/04/1917	08/04/1917
War Diary	Neuville Vitasse M (Sheet 51b)	01/05/1917	14/05/1917
War Diary	Boisleux St Marc (S 17.a. 8.4) (Sheet 51b)	15/05/1917	31/05/1917
Miscellaneous	Arrangements Made By 18th Divisional Signals For The Forthcoming Operations. "A".	01/05/1917	01/05/1917
Miscellaneous	Scheme For Divisional Signalling School. 16th Division.	26/05/1917	26/05/1917
Diagram etc	Pole Diagram Back To Signal Office.		
War Diary	Boisleux-St. Marc. (S.17.a. 8.14) (Sheet 51b)	01/06/1917	11/06/1917
Miscellaneous	Scheme Of Training To Be Carried Out By 18th Divisional Signal Company R.E. While The Division is in Rest. "A"	21/06/1917	21/06/1917
Diagram etc	Communications. 18th Division. "C"		
Diagram etc	Route Diagram Of Lines In Hindenburg Route. 10.6.17. "D".		
War Diary	Couin	01/07/1917	03/07/1917
War Diary	Steenvoorde	03/07/1917	06/07/1917
War Diary	Reninghelst	07/07/1917	29/07/1917
War Diary	H.27. B. 5.7	30/07/1917	31/07/1917
Miscellaneous	System Of Communications for Forthcoming Offensive Operations. A.	20/07/1917	20/07/1917
Miscellaneous	Scheme For Tank Detailed For Divisional Signals. B	26/07/1917	26/07/1917
Miscellaneous	Orders. For Runner Service, 18th Division. C	26/07/1917	26/07/1917
Miscellaneous	Orders For Cable Laying Bn "Z" Day. D	24/07/1917	24/07/1917
Miscellaneous	Account Of Buried Cable Route From Bedford House To Dormy House. F	10/08/1917	10/08/1917
Map	Map Shewing Buried Cable.		
Heading	Route Diagram Of Communications. 18th. Divisions.		
Map			
War Diary	Reninghelst	01/08/1917	03/08/1917
War Diary	H.27.b. 5.6 (Sheet 28 1/40000)	04/08/1917	12/08/1917
War Diary	Reninghelst	13/08/1917	14/08/1917
War Diary	Lederzeele	15/08/1917	31/08/1917

War Diary	Scheme of Training To Be Carried Out By 18th Divisional Signal Company R.E. While The Division Is In Rest. "A".	19/08/1917	19/08/1917
Miscellaneous	Lederzeele	02/09/1917	02/09/1917
War Diary	Esquelbecq	03/09/1917	23/09/1917
War Diary	Poperinghe	24/09/1917	30/09/1917
Diagram etc	Communications, 18th Division.		
War Diary	Poperinghe	01/10/1917	10/10/1917
War Diary	Canal Bank (C.19.c. 2.6 Sheet 28 NW)	11/10/1917	24/10/1917
War Diary	Poperinghe	25/10/1917	29/10/1917
War Diary	Proven	30/10/1917	30/10/1917
Miscellaneous	System Of Communications Of 18th Division For Forthcoming Offensive Operations-October, 1917 D	10/10/1917	10/10/1917
Map	Map "B".		
Map	Map "A".		
Heading			
Diagram etc	Diagram Of Communications. 18th Division.		
War Diary	Proven	01/11/1917	14/11/1917
War Diary	J. Camp (A.8.b. 1.5 Sheet 28 NE)	05/11/1917	10/11/1917
War Diary	Elverdinghe Chateau	11/11/1917	30/11/1917
Miscellaneous	System Of Communications 18th Divisional Defence Scheme. "A".	23/11/1917	23/11/1917
Miscellaneous	Report On Forward W/T And P.B.And A. Station. "B".	13/11/1917	13/11/1917
Map	Route Diagram Of Communications 18th Division.		
Heading	D		
Heading	18th Di Signal Vol 24		
War Diary	Elverdinghe Chateau	01/12/1917	17/12/1917
War Diary	Rousebrugge	18/12/1917	02/01/1918
War Diary	Elverdinghe Chateau	03/01/1918	29/01/1918
War Diary	Rousebrugge	30/01/1918	31/01/1918
Heading	18 D Signal Vol 27		
War Diary	Rousebrugge	01/02/1918	07/02/1918
War Diary	Salency (Orse)	08/02/1918	16/02/1918
War Diary	Baboeuf (Oase)	17/02/1918	25/02/1918
War Diary	Rouez	27/02/1918	28/02/1918
Miscellaneous	System Of Communications 18th Division. A	02/03/1918	02/03/1918
Diagram etc	Diagram Of Wireless Communications 18th Division. 2.3.18		
Miscellaneous	General Staff, 18th Division.	23/02/1918	23/02/1918
Map	18th Division.		
Map	Route Diagram Of Communications.		
Heading	A		
Miscellaneous	Communications 18th Division.		
Miscellaneous	3rd Corps Communications. 18th Divisional Defence Scheme.		
Map			
Heading	C		
Map	Visual Communications 18th Division 5.3.18		
Heading	D		
Heading	War Diaries Of A.D.M.S 36th Div 108th Fld Ambce February 1918		
Heading	War Diary 18th Divisional Signal Company. R.N. March 1918		
War Diary	Rouez	01/03/1918	21/03/1918
War Diary	Ugny-le-Gay	22/03/1918	23/03/1918
War Diary	Caillouel	23/03/1918	23/03/1918

War Diary	Baboeue	24/03/1918	24/03/1918
War Diary	Varesnes	25/03/1918	25/03/1918
War Diary	Caisnes	24/03/1918	31/03/1918
Heading	Appendices A,B,C & D.		
Miscellaneous	Work On Communications. Completed During Week Ending March, 9th, 1918 A.	10/03/1918	10/03/1918
Miscellaneous	General Staff, 18th Division. B	23/02/1918	23/02/1918
Miscellaneous	System of Communications-18th Division. C	02/03/1918	02/03/1918
Diagram etc	Diagram Or Wireless Communications 18th Division. 2.3.18		
Miscellaneous	Notes On Visual Communication 18th Divisional Area. D	08/03/1918	08/03/1918
Heading	18th Divisional Signal Company, R.E. April 1918		
War Diary	Boyes	01/04/1918	11/04/1918
War Diary	St Fuscien	13/04/1918	25/04/1918
War Diary	Cavillon	26/04/1918	30/04/1918
Diagram etc	Route Diagram Communications 18th Division. 7.4.18		
War Diary	Cavillon	01/05/1918	05/05/1918
War Diary	Bavelincourt	05/05/1918	20/05/1918
War Diary	Molliens-Au-Bois	25/05/1918	31/05/1918
Heading	Handing Over Notes Of 18th Divisional Signals In The Bavelincourt Sector.	23/05/1918	23/05/1918
Miscellaneous	Communications 18th Division.		
Miscellaneous	C		
Miscellaneous	D		
Miscellaneous	Allotment Of Lines. Appendix I.		
War Diary	U.21d 3.7 Contay	01/06/1918	29/06/1918
War Diary	Buried Cable Routes.		
Miscellaneous	18th Division Location Report-6a.m. June 11th 1916	10/06/1918	10/06/1918
Miscellaneous	18th Division G. 638 B	26/06/1918	26/06/1918
Miscellaneous	General Staff, 18th Division. B	28/06/1918	28/06/1918
War Diary	U21d 3.7 Contay	01/07/1918	13/07/1918
War Diary	Cavillon	14/07/1918	31/07/1918
Heading	18th Division Engineers. 18th Divisional Signal Company, R.E. August 1918.		
Miscellaneous	18th Division. "A".	10/09/1918	10/09/1918
War Diary	St Gratien	01/08/1918	11/08/1918
War Diary	Contay	12/08/1918	24/08/1918
War Diary	Henecourt	26/08/1918	26/08/1918
War Diary	Becourt	27/08/1918	29/08/1918
War Diary	S. 27.a. 2.8 (N.W. Mountauban)	31/08/1918	31/08/1918
Miscellaneous	Notes On Communications During Recent Operations. B		
Miscellaneous	Artillery Communications-August 23rd To September 5th, 1918	07/09/1918	07/09/1918
War Diary	Dugouts St S27. B 2.8 (N.W. Of Moitauban)	01/09/1918	03/09/1918
War Diary	Ref Map Sheet 57 Combles B.4. Cn 3.6	03/09/1918	04/09/1918
War Diary	8 27a 2.8 (N.W. Of Moment)	05/09/1918	15/09/1918
War Diary	Lieramont (D. 12d 6.6)	17/09/1918	24/09/1918
War Diary	Combles	25/09/1918	27/09/1918
War Diary	Lieramont	28/09/1918	01/10/1918
War Diary	Beaucourt	02/09/1918	16/09/1918
War Diary	Ronssoy Wood	17/10/1918	18/10/1918
War Diary	Serain	19/10/1918	19/10/1918
War Diary	Reumont	20/10/1918	22/10/1918
War Diary	Le Cateau (Q In C. 9.5)	23/10/1918	26/10/1918

Miscellaneous	Signal Instructions For Forthcoming Operations. "B".	22/10/1918	22/10/1918
War Diary	Lecateau	01/11/1918	11/11/1918
War Diary	Serain	13/11/1918	13/11/1918
Miscellaneous	Signal Instructions For Forthcoming Operations. "A".	31/10/1918	31/10/1918
Miscellaneous	Notes On Communications During Operations Leading Up to the Capture of Bousies and Robersart. "B"	09/11/1918	09/11/1918
Miscellaneous	Notes On Communications During Operations Between October 25th And November 7th, 1918. "C".	16/11/1918	16/11/1918
Miscellaneous	18th Division "A".	24/01/1918	24/01/1918
War Diary	Serain	01/12/1918	01/12/1918
War Diary	Ligny-en-Cambresis	17/12/1918	01/01/1919
Map			
Miscellaneous	A.		

18TH DIVISION

18TH SIGNAL COY R.E.

JLY 1915 - JAN 1919

DEC 17 — JAN 17

18th Typical Day
Vol I

121/7936

July
Aug
Sept 3
Oct 4
Dec 5

Army Form C. 2118

WAR DIARY
or
INTELLIGENCE SUMMARY
(Erase heading not required.)

18th Divnl. Signal Coy R.E.

Place	Date	Hour	Summary of Events and Information	Remarks and references to Appendices
HAVRE	25/7/15	Noon	Disembarked and completed equipment from Ordnance Base. Stayed night in No. 5 Camp.	
	26/7/15		Entrained at point 4, starting at No. 39 (French Time) arrived at LONGUEAU 23.05, detrained, marched to FLESSELLES arriving 6 a.m.	
FLESSELLES	27/7/15		Div H.Q in Chateau. Set up Signal office immediately and laid out lines to the following:-	
			53rd Inf Bde at MOLLIENS-AU-BOIS 7½ miles	
			54th Do. - NAOURS 3 "	
			55th Do - BERTANGLES 4½ "	
			-18th Divnl Arty " MONTONVILLIERS 2 "	
			Branch laid out by T off 55th Inf Bde line to 85th Bde R.F.A. (How?) to VAUX-EN-AMIENOIS.	
	28/7/15		Corps line through from QUERRIEUX.	
	30/7/15		Capt Bradley K.O.Y.L.I. joined Company	
	31/7/15		D.R.L.S. started within the Division. D.R. leaving H.Q at 7am, Noon and 6 pm. Daily, goes the round of Brigades and Divnl Artillery on fixed timetable. Considerable trouble caused at first by messages for units in Brigades being given to A.R. but this was stopped and after first day he ran to time.	

M. Norte
O.C. 18th SIGNAL Co. R.E.

Army Form C. 2118

WAR DIARY
or
INTELLIGENCE SUMMARY
(Erase heading not required.)

18th Divnl Signal Coy R.E.

Place	Date	Hour	Summary of Events and Information	Remarks and references to Appendices
FLESSELLES	2/8/15		53rd Bde left Divnl area, moved to LAVIÈVILLE, attached to 51st (Highland) Divn. Gave them their 2 DRs Motor Cyclists for communication.	
	4/8/15		Their move took place on nights of 2/3/8/15 and 3/4/8/15.	
	9/8/15		On nights of 6/7/8/15 to 8/9/8/15 Division moved to area BEAUCOURT – ST. GRATIEN – PONT NOYELLES – LA NEUVILLE – BONNAY – LA HOUSSOYE – BEHENCOURT. 55th Bde took Southern area and marched straight through in 2 nights having their H.Q. at BONNAY on night of 8th and next night on to BRAY attached to 13th Bde 5th Divn. 13th Bde opened at Chateau MONTIGNY at noon on 8/8/15 closing at Divnl H.Q. FLESSELLES at same time. 54th Bde established H.Q. at LA NEUVILLE on night of 8/9/8/15 and moved to FM DU QUAI-À-FAGOT on 10th moving again to CORBIE on 11th 8/15. They were in cable communication with Divn the whole time except when actually on the march. Divnl Arty H.Q. were established at EBART FM at N end of BEAUCOURT when Divn moved to MONTIGNY and were in cable communication. X Corps had cable ready for Division when above move took place. They also had a telephone line through to Divn. Trench telephones were fitted in to "A" and "G" offices and 9c Signals this connected by exchange in the Signal Office on to 10th Corps H.Q.	
	10/8/15		2/Lt Robertson RE arrived for attachment to the Coy for instruction.	

1875 Wt. W593/826 1,000,000 4/15 J.B.C. & A. A.D.S.S./Forms/C. 2118.

W. Robb Captain
O.C. 18th SIGNAL Co. R.E.

(3)

Army Form C. 2118

WAR DIARY
or
INTELLIGENCE SUMMARY
(Erase heading not required.)

18th Divnl. Signal Coy R.E.

Instructions regarding War Diaries and Intelligence Summaries are contained in F.S. Regs, Part II. and the Staff Manual respectively. Title Pages will be prepared in manuscript.

Place	Date	Hour	Summary of Events and Information	Remarks and references to Appendices
HEILLY	19 8/15		Divnl. H.Q. moved to HEILLY on 19th Aug taking over Chateau previously occupied by 5th Divn.	
	20 8/15		53rd Bde. took over right of line CARNOY – MAMETZ road with H.Q. at BRAY. This was connected up by cable from HEILLY running along CORBIE – BRAY road. 55th Bde. on left of line with 3 Battns. in trenches and one in reserve establishes H.Q. at MEAULTE. Artillery right group at BRAY and left group at MEAULTE were connected up direct to Divnl. Artillery H.Q. at HEILLY by telephone. The permanent lines along AMIENS – ALBERT Railway were brought into use, the 12 lines on South side of poles being allotted by 10th Corps for use of this Divn. These were used as follows:– 2 for sounders and superimposed telephone to MEAULTE (55th Bde), 2 for ditto to BRAY (53rd Bde) one for telephone to each artillery group. Originally the artillery groups were given metallic circuits but owing to their great distance and the shortage of cable it was considered advisable to reassume one line and give them earth returns. The 54th Bde. was in Reserve at RIBEMONT, but after two days moved to Chateau at TREUX. Vibrator and telephone communication being established with them at both places.	
	26 Aug		On night of 26/27 Aug. O.C. was driving in light Lanchester car with 1/Lieut. Dacroft to visit H.Q. of right artillery group at BRAY with views to determining best route for cable. Car was driven into a large shell-hole on ALBERT – BRAY road about 12.30 am breaking front axle and damaging chassis. This was rescued on the following night by Divnl. Supply column.	

W. Roche Capt. R.E.
O.C. 18th SIGNAL Co. R.E.

Army Form C. 2118

WAR DIARY
or
INTELLIGENCE SUMMARY
(Erase heading not required.)

18th Divnl. Signal Company R.E.

Place	Date	Hour	Summary of Events and Information	Remarks and references to Appendices
HEILLY	1/9/15		Informed by Divnl. Staff that an Advd Divnl H.Q. were to be established at MORLANCOURT to be used in case of an advance or any minor operations. Three deep dug-outs with protection of over 12ft of earth were to be constructed and these were commenced forthwith; one of these dug-outs was for Signal office but in meanwhile a room in farm was taken and lines run from this to Brigades. This entailed complete duplication of vibrator circuits and it was decided to loop in Artillery telephone these loops being permanently connected through while HQ remains at HEILLY.	
	4/9/15		No. 46248 Sgt Chalkcott J. Despatch Rider met with accident on night of 4/5 when taking despatch to BRAY. He collided with a motor car on MEAULTE - BRAY road, the night being dark and roads muddy. He broke his ankle and was evacuated.	
	8/9/15		No 54140 Cpl Budd, Despatch Rider was accidentally shot in the thigh by C.Q.M.S. Lamb J. while handling a revolver. He was evacuated. Two men to replace the above 2 DRs joined 2 or 3 days later. 2/Lt Robertson R.E. left and 2/Lt R. O'Kelly R.E. arrived for attachment to the Coy for instruction.	
	11/9/15			
	12/9/15 to 19/9/15		General maintenance of lines and improvements.	
	20/9/15		Line buried from MORLANCOURT down MAIDSTONE AVENUE to MAPLE REDOUBT.	
	22/9/15		Two lines laid to 55th Bde. Advanced H.Q. down BERKSHIRE AVENUE	

W.P. [signature]
Capt. R.E.
O.C. 18th SIGNAL Co. R.E.

(5)

Army Form C. 2118

WAR DIARY
or
INTELLIGENCE SUMMARY
(Erase heading not required.)

18th Divnl. Signal Coy. R.E.

Instructions regarding War Diaries and Intelligence Summaries are contained in F.S. Regs., Part II. and the Staff Manual respectively. Title Pages will be prepared in manuscript.

Place	Date	Hour	Summary of Events and Information	Remarks and references to Appendices
HEILLY	23/9/15		Line laid to QUEENS Redoubt.	
	25/9/15		Line laid to 53rd Advanced H.Q. at CHAPES	
	30/9/15		Lateral line to 5th Divn at BRAY from MOULIN-DU-VIVIER. Comm. airline across country	
	2/10/15		2nd Lt. Kelly evacuated sick on 2/10/15	
	3/10/15 to 17/10/15		General maintenance of lines and some cable lines replaced by Comic Airline.	
	18/10/15 to 21/10/15		Line laid to Anti Aircraft observation post.	
	22/10/15 to 30/10/15		General maintenance of lines	

W. Parks Capt. R.E.
O.C. 18th SIGNAL Co. R.E.

Army Form C. 2118

WAR DIARY
or
INTELLIGENCE SUMMARY
(Erase heading not required.)

18th Divnl Signal Coy RE

Place	Date	Hour	Summary of Events and Information	Remarks and references to Appendices
HEILLY	31/10/15		Cpl Comford and M/Cpl Parker wounded and evacuated.	
	1/11/15		Exchange of N.C.O's with 5th Division for instructional purposes. S.M. Harrod, Cpl Hunt, 2nd Cpl Arnold, and 2nd Cpl West proceed to 5th Divn H.Q. and were replaced by Sgt Manzell, Cpl Flett and 2nd Cpl Snell from 5th Divn.	
	3/11/15		Sgt Cornish proceeded to 5th Divn and was replaced by Sgt Campbellon from 5th Divn.	
	8/11/15		Lieut Carter R.E. proceeded to 5th Divn and was replaced by 2 Lieut Parsons R.E. from 5th Divn.	
	9/11/15		Comic airline laid to ALBERT	
	11/15		2/Lt Jeeves R.E. transferred to 5th Divn and 55th Bde section taken over by 2/Lt Floyd R.E.	
	14/11/15		Officers and N.C.O's of 5th and 18th Divisns above mentioned rejoined their respective units	
	15/11/15 to 22/11/15		General maintenance of lines	

W Parth Capt RE
O.C. 18th SIGNAL Co. R.E.

(7)

Army Form C. 2118

WAR DIARY
or
INTELLIGENCE SUMMARY
(Erase heading not required.)

18th Divnl Signal Coy RE

Instructions regarding War Diaries and Intelligence Summaries are contained in F.S. Regs., Part II. and the Staff Manual respectively. Title Pages will be prepared in manuscript.

Place	Date	Hour	Summary of Events and Information	Remarks and references to Appendices
HEILLY	23/11/15		2/Lt C.R.Lynch RE attached for instruction.	
	24/11/15 to 30/11/15		Permanent line laid from HEILLY STATION to Signal office and general maintenance of lines.	
	1/12/15 to 7/12/15		General maintenance of lines.	
	8/12/15 to 15/12/15		Buried cable from ADS HQ at DERNANCOURT to all Brigade General maintenance of of lines and completing buried cable	
	16/12/15		2/Lt Weston A 1st E.Lancs attached for instruction.	
	17/12/15		2/Lt Laurie A.O. 20th Liverpools attached for instruction	
	18/12/15 to 25/12/15		General maintenance of lines	

M. Park Capt RE
O.C. 18th SIGNAL Co. R.E.

WAR DIARY or INTELLIGENCE SUMMARY

18th Divisional Signal Company

Place	Date	Hour	Summary of Events and Information	Remarks and references to Appendices
HEILLY	27/12/15		Lieut E.P. Oxcroft RE proceeded to 3rd Army H.Q. for Wireless course	
	28/12/15		Seven N.C.O.s and men from Inf. Battns in Divn attached to Signal Coy to be trained as short range wireless operators. All to be sent to 3rd Army H.Q. for course.	
	29/12/15 to 31/12/15		Laid lines from No. 3 Kite Balloon Sectn to Right Group Artillery.	

O.C. 18th Signal Co. R.E.

18th avril: S'quels
rot 6
VAN.

WAR DIARY or INTELLIGENCE SUMMARY

Army Form C. 2118

18th Divnl Signal Coy. R.E.

Place	Date	Hour	Summary of Events and Information	Remarks and references to Appendices
HEILLY	1/1/16 to 8/1/16		Burying line from Battle H.Q. at DERNANCOURT to Heavy Bde R.G.A. at BRAY. Party (1 N.C.O. 10 men) at TREUX preparing stables and billets in anticipation of H.Q. moving there. 4/1/16 Lorry sent to DOULLENS for fitting new types — Returned same day. 2/1/16 Guide R.G. ordered to proceed to 10th Corps Sigs.	
	9/1/16 to 16/1/16		Labelling all Divisional lines in accordance with 3rd Army Circulars. 11/1/16 Six men from Battns of 18th Divn sent to 3rd Army H.Q. for course of Wireless. 11/1/16 Lecture to Signal Sec officers at 3rd Army H.Q. by Capt. Dickinson attended by Capt. Porter R.E., Lt. Cutler R.E., Lt. Dearupp R.E. and Lt. Chute R.E. 3 a.m. 18th Divnl Signal Coy. General maintenance of lines.	
	17/1/16 to 24/1/16		All lines in Divnl and Brigade areas labelled in accordance with 3rd Army Circular. General maintenance of lines. 20/1/16 35 Men from Battns for course of instruction in Signalling. 23/1/16 One Bomber from Heavys 82nd 83rd and 84th Bde R.F.A. for short course of instruction in instrument repairing — DIII and French Telephone. It is anticipated that these men will be able to effect minor [repairs?]	

O.C. 18th SIGNAL Co. R.E. Capt. R.E.

Army Form C. 2118

(2)

WAR DIARY
or
INTELLIGENCE SUMMARY

(Erase heading not required.)

19th Divnl Signal Coy R.E.

Place	Date	Hour	Summary of Events and Information	Remarks and references to Appendices
HEILLY	23/1/16 (Contd)		the repairs to Artillery instruments and to relieve to some extent the work of the Signal Service.	
	23/1/16		Divnl Signal Coy. for instruction on practical working in the field. Six N.C.O's and men sent to each Bde Section for instruction in Brigade Section Signal work. The remainder were given instruction in H.Q. work and General Routine duties and some valuable hints were no doubt obtained.	
	23/1/16		Men returned from Wireless course and are temporarily attached to Signal Company with a view to being fully absorbed therein.	
25th to 31st			General maintainence of lines	
	27/1/16		Five NCO's and men from Inf. Battns listed as office Telegraphists in accordance with W.O. letter 115/Engrs/1175 (A.G.7). d/28.2.15. all passed out as proficient and their Commdg officers informed accordingly.	

W. Pole

O.C. 19th SIGNAL Co. R.E.

WAR DIARY
or
INTELLIGENCE SUMMARY

(Erase heading not required.)

18th Divnl. Signal Coy. R.E.

Army Form C. 2118

(3)

Place	Date	Hour	Summary of Events and Information	Remarks and references to Appendices
HEILLY	29/7		Second party consisting of 2 officers and 28 other ranks of 55th Divnl. Signal Coy arrived for instruction and first party returned to their own H.Q. same evening. Second party distributed similarly to their first party. Owing to hit but after two days at 5th Bde sector of their 6 men was found necessary to relieve these men owing to anticipated move of Brigade. Three of these men were sent to 53rd and 3 to 55th Bde. All were given a complete tour of signal work and any details which might be of resistance points out to them.	
	30/7			
	31/7		All available men laying new track at RIBEMONT.	

W.J. Parks
Capt. R.E.
O.C. 18th SIGNAL Co. R.E.

18 Div. Signal Coy

Vol 5

Army Form C. 2118

WAR DIARY
or
INTELLIGENCE SUMMARY

(Erase heading not required.) 18th Divnl Signal Coy RE

(1)

Place	Date	Hour	Summary of Events and Information	Remarks and references to Appendices
HEILLY	1/2/16 to 4/2/16		1.2.16. Laying line to new H.Q. of 54th Bde. (in rest) at BOIS ESCARDONNEUSE 2/2/16 line completed.	
			3/2/16 Laying new 8-line track from Railway to new Divnl. H.Q. at Chateau RIBEMONT. Cable from terminal pole to Chateau – about 300 yards – made with 8 strands of "S" Substitute cable twisted together. Wires were found to be very satisfactory and lasted ~ very next job. Everything was complete and all lines through on morning of 5th.	
			3/2/16 2/Lt. J. Boyd RE granted short leave to England and was detained in hospital in London suffering from shell-shock. 55th Brigade Section temporarily in charge of 2/Lt Turner, 20th Kings Liverpool Regt., attached 18th Divnl Signal Coy to instruction.	
RIBEMONT	5/2/16		Divnl. H.Q. moved from HEILLY to RIBEMONT. Signal Office closed at one former place at 10 a.m. and new office opened at RIBEMONT at same time all lines being through and ready to work when staff arrived. Signal office in small garage next attached to Chateau. Lines in divisional comms at mill.	

M D Putts Capt. RE
O.C. 18th SIGNAL Coy R.E.

Army Form C. 2118

WAR DIARY
or
INTELLIGENCE SUMMARY

(Erase heading not required.)

19th Divl Signal Coy RE

Place	Date	Hour	Summary of Events and Information	Remarks and references to Appendices
RIBEMONT	6/7/16	7 am	Building new standings for horses and smoking shelters. No. 43886 Sapper Trebban W.T. and No. 43882 Sapper Roberts T. accidentally suffocates by fumes from coke brazier in dug out at F.A.B.R.A. When discovered by Motor Cyclist Sr. Hill at 7.0 am Sapper Trebbans was found to be dead and artificial respiration had to be resorted to for some time before Sapper Roberts recovered consciousness. Enquiry held by 54th Bde. Sapper Trebbans was buried at CORBIE on 7th Feby in the part of the cemetery reserved for British Military purposes.	
	8/7/16 9/7/16		Wiring out new Signal office, clearing up cable so far as possible and refaceing with air-line through villages.	
	10/7/16		2/Lt A.O. Laurie (20th Kings Liverpool) transferred to 39th Divn Signals and replaced at 57 Bde by 2/Lt J.A. Sexton (1st Cheshires) who remains temporarily in charge of the Brigade Section.	

M. J. Parle
Capt. R.E.
O.C. 19th SIGNAL Co. R.E.

WAR DIARY
or
INTELLIGENCE SUMMARY

Army Form C. 2118

(Erase heading not required.) 18th Divl. Signal Co RE

(3)

Place	Date	Hour	Summary of Events and Information	Remarks and references to Appendices
RIBEMONT	10/2		One mile each of Mark I* and Mark II new experimental cables sent to Ingrah.	
	13/2		53rd and 55th Bdes R.F.A. Replacing cable line from MEAULTE to 8th Bde R.F.A. Dug-out by air-line. Completed and working on 15th Feb.	
	16/2		Completed clearing up horses and built forage shelters. Poles to on to 53rd Visitation line.	
	17/2		Reeled in part of old 53rd Visitation line between RIBEMONT and HEILLY.	
	18/2		Party cutting poles at HEILLY. Arrangements were made to get these poles before heavy leaving HEILLY and CE 13th Corps approved to their being taken out.	

M. L. Pink Capt RE
O.C. 18th SIGNAL Co. R.E.

Army Form C. 2118

WAR DIARY
or
INTELLIGENCE SUMMARY

(Erase heading not required.) 18th Divl Signal Coy. R.E.

Place	Date	Hour	Summary of Events and Information	Remarks and references to Appendices
RIBEMONT	18/7/16		Seven men from 6th Entrenching Battn taken for Office Telegraphists. These only proved and it was recommended that these be strenuously attached to Signal Coy for a short course of instruction. This was agreed to and they joined beginning class on 20th July.	
	18/7/16		Cleared up pole at Signal Office and labored lines.	
	19/7/16		Four permanent lines erected through village, one pair for telephone to C.R.E. and one pair for A/Q officer. Cable to R.A. Headqrs replaced by copper airline and line laid to Signal Office.	
	20/7/16 to 22/7/16		Starts laying part of four copper airline track to 5th Bde H.Q. at LA HOUSSOYE. Part from HEILLY to RIBEMONT laid by Headqr section and that from HEILLY to LAHOUSSOYE laid by 5th Bde Section. Work had to be discontinued on latter route of line owing to the track having to be laid [...] by Battn of 5th Bde which was being used as a rifle range.	

O.C. 18th SIGNAL Co. R.E.

Army Form C. 2118

WAR DIARY
or
INTELLIGENCE SUMMARY

(Erase heading not required.) 18th Devnl Signal Coy RE

Place	Date	Hour	Summary of Events and Information	Remarks and references to Appendices
RIBEMONT	23/7/16		Corps HQ moved from QUERRIEUX to BAZIEUX.	
	24/7/16		Ordinary routine work and general maintenance of existing lines.	
	26/7/16		Fourteen men returned to Battalions from Signal Coy as proficient Signallers.	

M.D. Pyke Capt RE
O.C. 18th SIGNAL Co. R.E.

WAR DIARY or INTELLIGENCE SUMMARY

Army Form C. 2118

March '16 18th Divnl. Signal Coy RE

(1)

Place	Date	Hour	Summary of Events and Information	Remarks and references to Appendices
RIBEMONT	1st March		Nil	
	2nd		Nil	
	3rd	9 am	Came under orders of A.D.A.S. 13th Corps. Sergt. and party of 4 men sent to MONTIGNY to arrange Billets, Horse-lines, etc., in anticipation of move.	
	4th	8.30	Two NCOs and 16 men sent to MONTIGNY to establish visual stations for communication between D.H.Q., Infantry Brigades and D.A.C. when Division moves into rest.	
	6th		Divnl. H.Q. moves into rest at MONTIGNY. Signal Office at RIBEMONT closed at 11.50am and communication established at MONTIGNY at same hour.	
MONTIGNY	7th to 19th		Division in rest. All communication done by visual with the exception of a Lander and Telephone line to 13th Corps H.Q. at HEILLY. Visual worked with complete success. D.R.L.L. services to Brigades etc performed by horse D.Rs. M. Cyclist DRs are Motor Cyclist DRs had no opportunity of overtaking their	M.T. Park/Capt RE

Army Form C. 2118

(2)

WAR DIARY
or
INTELLIGENCE SUMMARY
(Erase heading not required.)

March '16   18th Divnl Signal Coy R.E.

Place	Date	Hour	Summary of Events and Information	Remarks and references to Appendices
MONTIGNY	7th to 12th (Contd)		Bicycles. During rest period opportunity was taken to thoroughly overhaul all Cable, Cable Limber, Wagons and Horses, and all deficiencies were made good so far as possible. Stores were carefully checked and all deficiencies applies for.	
	13th		Started laying main a Coms air line from D.H.Q. at MONTIGNY Chateau to Divnl. School at BOIS ESCARDONNEUSE.	
	14th	10 am	Above line finished and communication established.	
	15th		Line to Divl School extended and any small deficiencies discovered made good.	
	17th		Informed that Division would move to new H.Q. at ETINEHEM and relieve 30th Division on 20th inst.	
	18th		One N.C.O. and four linesmen proceeded to new Divnl H.Q. for the purpose of going through lines and communications generally with 30th Divnl Sigs.	

M. ? Poke Captain R.E.

WAR DIARY or INTELLIGENCE SUMMARY

Army Form C. 2118

March 1916   16th Divnl. Signal Coy RE

Place	Date	Hour	Summary of Events and Information	Remarks and references to Appendices
MONTIGNY	19th	9 a.m.	Two cable detachments, in charge of Lieut OSCROFT, proceeded to ETINEHEM to take over Billets etc., and some stores from 30th Divnl. Sigs. On the same date a similar party was sent to MONTIGNY by 30th Divnl. Sigs.	
	20th		Divnl. Headqrs: moved from MONTIGNY to ETINEHEM. Signal Office closes at former place at 12.30pm and opened at new H.Q at same hour. Remainder of Company, with the exception of two N.C.O's and six men who were left behind to hand over and clear up stores etc., proceeded to ETINEHEM.	
ETINEHEM	21st to 24th		General overhauling and improving of lines	
	25th	7 a.m.	Line to 9th Image Battery reported d.i.s. On investigation it was found that about 150 yards has been blown out of that part of the line which was laid on river.	

W. ?. ?????? — Capt RE

Army Form C. 2118

(4)

WAR DIARY
or
INTELLIGENCE SUMMARY

(Erase heading not required.)

March /16   18th Divnl Signal Coy RE

Place	Date	Hour	Summary of Events and Information	Remarks and references to Appendices
ETINEHEM	25th (Contd)		This was probably caused by French soldiers throwing explosives into the river for fish. destruction of fish. Put in 150 yards of four kind-covered as an experiment	
	26th		Laid pair D5 twist cable to CRE. On the night 25/26th a new testing table was installed and the 30-line exchange was replaced by one 15-line and one 10-line (now). Artillery lines so far as possible on 10-line (now) and others on 15-line	
	27th		Eight-way cable was at RIBEMONT again brought into use to replace some buried lines leading into by the Eight lines on permanent track along ETINEHEM —BRAY-CORBIE ROAD (near Camp) broken by shell-fire. Communication not interrupted through other lines. Broken wires repaired at 2.45pm. (Shelling ceased 2.15pm)	
	29th	2.0pm		
	30th		Line to Artillery Right group found to be "earthy". New cable laid between CAPPY CORNER and SUZANNE Chateau gale— about 2 miles. D5 substitute on trees.	
	31st			M. T. Pope Capt RE

1875 W; W593/826 1,000,000 4/15 J.B.C. & A. A.D.S.S./Forms/C. 2118.

Army Form C. 2118

WAR DIARY
or
INTELLIGENCE SUMMARY

(Erase heading not required.)

18th Divis'l Signal Coy R.E. Vol 5

April 1916

Place	Date	Hour	Summary of Events and Information	Remarks and references to Appendices
ETINEHEM	1st April		Nil	
	2nd		Nil	
	3rd		Nineteen men returned to Battalions as proficient linesmen.	
	4th		NFB½ - line to fels group artillery. Buried portion replaced by poles cable for about 600 yards from R.E. Dump Test Box	
	5th to 14th		Nil	
	15th		Studies laying of 4-way air-line trunk from CHIPILLY to BRAY.	
	16th to 19th		Still working on above line	
	17th at 4.5pm		N.D.11.A and N.B.11.B - Telephone pair to 55th Bde broken at point 80 on BRAY-CORBIE Road by shell fire. Line repaired and communication restored at 4.30pm	

M Lee Capt. R.E.
for O.C. 18th Signal Co. R.E.

Army Form C. 2118

WAR DIARY
or
INTELLIGENCE SUMMARY

(Erase heading not required.) 18th Division Signal Co. R.E.

April 1916

Place	Date	Hour	Summary of Events and Information	Remarks and references to Appendices
ETINEHEM	20th to 24th		Divisions 1 mile of line from CHIPILLY – BRAY track to clear landing ground for aircraft.	
	22nd		Started buried communications for Advanced H.Q. Twelve lines in trench 6ft deep. Working party from 19th Kings furnished augmented by 2 N.C.O's from Signal Co.	
	24th		Sergt Burr sent to Anti-Gas School at CHIPILLY for course of instruction.	
	25th & 26th		Still working on Advanced H.Q. buried communications.	
	27th to 29th		Work on Advanced H.Q. buried communications still proceeding.	

M?Arthur
Lieut R.E.
O.C. 18th SIGNAL Co. R.E.

WAR DIARY or INTELLIGENCE SUMMARY

Army Form C. 2118

(3)

April 1916   16th Division Signal Coy RE

Place	Date	Hour	Summary of Events and Information	Remarks and references to Appendices
ETINEHEM	30th	3:30pm	Fallen lines from ETINEHEM to BRAY-CORBIE road broken by shell fire. Lines repaired and communication restored at 4.35pm.	
	26th to 30th		Capt. M.T. Porter, R.E. O.C. on leave to UK. Lieut J.P. Baxter R.E. acting O.C. during absence.	

J P Baxter Lieut RE
for O.C. 16th SIGNAL Co. R.E.

18/SYR/75.

Officer i/c.,
A.G's Office, BASE.

Herewith War Diary for May 1916.

M.L. Poole.

Captn. R.E.
O.C. 18th Divn. Signal Coy. R.E.

4-6-16.

Army Form C. 2118

18 D Sig 24
V6 b

WAR DIARY
or
INTELLIGENCE SUMMARY
(Erase heading not required.) 18th Divnl. Signal Coy R.E.

May 1916

Place	Date	Hour	Summary of Events and Information	Remarks and references to Appendices
ETINEHEM	1st	6.30pm	Lorry sent to CAVILLON with stores.	
		1.30pm	Shell fire. Lines communication through at 2.5pm broken by barge. Two NCOs and 33 men sent forward to PICQUIGNY en route to CAVILLON to establish wireless communications and prepare billets in view of the Divn'n moving into rest at Moreuil the latter place.	
	2nd		Replacing one bay of permanent track at K.19 a 2.6 by buried cable to clear track for Kite Balloon lorry.	
	3rd		Drotting comic air line track between K.24 c 2.7 and K.24 c 10.9 to clear track for Kite Balloon lorry	
	4th		Parties finishing off above two jobs.	
	4th	3.30pm	Company marches out of its HQ in route to CAVILLON for night of 5/6 at CURBIE for Divnl. rest. Halted for night of 5/6 at CURBIE	

M? Park
Capt RE
O.C. 18th SIGNAL Co. R.E.

WAR DIARY or INTELLIGENCE SUMMARY

(Erase heading not required.) 18th Divnl. Signal Coy RE

Army Form C. 2118

(2)

May 1916

Place	Date	Hour	Summary of Events and Information	Remarks and references to Appendices
CORBIE	5th	8.30am	Proceeded from CORBIE en route to CAVILLON reaching the latter place at 3.35pm. Telephonic and visual communication established at 11.30pm - former to Brigades and Corps and latter to Brigades. Sounder working to Corps at 11.30am	
CAVILLON	6th	—	Nil.	
	7th	—	Party of horsemen regulating and overhauling escorting lines which were found to be in a very bad condition. Horses again out on overhauling of lines.	
	8th	—	Nil	
	9th	—	Nil.	
	10th		One cable detachment sent to BRAY to supervise and assist infantry working parties in laying buried communications which were commenced in April.	
	11th			

WAR DIARY
or
INTELLIGENCE SUMMARY

Army Form C. 2118

May 1916   18th Divl Signal Coy RE

Place	Date	Hour	Summary of Events and Information	Remarks and references to Appendices
CAVILLON	12th to 31st		Division in rest. All cable carts, wagons, limbers etc thoroughly overhauled and necessary repair effected. All stores checked and deficiencies applied for. Cable drill and flag drill daily so far as possible.	

M.? Duke Capt RE
O.C. 18th SIGNAL Co. R.E.

Army Form C. 2118

June
18 Div
Signals
Vol 7

WAR DIARY
or
INTELLIGENCE SUMMARY

(Erase heading not required.)

18th Divnl. Signal Coy RE

June 1916

Summary of Events and Information

Place	Date	Hour	Summary of Events and Information	Remarks and references to Appendices
CAVILLON	3rd		No. 54118 M/Cpl Patterson, J.E. fatally injured on FOURDINROY — BREILLY Road. Cpl Patterson was returning from trial run which he undertook in order to test some change which had he affected to his machine when he collided with a French cart with fatal results. Buried with full Military Honours at PICQUIGNY	
(SOMME)	5th		on 5th June 1916	
CORBIE	22nd		Company marched from CAVILLON to CORBIE. Advanced party sent on to prepare Signal Office in Battle Dug-Outs	
BATTLE H.Q. (L.16. a.8.2)	23rd		Company marched from CORBIE to ETINEHEM. Signal Office opened at BATTLE DUG-OUTS. Only supervising orderlies and men actually required to work were brought up to Battle HQ and a horse line and remainder of Company remained at ETINEHEM. Cable Carts etc were standing by at later place ready to move up at short notice but they were not required.	

M.J. Pate
Captn. R.E.
O.C. 18TH DIVNL. SIGNAL COY. R.E.

(2)

Army Form C. 2118

WAR DIARY
or
INTELLIGENCE SUMMARY

(Erase heading not required.)

18th Divnl. Signal Coy. R.E.

June 1916

Place	Date	Hour	Summary of Events and Information	Remarks and references to Appendices
BATTLE HQ 24th (L 14 a 6 2)			Sergt Hughes with 5 men at Visual transmitting station at (L 5 b 2.3) 2nd Cpl Knight with 3 men to Lieven's Dug-Out at L 6 a 1.1 Cpl Hughes and 12 men at forward visual station at A.19 b 3.9 All lines to Bdes and Artillery tested through correctly and all remained in good order during operations	

M. P.

Captn. RE

O.C. 18TH DIVNL. SIGNAL COY. R.E.

18/ Signals

18th Divisional Signal Company.

WAR DIARY
or
INTELLIGENCE SUMMARY

(Erase heading not required.)

18TH DIVNL. SIGNAL COY. R.E.

Army Form C. 2118

Place	Date	Hour	Summary of Events and Information	Remarks and references to Appendices
BATTLE H.Q. (BRAY-sur-Somme)	1st		Preparations for attack were all completed by this date; Divisional lines to Brigades and Artillery lines were all buried in 6 ft trenches, tested through and worked well. They had been in use for 8 days previous and had not given any trouble. The 3 Brigades, each with its affiliated Group of Artillery, were at following points respectively:— A.25.d.6.5; A.25.b.5.9; F.24.c.5.5 Sergt. J.E. Hughes with 5 men was stationed at transmitting visual station at point L.5.b.2.3. They called up all 3 Brigades, Divnl. H.Q. and 7th Divn at GROVETOWN three times a day, but were never required for messages as all lines remained through the whole time. 2nd/Cpl. Knights and 3 men were stationed at Firemen's Dug-Out at point L.b.c.1.1; they were very useful for keeping all lines tested. Corporal Hughes and 12 Infantry Brigades had been stationed at forward visual station at point A.19.b.2.9. for 5 days for the purpose of receiving visual messages. During the attack from this point the whole area between MAMETZ and MONTAUBAN as far up as the top of POMMIERS RIDGE could be seen.	

W.R. Pink
Capt. R.E.
O.C. 18th Div. Signal Coy. R.E.

Army Form C. 2118 (2)

WAR DIARY
or
INTELLIGENCE SUMMARY

(Erase heading not required.)

18TH DIVNL. SIGNAL COY. R.E.

JUL 1916

Place	Date	Hour	Summary of Events and Information	Remarks and references to Appendices
	1st (Cont'd)		Captn. J.R. Cater went to this visual station on morning of 30th and took charge. This station was manned in a most efficient manner during the battle of the 1st, and a large number of important messages were received. Touch was maintained continuously with Battalions, and the greatest energy and disregard of danger was displayed by all ranks in Brigade Sections. Light lines were run out to Battalions as they advanced, but these were continuously cut and were maintained with great difficulty. Shortly after the advance the Brigade Sections ran out more lines and made these as safe as possible. They were mostly laid in the remnants of the German trenches, and consisted of D.3, armoured cable and a certain amount of captured German cable.	
	2nd		Lines were maintained in good order. Patrols reached CATERPILLAR WOOD. Wireless communication was established with Battalion H.Q. in the LOOP, A.2.c.7.b. about 1 mile N. of CARNOY. A number of Pigeon messages got through from MONTAUBAN ALLEY and WHITE TRENCH	

W.R. Palmer / Captn. RE
O.C. 18th Div. Signal Coy RE

Army Form C. 2118

(3)

WAR DIARY
or
INTELLIGENCE SUMMARY

(Erase heading not required.)

18TH DIVNL. SIGNAL COY. R.E.

JULY 1916

Instructions regarding War Diaries and Intelligence Summaries are contained in F. S. Regs., Part II. and the Staff Manual respectively. Title Pages will be prepared in manuscript.

Place	Date	Hour	Summary of Events and Information	Remarks and references to Appendices
	3/7/16		CATERPILLAR WOOD was captured and Advanced Post established in MARLBORO WOOD. 53rd Brigade Rd line and maintained it from the LOOP along CATERPILLAR TRENCH in to CATERPILLAR WOOD.	
	4/5th		Battalions of 55th Brigade withdrew to RAIL AVENUE and BRONFAY FARM, Brigade HQ remaining at the same place. 53rd and 54th Brigades appeared to their right and took over the whole front between them, from WHITE TRENCH to MONTAUBAN.	
	7/7/16		8th Brigade relieved 53rd Bde who went to GROVETOWN. Communication to 53rd obtained by lines previously used to Brigade Transport Office of which has been run by 3 Signallers & Brigade Pioneers and an orderly from each transport unit.	
	8/4/16		9th Brigade relieved 54th Bde who went to BOIS DES TAILLES. Divnl HQ moved to GROVETOWN and cable was run out	
GROVETOWN	9th		to 54th at BOIS DES TAILLES	

W.P Rowe Capt. RE
O.C. 184 Div Signal Coy RE

Army Form C. 2118

WAR DIARY
or
INTELLIGENCE SUMMARY
(Erase heading not required.)

18TH DIVNL. SIGNAL COY. R.E.

Instructions regarding War Diaries and Intelligence Summaries are contained in F. S. Regs., Part II. and the Staff Manual respectively. Title Pages will be prepared in manuscript.

JUL 1916

Place	Date	Hour	Summary of Events and Information	Remarks and references to Appendices
	9th (Contd)		55th Bde moved to BOIS CELESTINES. Communication by telephone was obtained with them through XIII Corps R C at CHIPILLY. 18th Divnl Arty remained at LD Battle H.Q. and came under orders of 3rd Divn.	
GROVETOWN	10th/12th		At GROVETOWN — overhauling stores etc – general duties.	
COPSE RAVINE	13th		Divnl H.Q. moved to COPSE RAVINE, taking over from 30th Divn at point A. 21 R.5.4 at 10.0 am. 55th Brigade moved H.Q. to COPSE "C" and took over from 89th Bde. 54th Brigade moved to TRIGGER WOOD. 53rd Brigade remained at GROVETOWN. Existing line to COPSE "C" was used but a line had to be constructed to TRIGGER WOOD by 54th Bde and was through at 3pm. 55th Brigade had orders to capture TRONES WOOD; commencing the attack at 6.0pm	

W P G / Capt RE

O.C. 18th Div Signal Coy RE

WAR DIARY or INTELLIGENCE SUMMARY

Army Form C. 2118

18TH DIVNL. SIGNAL COY. R.E.

JUL 1916

Place	Date	Hour	Summary of Events and Information	Remarks and references to Appendices
	10th		55th Brigade attacked TRONES WOOD and found it so strongly defended that at 12.30am the 54th Bde were called up from TRIGGER WOOD in support and took over COPSE "C" from 55th. 53rd Brigade were ordered up from GROVETOWN to relieve the 54th at 4.30am on 11th and made their Brigade H.Q. at MARICOURT CHATEAU. A line was run out to MARICOURT CHATEAU from Div. H.Q. at about 5.0am by Lt. Oscroft as well as a line from there to COPSE "C". These were tested through and starts working immediately. The 55th Bde then withdrew and established their H.Q. at GROVETOWN.	
	11th		The 53rd Bde. consolidates positions in BERNAFAY WOOD and the HAIRPIN, and the captures positions in front were still held by the 54th Bde. Visual communication was established from the BRIQUETERIE to 2 points on the W. End of MARICOURT; one for 53rd and one for 54th Bde. A number of pigeons were successfully flown from BERNAFAY and TRONES WOODS on this day, an extra large number, viz 36 being sent up in rear of the difficult positions occupied by the leaving Coys.	Capt. R.E.

M.J. Powle
O.C. 18th Div. Signal Coy R.E.

Army Form C. 2118

WAR DIARY
or
INTELLIGENCE SUMMARY
(Erase heading not required.)

18TH DIVNL. SIGNAL COY. R.E.

JUL 1916

(6)

Place	Date	Hour	Summary of Events and Information	Remarks and references to Appendices
	14th (contd)		The Company has been moved up and were encamped in valley at the South end of COPSE RAVINE.	
	15th/16th		Maintaining lines in positions shown above; no new work took place but heavy fighting continued in TRONES WOOD	
	17th		Instructions received that Divn to be prepared to take over modified front and front from S. of DELVILLE WOOD to near GUILLEMONT. MINDEN POST, and front from S. of DELVILLE WOOD to near GUILLEMONT. This meant a new system of lines and arrangements were made to take over a number of phone lines used by 13th C.H.A. to was which it was proposed to build a permanent line to C.H.A. Dug-outs, 1000 yards S. of MINDEN POST. Work was started on this, and line was fell constructed when orders were received that Divn were coming right out of the line. This work was, however, not wasted as the 9th(?) Division (newly here to take over its H.Q. and lines in this direction. 53rd Bde was relieved by 105th Bde at MARICOURT and 53rd Bde moved to TALUS BOISE coming under order of 9th Divn for the purpose of the attack on LONGUEVAL and DELVILLE WOOD	

M.J. Polo (?)
Capt RE
O.C. 18th Div. Signal Coy RE

Army Form C. 2118

(7)

WAR DIARY
or
INTELLIGENCE SUMMARY
(Erase heading not required.)

18TH DIVNL. SIGNAL COY. R.E.

JUL 1916

Instructions regarding War Diaries and Intelligence Summaries are contained in F. S. Regs., Part II. and the Staff Manual respectively. Title Pages will be prepared in manuscript.

Place	Date	Hour	Summary of Events and Information	Remarks and references to Appendices
GROVETOWN	16th		5th Div came out of the line that position on the line being taken over by 106th who made that H.Q. at the BRIQUETERIE 5th moved to BOIS DES TAILLES.	
	19th		Div was relieved by 35th Divn who took over the H.Q. at COPSE RAVINE. Divnl. H.Q. moved to GROVETOWN; the 53rd still remaining under orders of 9th Divn. Company made camp on its site in GROVETOWN. Orders received for transport to commence to march to HALLENCOURT next day, and all attachments were made. Store in BRAY was rearranged so that all stores required could be easily removed.	
	20th		Company marched out and halted for night near D'HOURS.	
HALLENCOURT	21st		Divnl. Hdqrs. moved to HALLENCOURT.	
	22nd/23rd		In billets at HALLENCOURT, brigades being in villages around, and some existing lines laid by Signal Depot Staff ABBEVILLE were picked up and new Artillery lines came up on 23rd and 24th.	
	24th		Company marched to PONT REMY — entrained and arrived at ST. OMER, marching from there to RENESCURE.	

W.J. Parke /Capt. R.E.

O.C. 18th Divn. Signal Coy R.E.

Army Form C. 2118

WAR DIARY
or
INTELLIGENCE SUMMARY

(Erase heading not required.)

18TH DIVNL. SIGNAL COY. R.E.

JUL 1916

Place	Date	Hour	Summary of Events and Information	Remarks and references to Appendices
RENESCURE	25/27th		At RENESCURE, the Brigades were as follows:- 53rd at BLARINGHEM; 54th at WALLON CAPPEL and 55th at WARDRECQUES. It was found that the back area in 2nd Army had a large number of exchanges in villages and by means of these communication was established without any difficulty. On 26th orders were received for Divn HQ to move to FLETRE, and Bdes to villages around in 54th Corps reserve area. Arrangements were accordingly made for lines to be laid on to this place, but as news arrived from II Anzac Corps that Divn would move in the course of a day or two to their area, and come under their orders, it was decided not to move Divn HQ. The arrangements were accordingly modified, Bdes being as follows:- 53rd Point S. of MONT DES CATS; 54th near METERN; 55th at THIESHOUK, with Divl. Arty at EECKE. Lines from these were run to nearest existing exchanges and by sending a few men to assist the operators at CAESTRE, exchange communication was kept up the whole time with Divn at RENESCURE.	
	29th		6 Wireless operators to 2nd Army Signal School at ZUYTPEENE	
	30th		Kept Roger and detachment to CROIX DU BAC to get lines all ready	

M.I.P.K
O.C 18th Divl Signal Coy RE

18th Div Signal Coy RE
April 1916

Vol 9

Army Form C. 2118

WAR DIARY
or
INTELLIGENCE SUMMARY

(Erase heading not required.)

18TH DIVNL. SIGNAL COY. R.E.

AUG. 1916

Place	Date	Hour	Summary of Events and Information	Remarks and references to Appendices
CROIX-DU-BAC	2nd		Company moved from RENESCURE to new HQ at CROIX-DU-BAC. Signal Office closed at former place at 12 Noon and opened at latter place at same hour. Found lines in this area were laid on the funnel system. Trunk lines (buried) forward from two points in front of Div. H.Q. forward, and finally up to front line. These were cross-connected at different distances along their length by laterals. Where these "crosses" test points were made, manually in built up shelters where terminal boards were installed for the purpose of cross-connecting. Each of these points was given a distinguishing letter and bore the name of "land front". This system was found to be incomplete owing to insufficiency of laterals and was extended while the Division was in the area.	
	4th		Sergt Palmer and Party constructing 12-way track from FORT-ROMPU to ERQUINGHEM.	Brig. P. Vernon /h maint RE CORPS RE O.C. 18th Divl. Sigl. Coy RE

WAR DIARY or INTELLIGENCE SUMMARY

Army Form C. 2118

18TH DIVNL. SIGNAL COY. R.E.

AUG 1915

Place	Date	Hour	Summary of Events and Information	Remarks and references to Appendices
	8th		Pegged out route for cable trench from ROLANDERIS to RUE MARLE.	
	9th		Two companies of Infantry digging above trench 6 days for 10 prs. cables	
	10th		Major Serra states from 2 Brigades on line to Lefas at BAC. ST MAUR. Reports on ditches in fair permanent track through communes states on 4th Inniskes and tested through control Airline.	STEENWERCK
	19th		Advance party of 1 officer and 7 OR. from 34th Divn. (relieving Division) arrived to take over lines etc.	
BAILLEUL	21st		Company moves from CROIX DU BAC to BAILLEUL by march route	

Jn. P. Vanolf Lieut. R.E.
for Col. R.E.
O C 18th Divnl Signal Coy R.E.

(3.)

Army Form C. 2118

WAR DIARY
or
INTELLIGENCE SUMMARY
(Erase heading not required.)

18TH DIVNL. SIGNAL COY. R.E.

AUG 1916

Place	Date	Hour	Summary of Events and Information	Remarks and references to Appendices
ROELLECOURT	25th		Company moved from BAILLEUL to ROELLECOURT. Entrained BAILLEUL (WEST) 10.20am for ST. POL. ST POL to ROELLECOURT by march route.	
	26th		Cable line to 55th Bde. to be replaced by air-line.	
	27th		Line single copper - air-line from Div. Hqrs. to 55th Bde at MONCHY BRETON and L.J. 55th line utilised for telephone to CRE at BOIRIN.	

Lui. P. Cheney
Lieut R.E.
for Captain R.E.
O.C. 18th Div. Signal Coy R.E.

War Diary

18th Div. Sig. Coy

Army Form C. 2118

WAR DIARY
or
INTELLIGENCE SUMMARY

(Erase heading not required.)

Vol / 0

18th Divl. Signal Coy RE

September 1916

Place	Date	Hour	Summary of Events and Information	Remarks and references to Appendices
ROELLECOURT	8th		2nd Lieut C.V. RILEY, RE appointed for duty as Intermediary Officer to Divnl. Artillery as Artillery Signal Officer.	
DOULLENS	9th		Company moved from ROELLECOURT to DOULLENS by march route. Signal Office closed at former place and opened at Tribunal DOULLENS at same hour.	
ACHEUX	10th		Company moves from DOULLENS to ACHEUX by march route. Signal Office closed DOULLENS 10.30am and opened at ACHEUX at same hour.	
	12th		2nd Lieuts N.E. Davies and T. C. Morgan RE attached down Reserve Army Signals for instruction.	
	14th		Sent Reays and party of 10 men to Divnl. H.Q. at TARA to assist with communications.	
	16th		53rd Div. moved forward to BOUZINCOURT	A.J. Porter Capt. RE O.C. 18th Div. Sig. Coy. R.E.

Army Form C. 2118

(2)

WAR DIARY
or
INTELLIGENCE SUMMARY

(Erase heading not required.) 18th Divnl. Signal Coy RE.

Sept. 1916

Place	Date	Hour	Summary of Events and Information	Remarks and references to Appendices
	19th		One cable section completed to Divnl Arty in accordance with A/HQ instruction SB/1299	
	22nd		Party of 1. humen sent to 147th Divn to look over lines in anticipation of relief	
	23rd		53rd and 55th Bdes relieved 147th Bde (49th Divn) on line opposite THIEPVAL.	
	24th		54th Bde to relieve 55th on night of 24/25th. 55th Bde to be in Divnl. Reserve at HEDAUVILLE	
HEDAUVILLE	25th		Company moved to HEDAUVILLE by march route Signal Office closed 10:0 am at ACHEUX and opened at HEDAUVILLE at same hour. "A" Cable Section (2nd Lt GODDARD RE) attached to us to assist with general maintenance of lines during proposed attack on THIEPVAL.	

M.T.Parle
Capt. RE
O C 18th Div Signal Coy RE

WAR DIARY or INTELLIGENCE SUMMARY

Army Form C. 2118.

(3)

Sept. 1916   1/8th Divisional Signal Coy R.E.

Place	Date	Hour	Summary of Events and Information	Remarks and references to Appendices
	25th		146th Bde (49th Divn) were left in the line under 18th Divn, and held the left of the line N. of THIEPVAL WOOD, up to the ANCRE.	
	25th		Sergt. Hughes, with 8 men (Infantry Signallers), was stationed at Visual receiving station on hill behind AVELUY. Corpl Hughes, with 4 linesmen and 1 b operator, was in charge with 4 men to the MEUUES. Left Coprl R.B.Simm L.V.R. station near MARTINSART, through which station all the forward lines pass. 4 linesmen and 2 operators at STR station on Railway ½ mile S. of PASSERELLE DE MAGENTA. This last station experienced much trouble with the lines under shell fire, was particularly the main crossings which were continually heavily shelled. Two casualties were sustained in this party.	
	26th		Attack on and capture of THIEPVAL carried out by 53rd and 54th Inf. Bde. All Divisional lines remained through out and in good working order during the attack. The attack commenced at 12.35 pm and position N. of THIEPVAL was consolidated that evening except for N.W. corner which was carried successfully to the Pope's Nose by 6 pm next morning.	

O.C. 1/8th Div. Sig. Coy R.E.
N L Rodney Cyfre

Army Form C. 2118.

WAR DIARY or INTELLIGENCE SUMMARY

(Erase heading not required.)

18th Divnl Inf Co RE

Sept 1916

Place	Date	Hour	Summary of Events and Information	Remarks and references to Appendices
	27th		53rd Bde has 6 lines through to N.E. corner of THIEPVAL and 54th Bde has 3 lines to Chateau. These were maintained without the greatest difficulty.	
	28th		7th Bde relieved 146th Bde on the left. A further attack was carried out by 53rd and 75th Bdes on SCHWABEN REDOUBT at 1.0pm. The North portion of this position was captured and consolidated that evening. The 7th Bde was withdrawn and left 2 battalions with 53rd Bde and 55th Bde flew 6th R.B. etc relieved 53rd and 57th Bdes and 2 Battalions of 7th Bde, making their H.Q. at BRIGHTY VALLEY. Thus H.Q. was changed early next morning to PASSERELLE where the 51st Bde has been.	
	29th		Infantry was consolidating positions gained. Parties from "H" Cable Section were sent out to recover its cables, which was overheated and re-issued. Very little wire was made of thoread as all lines were kept through. Wireless which was erected at B.V. with forward set on THIEPVAL was not much use at all, but pigeons were found very useful all through the operations.	
	30/31st			

W R Pinkerton RE
O. C. 18th Divnl Inf Co RE

WAR DIARY or INTELLIGENCE SUMMARY

Army Form C. 2118.

(5.)

Septr 1916   178th Divnl Signal Coy R.E.

Place	Date	Hour	Summary of Events and Information	Remarks and references to Appendices
			The following honours were awarded to N.C.O.'s and men of the Company for the operations on the Somme during July.	
			No 43893 Sergt W. GREY D.C.M.	
			" 59462 Corpl. W. HURST D.C.M.	
			" 48769 Sergt. T.E. PALMER D.C.M.	
			No 58357 Sapper E. AVERILL M.M.	
			" 47082 La/Cpl F. CLARKSON M.M.	
			" 55188 Corpl. H.E. HUGHES M.M.	
			" 57165 2nd Cpl H. KNIGHTS M.M.	
			" 47234 2nd Cpl D. MILLAR M.M.	
			" 49540 La/Cpl S. POXON M.M.	
			" 43880 Sapper A. WHITEHEAD M.M.	

W. Park

"A" Form.
Army Form C. 2121.

MESSAGES AND SIGNALS.

No. of Message _____

Prefix ____ Code ____ m.	Words	Charge	This message is on a/c of:	Recd. at _____ m.
Office of Origin and Service Instructions.				Date _____
	Sent At _____ m.		_____ Service.	From _____
	To			By
	By		(Signature of "Franking Officer.")	

TO | 18th Signals | | |

| Sender's Number. | Day of Month | In reply to Number | AAA |
| A 221. | Nov 10th | | |

Car away for Octrud

From 18th A
Place
Time 11.30 am

WAR DIARY or INTELLIGENCE SUMMARY

Army Form C. 2118.

Vol 11

18TH DIVNL. SIGNAL CO R.E.

OCT 1916

Place	Date	Hour	Summary of Events and Information	Remarks and references to Appendices
HEDAUVILLE	1st to 5th		Divnl. H.Q. at HEDAUVILLE. This was the period immediately following the THIEPVAL and SCHWABEN REDOUBT operations. There was no new work done on Divisional communications but considerable work in the forward area, where the lines to THIEPVAL were renewed and strengthened by the 55th Bde. Section. This Brigade was holding the Divisional front previously held by 53rd, 54th and 7th Bdes while Divnl artillery came to Divnl Corps at On the 1st the 18th Divnl Artillery came to 39th Division Advantage was taken of this to call in the 2 Cable Detachments who were with them, and replace them by 1 detachment under 2nd Lieut CA. Riley with Sergt. Rogers.	
BERNAVILLE	6th		Divnl. H.Q. moved to "rest" area at BERNAVILLE and Signal office stands there at 11.0 a.m., having closed at HEDAUVILLE at the same hour. The whole Division was in rest; Brigades being as follows:-	
	7th to 13th		53rd at LE MEILLARD; 54th at RIBEAUCOURT and 55th at FIENVILLERS. Permanent lines were picked up to all these places from BERNAVILLE, the arrangements being made by Reserve Army Signals. At BERNAVILLE a G.C.P. Office is established and the Divnl Signal Office, about 1/4 mile away, works through the front and 53rd Bde came under orders M.D.R. F. Canadian Corps.	

O.C. 18TH DIVNL. SIGNAL CO.

Army Form C. 2118.

WAR DIARY or INTELLIGENCE SUMMARY

(Erase heading not required.)

18TH DIVNL. SIGNAL CO. R.E. (2)

OCT 1916

Place	Date	Hour	Summary of Events and Information	Remarks and references to Appendices
ALBERT	13th		An Advanced Divl. H.Q. was established at ALBERT and 53rd Bde moved up to forward area from 12th to 15th.	
	14th–15th		53rd Bde took over the front line N. of POZIERS in KENORA TRENCH. Preparations had been in hand since 12th October for an attack by this Brigade to form a defensive flank to the Canadian Corps. on its right attacking PYS.	
	15th to 20th		During 15th, 16th and 17th October the remainder of 18th Division moved from the BERNAVILLE area to the vicinity of ALBERT by march route. On 16th remainder of Divl. H.Q. joined Advanced H.Q. at ALBERT, the Imperial Office being closed at BERNAVILLE at 8 a.m. On 17th the 18th Division was transferred from the Canadian Corps to 2nd Corps. It was originally intended to carry out the attack on REGINA TRENCH on the 19th but owing to bad weather this date was altered to 21st Oct.	
	21st		The 53rd Bde H.Q. has been established at POZIERS CEMETERY, and communication with them was obtained by a pair of lines in the Canadian Corps buried route, running from USNA HILL past POZIERS, and then ready to the front line via KENORA TRENCH.	

W.D.N.S.
Captain R.E.
O.C. 18TH DIVNL. SIGNAL CO. R.E.

WAR DIARY or INTELLIGENCE SUMMARY

Army Form C. 2118.

18TH DIVNL. SIGNAL CO. R.E.

OCT 1916

(3)

Place	Date	Hour	Summary of Events and Information	Remarks and references to Appendices
	22nd		53rd Bde. attacked and took REGINA TRENCH from COURCELETTE Road to TWENTYTHREE Road. The same evening the 55th Bde. took over the front to the left of 53rd Bde. - previously occupied by 7th Bde. (25th Divn.) - making their H.Q. at MOUQUET FARM, a line being taken over from 25th Divn. through USNA REDOUBT and JONNET'S POST. Another line was arranged from PZ (POZIERS Exchange) on the PZ-MNQ route. This latter has 5 pairs originally, all in good order, but these soon became unworkable and after a week not one line remained through.	
	23rd		54th Bde. relieved 53rd and made their H.Q. at R.29 Central W of COURCELETTE. Three pairs were laid to them from point 'E' on buried route, these being an an drained trench, but were continually cut and gave much trouble. The 53rd Bde. moved back to billets in ALBERT.	
TARA HILL	23rd		On this day Divnl H.Q. was established at TARA HILL, the Automatic being taken over from Canadian Corps R.O.	

M. D. Wh. Captain R.E.
O.C. 18TH DIVNL. SIGNAL CO. R.E.

Army Form C. 2118.

WAR DIARY
or
INTELLIGENCE SUMMARY

(Erase heading not required.)

18TH DIVNL. SIGNAL CO. R.E.

OCT 1916

Place	Date	Hour	Summary of Events and Information	Remarks and references to Appendices
	24th to 31st		Much work was done in improving forward communications, which were continually being broken. Only 1 through line was allotted to the Division by 2nd Corps on the buried route, resulting in many lines being broken and known out continuously. An airline partly from the Corps wired up a trestle route to 1 pair from TARA HILL to POZIERS. This has been blown down and cut frequently by shell fire but has been kept through practically the whole time. Another line was laid from P2 to MQ (MOUQUET FARM) and as this was frequently cut, a loop was made and one leg of the loop has been found fairly satisfactory.	

W. Price
O.C. 18TH DIVNL. SIGNAL CO. R.E.

Army Form C. 2118.

WAR DIARY
or
INTELLIGENCE SUMMARY

(Erase heading not required.)

18th DIVL. SIGNAL CO, R.E.

HEAD QUARTERS
9 DEC. 1916
18TH DIVISION

Vol 12

Instructions regarding War Diaries and Intelligence Summaries are contained in F. S. Regs., Part II. and the Staff Manual respectively. Title Pages will be prepared in manuscript.

NOV 1916

Place	Date	Hour	Summary of Events and Information
ALBERT. (TARA HILL)	1st to 7th		Relaying and improving Divisional lines. Forward lines were continuously being broken by shell fire and linesmen were constantly out on repairs. Though the Trestle route from TARA HILL to POZIERS was frequently broken by shell fire, communication was rarely interrupted for any length of time.
	8th to 15th		Operations postponed owing to persistent wet weather and time was for the most part occupied in carrying out improvements to existing communications. On the 12th, a line was laid from TARA HILL to the Auts in MASH VALLEY to provide divisional communication between B.H.Q. and battalions during the huts. On the 11th a line was laid from Red Cross Corner to the Wireless Station at X.11.c.88. This was connected up to PZ (Forward Exchange).

M Wenton
Captain RE
for Major RE
O C 18th Divnl. Signal Coy RE

Army Form C. 2118.

(2.)

WAR DIARY
or
INTELLIGENCE SUMMARY
(Erase heading not required.)

18th DIVL. SIGNAL CO., R.E.

— NOV 1916

Place	Date	Hour	Summary of Events and Information	Remarks and references to Appendices
	16th to 21st		It was found increasingly difficult to maintain constant communication between PZ (Forward Exchange) and MOUQUET FARM owing to lines being continually broken by shell fire. A Trench Wireless Set was erected at PZ and a similar set was placed in the vicinity of MOUQUET FARM. These sets proved very useful in maintaining communication when other means failed. 54th Bde relieved by 11th Canadian Bde on night of 16th; the former moving into huts at NASH VALLEY. On the same night the 55th Bde took over the front from SIXTEEN ROAD (exclusive) to STUMP ROAD (exclusive) from 19th Divn. On the 19th an attack by 18th Divn (55th Bde only) was made, having for its objective the approx line M.18.a.05.95 — (COURCELETTE TRENCH inclusive) — R.11.d.3.2.5 — R.11.c.o.5 — R.15.a.9.9. This was only partly successful owing to the 19th Divn on left having failed to secure all their objectives.	

M. ....
Captain RE
for Major OC
O.C. 18th Divnl Signal Coy R.E.

Army Form C. 2118.

WAR DIARY
or
INTELLIGENCE SUMMARY

(Erase heading not required.)

18th DIVL. SIGNAL CO., R.E.

NOV 1916

Place	Date	Hour	Summary of Events and Information	Remarks and references to Appendices
	21st		On the night of the 21st the HZ dug out received two direct hits which completely destroyed it, wounding two men and breaking all forward lines. The staff (operators and linemen) in this dug out with great promptitude and coolness immediately set to work to restore communication and all lines were again through and working in about half an hour.	
	21/22		18th Divn relieves by 61st Division on night of 21/22nd	
CONTAY	22nd		Divl. H.Q. established at CONTAY at 9am having closed at TARA HILL at same hour. All work (tanks) over to 54th Army Sub Office. Telephonic communication with 54th Bde through HERISSART Exchange. No telephonic communication with other two Brigades. Company moved from ALBERT to CONTAY by march route.	

M West Captain RE
to Major RE

O.C. 18th Divnl. Signal Coy RE

Army Form C. 2118.

WAR DIARY
or
INTELLIGENCE SUMMARY

(Erase heading not required.)

18th DIVL. SIGNAL CO., R.E. (4.)

Instructions regarding War Diaries and Intelligence Summaries are contained in F. S. Regs., Part II. and the Staff Manual respectively. Title Pages will be prepared in manuscript.

Place	Date	Hour	Summary of Events and Information	Remarks and references to Appendices
DOULLENS	23rd		Divnl H.Q. established at DOULLENS at 10.15am. From that time to Noon work was done through YDZ, lines afterwards being taken over and communication established with 53rd Bde through GEZAINCOURT (DOULLENS Civil Ex.); to 54th Bde direct and to 4th Corps. No communication with 55th Bde. Company moved from CONTAY to DOULLENS by march route.	
BERNAVILLE	24th		Divnl. H.Q. established at BERNAVILLE at 11:15 am. Existing lines taken over and communication established with ACo — sounder superimposed Direct telephonic communication with 53rd and 54th Brigades. No communication with 55th Bde.	
YVRENCH	25th		Divnl. H.Q. established at YVRENCH at 11:15 am. From that time to 1-0pm combined office with 2nd Division. Afterwards separate lines allotted and direct communication with Fourth Corps — sounder superimposed — established. No telephonic communications with any of the Brigades. Company moved from BERNAVILLE to YVRENCH by march route and occupied billets in YVRENCHEUX.	

M Watt Captain RE
for O.C. 18th Divnl Signal Co. RE.

O.C. 18th Divnl Signal Co. RE.

Army Form C. 2118.

WAR DIARY
or
INTELLIGENCE SUMMARY

(*Erase heading not required.*) 18th DIVL. SIGNAL CO., R.E.

NOV 1916

(5.)

Place	Date	Hour	Summary of Events and Information	Remarks and references to Appendices
BUIGNY-St Maclou	26th		Divnl H.Q. established at BUIGNY-ST-MACLOU. Direct communication with Fourth Corps. No news with Brigades. Company moved from YVRENCHEUX to BUIGNY-ST-MACLOU by march route.	
	27th		All Brigades reached their allotted areas and communication established with them.	

McLaws(?)
Captain R.E.
for Major R.E.
O.C. 18th Divnl Signal Coy R.E.

Army Form C. 2118.

WAR DIARY
or
INTELLIGENCE SUMMARY
(Erase heading not required.)

18th DIVL. SIGNAL CO., R.E.

DEC 1916

No 13

Place	Date	Hour	Summary of Events and Information	Remarks and references to Appendices
BUIGNY-ST-MACLOU	1st		Divisional Headquarters at BUIGNY-ST-MACLOU. 53rd Brigade Headquarters at LE TITRE. 54th Brigade Headquarters at DRUCAT. 55th Brigade Headquarters at CANCHY. During the whole month the Division was in rest in Fifth Army "K" Training Area. All cable carts, wagons, limbers, etc, were thoroughly overhauled, and necessary repairs to instruments and equipment carried out. Training consisting of Squad and Rifle Drill, and Riding exercise every alternate day, was given to all available personnel, and additional linemen were trained in permanent and comic air-line work.	
	2nd		A Divisional Signal School was established at LE PLESSIEL, to which each Infantry Battalion sent six men. These men were given a complete course in all branches of Signalling, and specially instructed in the use of the Fullerphone. In addition to this, each Brigade Section established a Signal School in which further personnel from Battalions was trained.	

M.J.P.G.
Major R.E.
OC. 18th Divnl. Signal Coy R.E.

WAR DIARY

INTELLIGENCE SUMMARY

18th DIVL. SIGNAL CO., R.E.

DEC 1916

Place	Date	Hour	Summary of Events and Information	Remarks and references to Appendices
	6th		On the sixth of December the 18th Divisional Artillery arrived in the training area and established their H.Q at PORT LE GRAND. 33 men from Artillery Brigades and D.A.C. were sent to the Divisional Signal School, and a small Signal School under the supervision of Artillery Signal Officer was run in addition.	
	14th		54th and 55th Brigades exchanged areas, the 54th moving to CANCHY area and the 55th to DRUCAT area.	
	29th		53rd and 55th Brigades exchanged areas, the 53rd moving into DRUCAT area, and the 55th to LE TITRE area.	

M. Park
Major R.E.
OC 18th Divnl Signal Coy R.E.

WAR DIARY or INTELLIGENCE SUMMARY

Army Form C. 2118.

18 D Signals

Vol 14

Place	Date	Hour	Summary of Events and Information	Remarks and references to Appendices
BUIGNY-ST-MACLOU	2ND		18th Divisional Artillery moved from BUIGNY-ST-MACLOU area to BRAILLY-YVRENCH area accompanied by No.3 Detachment, 18th Divisional Signal Company.	
	3RD		18th Divisional Artillery moved from BRAILLY-YVRENCH area to OUTRE-BOIS area.	
	4TH		18th Divisional Artillery moved from OUTRE BOIS area to MARIEUX-AMPLER-AUTHIEULE-SARTON area.	
	5TH		18th Divisional Artillery moved from MARIEUX-AMPLER-AUTHIEULE-SARTON area to IVth Corps area at W.7.&.Y.1. to reinforce Artillery on Corps front.	
YVRENCH	11TH		18th Divisional Headquarters moved from BUIGNY-ST-MACLOU to YVRENCH. Communication with IInd Corps at CRECY on BCO-CCY permanent track on new Nos 7 and 8 superimposed. Communication opened at YVRENCH at 12 noon. A small Signal Office was maintained at BUIGNY-ST-MACLOU for communications of BADOS, ADMS, Claims Officer and No.3 A.S.C, none of whom moved with the Division. This office was closed at 9.0 pm on 14th.	

Willc Captain RE.
OC 18th Divl Signal Cy RE.

JAN 1917

Army Form C. 2118.

WAR DIARY
or
INTELLIGENCE SUMMARY.
(Erase heading not required.)

JAN 1917 (2.)

Place	Date	Hour	Summary of Events and Information	Remarks and references to Appendices
YVRENCH (contd).	11TH		53rd Brigade Headquarters at PROUVILLE Telephone pair on permanent track CCY 1+2	
			54th Brigade Headquarters at LE PLOUY Telephone pair on French permanent line from LE PLOUY post office to YVRENCH.	
			55th Brigade Headquarters at CRAMONT Telephone pair on permanent track YCT a and b.	
BERNAVILLE	12th		Divisional Headquarters moved from YVRENCH to BERNAVILLE (area of IVth Corps) Communication established at 12 noon with IVth Corps at DOULLENS.	
			A permanent Signal Office is maintained at BERNAVILLE by IVth Army and lines to Brigades were allotted on permanent tracks	
			53rd Brigade Headquarters at GEZAINCOURT Telephone pair FL 1 and 2.	
			54th Brigade Headquarters at FIENVILLERS Telephone pair FL 13 and 14.	
			55th Brigade Headquarters at MON PLAISIR Telephone pair BE-RU 1 and 2.	

[signed] Captain R.E.
O.C. 18th Divnl Signal Coy R.E.

Army Form C. 2118.

Instructions regarding War Diaries and Intelligence
Summaries are contained in F. S. Regs., Part II.
and the Staff Manual respectively. Title pages
will be prepared in manuscript.

WAR DIARY
or
INTELLIGENCE SUMMARY. (3).
(Erase heading not required.)

JAN 1917

Place	Date	Hour	Summary of Events and Information	Remarks and references to Appendices
MARIEUX	14th		Divisional Headquarters moved from BERNAVILLE to MARIEUX. Communication established with IVth Corps at DOULLENS at 12 noon and lines to Brigades allotted by Corps. 53rd Brigade at PUCHEVILLERS. Telephone pair through PUCHEVILLERS exchange. 54th Brigade at RUBEMPRÉ. Telephone pair through Fifth Army Trunks and PUCHEVILLERS exchange. 55th Brigade at BEAUQUESNE. Telephone pair through BEAUQUESNE exchange.	
BOUZINCOURT W.T. P.3.7	16th		Divisional Headquarters moved from MARIEUX to Huts North of BOUZINCOURT and took over from 61st Division. Communications all in position and taken over as they stood. 54th Brigade in Line. 53rd Brigade in Support (MARTINSART). 55th Brigade in Reserve (HEDAUVILLE). Sounder superimposed to IInd Corps at SENLIS and sounders superimposed to all Brigades.	

J Millho Capt. RE
OC 18 Divnl Sigl Coy RE

Army Form C. 2118.

WAR DIARY
or
INTELLIGENCE SUMMARY. (4)

(Erase heading not required.)

Instructions regarding War Diaries and Intelligence Summaries are contained in F. S. Regs., Part II. and the Staff Manual respectively. Title pages will be prepared in manuscript.

JAN 1917

Place	Date	Hour	Summary of Events and Information	Remarks and references to Appendices
BOUZINCOURT cont'd	17th to 26th		All spare men employed on constructing new covered Horse Standings. Lorry employed daily for transport of material from C.R.E's Dump AVELUY.	
	27th/28th		52nd Brigade relieved 5th Brigade in line, and 58th Brigade moved into support area, MARTINSART.	

Honours and Awards.

Major M J Porter — Military Cross
Lieut (Temp Captain) J R Carter — Mentioned in Despatches 1-1-17.

Sergeant E V Beer — Military Medal
Lance Corporal A McKinn — Military Medal
Sapper J Cuthbert — Military Medal

A White Capt R.E.
O/C 1st Devonwat (by Capt R.E.)

Army Form C. 2118.

WAR DIARY
INTELLIGENCE SUMMARY

(Erase heading not required.)

18th DIVL. SIGNAL CO., R.E.

FEB 1917

Place	Date	Hour	Summary of Events and Information	Remarks and references to Appendices
BOUZINCOURT (W.7.b.3.7)	1st		Captain J.C. WILLIS, M.C., R.E. arrived to take over command of Company from Major M.T. PORTER, M.C., R.E. who has been transferred to First Army Signal Company R.E.	
	1st		Command of 18th Divisional Signal Company R.E. assumed by Captain WILLIS.	
	7th		Permanent track from Div. H.Q. to T.D.O. Test Point (W.8.a.6.2) overhauled and regulated.	
	8th		Artillery permanent lines from Div. Arty. H.Q. to T.D.O. Test Point overhauled and regulated.	
	9th		53rd Infantry Brigade in line relieved by 54th Inf. Bde. on night of 9/10th. 33rd Bde. to move into MARTINSART area. Communications taken over on site.	

Willis
Captain
O.C. 18th DIVL. SIGNAL CO., R.E.

Army Form C. 2118.

(2)

WAR DIARY
or
INTELLIGENCE SUMMARY.
(Erase heading not required.)

18th DIVL. SIGNAL CO., R.E.

FEB 1917

Place	Date	Hour	Summary of Events and Information	Remarks and references to Appendices
	10th		One armoured quad laid overground from MOUQUET FARM. to "E" Test Point (R.28.c.92.)	
	11th		One armoured twin laid overground from MOUQUET FARM to "Z" Test Point (R.28.b.3.8) for communication to Brigade at "Z"	
	12th		Laid 2 armoured quads overground from "Z" to M.G.12. (R.23.c.37) and one armoured twin from "E" to M.G.12 to provide laterals between Brigades	
	13th		One armoured twin laid overground from R.27. central to M.G.12 (Right Brigade) and also one pair D.V. twisted. One armoured twin from "E" to "Z" and one pair D.V. from MOUQUET FARM to "Z" all to provide duplicate lines to Brigades	
	14th		Four linemen to MOUQUET FARM and two to T.S Test Point (X.2.b.0.1) to maintain forward lines. In view of impending active operations an Advanced Divn. H.Q. is to be established in old German dugouts at X.2.a.32. on NAB ROAD and preparations were put in hand for necessary wiring for electric	

Mallin Captain R.E.
O.C. 18th DIVL. SIGNAL CO., R.E.

WAR DIARY
INTELLIGENCE SUMMARY

FEB 1917 — 18th DIVL. SIGNAL CO., R.E.

Army Form C. 2118. (3)

Place	Date	Hour	Summary of Events and Information	Remarks and references to Appendices
	14th (contd)		light system and telegraphic and telephonic communication.	
	15th		55th Brigade relieved by 53rd and 54th Brigades on night of 15/16th. 54th Bde. H.Q. in SUDBURY TRENCH at R.28.b.3.8 and 53rd Bde. H.Q. in ZOLLERN TRENCH at R.23.d.0.4. Communication established with 54th Bde through MOUQUET FARM and thence on armoured twin laid on 11th inst.	
THIRD STREET (X.2.a.3.2)	16th		Advanced Divl. H.Q. established at X.2.a.3.2 (THIRD STREET) old German dug outs. Communication established with all Brigades and units at 12:0 Noon. A small office staff was left at Rear Divnl. H.Q. to maintain communication with D.A.D.O.S. and others in rear.	
	17th		On this date an attack was made by IInd Corps (2nd, 18th and 63rd Divisions) with the object of capturing SOUTH MIRAUMONT TRENCH. The attack of the 18th Division was carried out by the 54th Inf. Bde (Right) and 53rd Inf. Bde (Left); 55th Inf. Bde being in Reserve. A telepl. line to Right Bde of Left Division (63rd) was laid early in the morning, but this	

M. Willis Captain R.E.
O.C. 18th DIVL. SIGNAL CO., R.E.

Army Form C. 2118.

WAR DIARY
INTELLIGENCE SUMMARY.
(Erase heading not required.)

FEB 1917   18th DIVL. SIGNAL CO., R.E.   (4.)

Place	Date	Hour	Summary of Events and Information	Remarks and references to Appendices
	17th (contd)		Line was very little used. There was a very heavy ground mist during the greater part of the day and it was found impossible to use visual, pigeons or aeroplanes. Power Buzzers were installed at R.16.d.9.8. and R.17.d with an "IT" set at R.28.a.8.9 and several important tactical messages from attacking battalions were transmitted back by this means. Wireless was very little used. A Post of 10 runners was established near NAB VALLEY JUNCTION (R.32.b.9.8). All despatches were taken to this post from Advanced Div. Sig. by Motor cyclist and thence to Brigade H.Q. by runners.	
BOUZINCOURT (W.7.d.37)	18th		Advanced Div. H.Q. closed at X.2.a.3.2. at 2.0 pm and all communications were transferred to Rear H.Q. at that hour. An advanced Exchange was left at X.2.a.3.2. for communications to Artillery Brigades and two R.E. Field Companies, and this point was also used as a testing station for forward lines.	
	19th		54th Brigade in line relieved by 55th Inf. Bde. on night of 18/19th. Communications taken over in situ.	

O.C. 18th DIVL. SIGNAL CO., R.E.

Army Form C. 2118.

(5)

WAR DIARY
INTELLIGENCE SUMMARY.
(Erase heading not required.)

18th DIVL. SIGNAL CO., R.E.

Instructions regarding War Diaries and Intelligence Summaries are contained in F.S. Regs., Part II. and the Staff Manual respectively. Title pages will be prepared in manuscript.

FEB 1917

Place	Date	Hour	Summary of Events and Information	Remarks and references to Appendices
	21st		One metallic pair of poled D. Twin laid from "NV" Test Point on IInd Corps bury to Runners Post at NAB VALLEY JUNCTION.	
	22nd		55th Inf. Bde. took over that part of the line held by 53rd Bde and on completion of relief 53rd Bde H.Q. established at WELLINGTON HUTS. One metallic pair of poled cable laid from R.29 Central to 55th Brigade at R.23.C 100.95. This line was finished on 23rd. A poles cable route of two pairs was also laid from MOUQUET FARM to "E" Test Point. This was also finished on 23rd inst.	
	23rd		Two pairs twisted D.V cable laid from "BV" Test Point on IInd Corps bury to WELLINGTON HUTS – new H.Q. of 53rd Inf. Bde. Lines through and communication established at 10.0am. Route poles afterwards. One lineman sent to "QP" Test Point and one to "SB" Test Point for maintenance	
	27th		Party of men from IInd Corps Signals, supplemented by 2 men from company, built a trestle route of 12 pair twisted D.V cable from "QP" Test Point to WARWICK HUTS – proposes new Divnl. H.Q. All	

M.Miller Capt. RE
O. C. 18th DIVL. SIGNAL CO., R.E.

Army Form C. 2118.

WAR DIARY
or
INTELLIGENCE SUMMARY.
(Erase heading not required.)

18th DIVL. SIGNAL CO., R.E.

FEB 1917

Place	Date	Hour	Summary of Events and Information	Remarks and references to Appendices
	27th (contd)		local circuits at these Huts were wired, and interior wiring of new Signal Office, and erection of one 20-line exchange put in hand. Some necessary constructional alterations were made on Signal Office (NISSEN HUT) and electric light mains of D.VI cable laid to the various Headquarters Offices	
	28th		Electric light wiring and interior communication wiring of (WARWICK HUTS) completed and 2 20-line exchanges erected. Party to continue work on poles cable route from MOUQUET to "E"	

ENCLOSURES.

A. Communication arrangements issued by General Staff for operations on 17th February 1917

B. Copy of arrangements made by 18th Divnl. Signal Coy R.E. for communications on 17th February 1917

C. Straight line diagram of Telephonic communications 18th Divn 21-2-17

[signature] Captain R.E.
O.C. 18th DIVL. SIGNAL CO., R.E.

SECRET.   Copy No. 12

                                                                X.118.

"D" SIGNAL COMMUNICATIONS ISSUED WITH
18TH DIV. INSTRUCTIONS OF FEBRUARY 11TH, 1917.
----

1. The following means of communication will be available for use during the forthcoming operations :-
   (a) Telegraph and Telephone.
   (b) Aeroplane.
   (c) Wireless.
   (d) Visual.
   (e) Pigeons.
   (f) Orderlies.

2. Telegraph and Telephones.

   Advanced Divisional Headquarters at X.2.a.3.3. will be in telephonic and telegraphic communication with

   53rd Bde. H.Q. in ZOLLERN   R.28.b.3.8.
   54th Bde. H.Q. in SUDBURY   R.23.d.0.4.
   (55th Bde.H.Q. is at X.2.a.3.3.)
   The three Field Artillery Brigades of the 18th
      Divisional Artillery,
   The two Field Artillery Brigades of the 31st
      Divisional Artillery.
   2nd Division W.24.b.8.8.
   63rd Division (through Rear Div.H.Q.) W.26.c.1.4.

   The 54th Infantry Brigade will be in communication with the left Brigade of the 2nd Division at R.24.c.5.4.
   The 53rd Brigade with the right Brigade of the 63rd Division (through Advanced Div. H.Q.) at Q.18.a.7.3.

3. Aeroplanes.

   An aeroplane (contact patrol) will be up during the attack.
   The distinguishing mark of this aeroplane will be a black square attached to the rear edge of both wings.

   Communication will be established by means of
(i) Flares. Every man will carry a flare. These will be lit half way through the halt on the first objective, and as soon as the 2nd and 3rd objectives are reached.
   Men of the different waves will be told off to light flares on the different objectives; the mopping up parties might do this on the 1st objective.
   Flares are not required to be lit closer than 50 yards apart.
   A series of "A"s on the Klaxon Horn or white light signals from the aeroplane means that it has not picked up the line, and requires more flares lighting.

(ii) Dropping messages. The aeroplane will drop messages at Divisional Headquarters X.2.a.3.3. which will be marked with a white "K" which will be altered to a white "F" to acknowledge receipt of a message.
   An orderly will be constantly on the look-out for messages.

- 2 -

4. Wireless.

The IInd. Corps Wireless Station at No.10 M.G.Post R.28.a.8.9. will be in communication with the 18th Division Wireless Station at Divisional Headquarters, X.2.a.8.3.
A power buzzer is allotted to each Brigade; they will be in communication with a receiving station established at R.28.a.8.9. The power buzzers will be installed by the signallers of the battalions to which they are allotted, as near the present front line as possible (preferably at Company Headquarters).
The exact locality of these sets should be made known to all runners, in order that, in the event of other methods failing, messages may be transmitted back by this means.

5. Visual Signalling will be established between Battalion and Brigade Hd.Qrs. Brigades will notify Div. Hd.Qrs. of the positions of these Visual Stations.

6. Pigeons.

10 pigeons are allotted to each Brigade. These will be delivered to Brigade Hd.Qrs. under Divisional arrangements.
Brigades will allot them to Battalions, and the pigeons should be sent forward with Company Hd.Qrs. under the charge of the trained pigeon men. Birds will be exchanged every 48 hours, if not required for use. Every effort will be made to bring back all Pigeon Equipment and hand it over to Brigade Hd.Qrs.

7. Runners.

A post of 10 runners will be established near NAB VALLEY junction at R.32.b.9.0.
Despatches will be taken by Motor Cyclist from Advanced Divisional Headquarters to this post and thence by runner to the two Brigade Hd.Qrs. This post will be in telephonic communication with Advanced Div. Hd.Qrs.

8. ACKNOWLEDGE.

February 14th 1917.

Guy. Blewitt Maj
for Lieut-Colonel,
General Staff, 18th Division.

Arrangements made by 18th Divisional Signal Company R.E.

Operations on the 17th February 1917.

1. Lines as in attached diagram.
   (a) Forward Dump of Cable will be established at Runners' Post NAB VALLEY JUNCTION, R.32.b.9.8. This Dump will be in charge of 2nd Lieut Henderson, R.E., who will distribute the Cable as necessary.

   The Dump will consist of:-

   2 miles twisted D.V. Cable. (Portion on D.I. reels.)
   2 miles twisted D.III cable.
   2 miles armoured Twin.
   6 miles D.I. or D.II cable.

   (b) Distribution of personnel according to Table I.

2. **D.R.L.S.** D.R's will run between YRR and NAB VALLEY JUNCTION Runner's Post (R.32.b.9.8.) At this point there will be 10 runners who will take all despatches on to the two Brigades in the line, and the F.A.Brigades according to the following Time Table:

D.R. will leave YRR at	8.0am.	12.30pm.	4.30pm.	8.0pm.
Arrive at Runners Post	8.10am.	12.40pm.	4.40pm.	8.10pm.
Arriving at Brigades	8.40am.	1.10pm.	5.10pm.	8.40pm.
Arriving back at YRR at	9.20am.	1.50pm.	5.50pm.	9.20pm.

   D.R's will leave for Rear Divisional Headquarters, IInd Corps and minor units of the Division according to the following table:-

Leave YRR	7.00am.	12.00 Noon.	6.30pm.
Arrive YR	7.45am.	12.45pm.	7.15pm.
Arrive YRR(on return journey)	8.30am.	1.30pm.	8.00pm.

   Times of D.R.L.S. to IInd Corps will not be altered.

3. **PIGEONS.** Ten pairs of birds will be delivered by Corps Signals each day at 12.30pm at YRR, starting on the 16th. Five pairs of birds will be taken by Despatch Rider and Runner to each Brigade in the Line, and Brigade Signalling Officers will arrange that the birds are sent out to the Battalions the same night.
   Pigeon equipment will be drawn by 53rd and 54th Brigade Signals from MOUQUET FARM.

4. **AEROPLANES.** No signalling to aeroplanes, other than the lighting of flares, will be attempted. Messages will however be dropped by aeroplane (aeroplane contact patrol) at Advanced Divnl. Headquarters. A large "K" of white American cloth will be put out at this point. Two orderlies will be constantly on the lookout for messages throughout the day. When a message has been dropped and safely picked up, the "K" will be altered to "F" as a sign of acknowledgment. The message will be taken straight in to the General Staff.

5. **VISUAL.** No visual will be attempted in rear of Brigade Headquarters.

6.   A system of Power Buzzers and Wireless has been installed in the forward area, with Power Buzzers near the front line at R.16.d.9.8. and R.17.d., working back to an "IT" receiving set at R.28.a.8.9. which is connected by wire to Left Brigade H.Q.s. The Power Buzzer at R.17.d. will be known as ZA, and that at R.16.d.9.8. as ZB, and as these are tuned to the same pitch, ZA will only send between the following times :-

    Zero hour   to Zero plus 10 minutes.
    Zero plus 20 to Zero plus 30 minutes.
    Zero plus 40 to Zero plus 50 minutes etc.

while ZB will also only send between

    Zero plus 10 to Zero plus 20
    Zero plus 30 to Zero plus 40 etc.

Both these sets are complete with buzzers, D.VI leads and good earths, accumulators, and watches which were synchronised before starting. There is also a Wireless station at R.28.a.8.9. which will work back to the receiving station at Advanced Divisional Head Quarters.

7.   Electric Light at Advanced Divisional Headquarters will be installed and in working order by 12-00 noon on 16th. The set will work between the hours of 6-30 a.m. and 12-30 a.m.

15_2_17.

(sd) J.C.Willis, Captain R.E.
O.C. Signals, 18th Division.

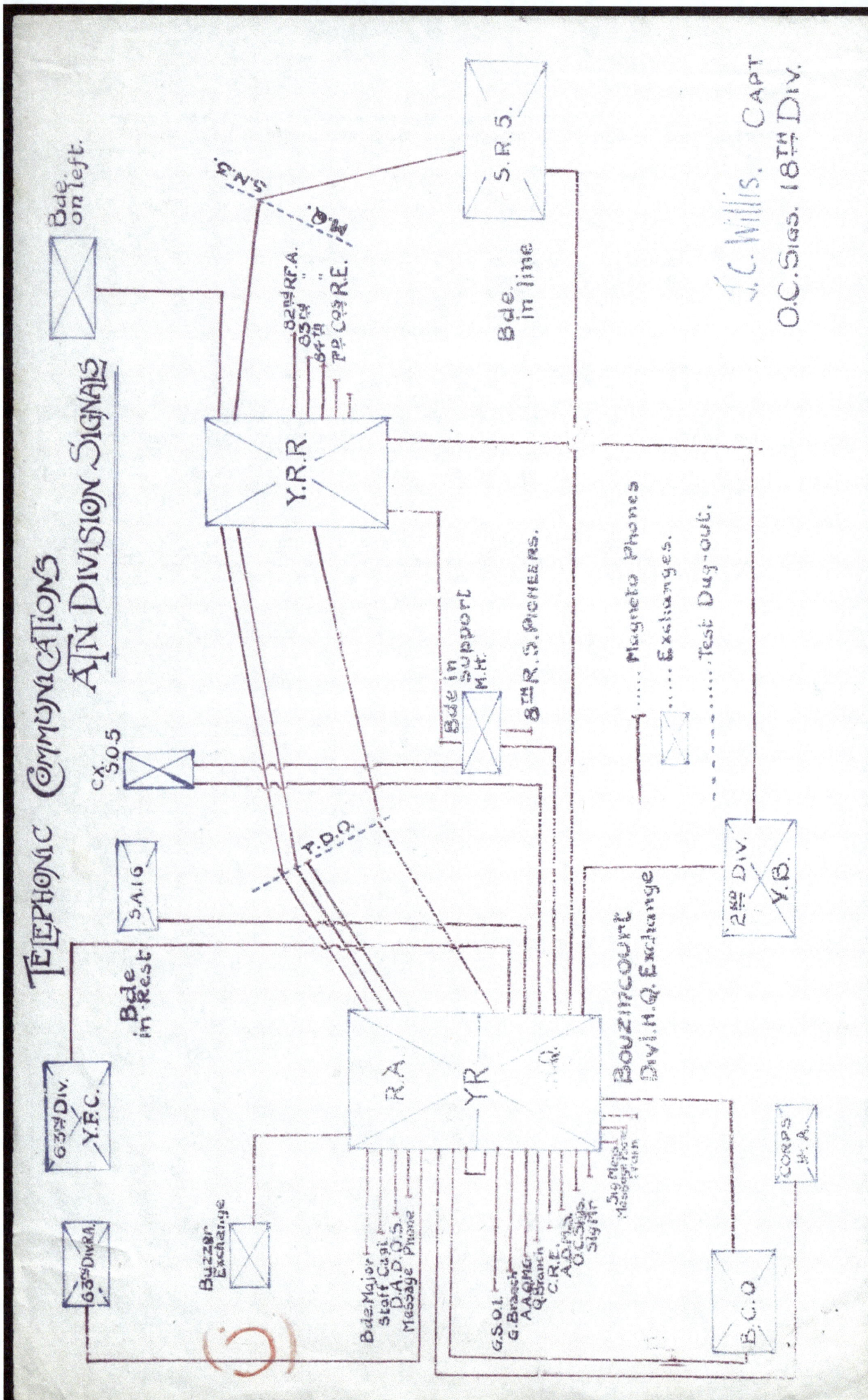

Army Form C. 2118.

WAR DIARY
or
INTELLIGENCE SUMMARY.
(Erase heading not required.)

18th DIVL. SIGNAL CO., R.E.

MAR 1917

Vol-16

Place	Date	Hour	Summary of Events and Information	Remarks and references to Appendices
BOUZINCOURT (W.7.b.7.1)	1st March	10½	Two pairs airline laid on existing 16 line permanent track from CRUCIFIX CORNER to new Divnl. H.Q. at WARWICK HUTS — one pair for Brigade in support at WELLINGTON HUTS. Exchange at CRUCIFIX CORNER closed.	
	2nd "		Started laying two armoured quads from "Z" Test Point to BOOM RAVINE — proposed new Brigade H.Q. Two pairs airline to WARWICK HUTS completed. Work continued on armoured quads from "Z" to BOOM RAVINE.	
	3rd "		All multicore and single cables at entrance to "Z" to be replaced by proper lead-covered lead in. All lines from CRUCIFIX CORNER to WARWICK HUTS overhauled and regulated. Two linemen to "Z" for maintenance. Work continued on armoured quads from "Z" to BOOM RAVINE. Divnl. H.Q. moved from BOUZINCOURT to WARWICK HUTS. Signal Office closed at BOUZINCOURT at 12 Noon and opened at WARWICK HUTS at same hour.	
WARWICK HUTS (X.1.c.9.2)	4th "		Owing to shortage of accommodation at new H.Q. Signal Camp to remain at BOUZINCOURT. Work continued on armoured quads from "Z" to BOOM RAVINE. New lead in at "Z" dug-out continued and all old cable recovered.	

18th DIVL. SIGNAL CO., R.E.

Army Form C. 2118.

(2)

WAR DIARY
or
INTELLIGENCE SUMMARY.
(Erase heading not required.)

18th DIVL. SIGNAL CO., R.E.

MAR 1917

Place	Date	Hour	Summary of Events and Information	Remarks and references to Appendices
Power Buzzr	4th Mar (contd)		Four men from Norfolks and 4 from Essex Regt instructed in use of Power Buzzr.	
	6th "		Armoured guards from "Z" to BOOM RAVINE completed. Exchange at old Advanced Div. H.Q. THIRD STREET closed and a 10-line exchange established at "Z" proposed new Advd Div. H.Q. C.S.M. Palmer proceeded to Fifth Army Signals to take up commission.	
	7th –		Started laying 3 new guards from "Z" to BOOM RAVINE. These are to be laid alongside existing guards on right hand side of railway. One lineman to "Z" Test Point in extra Artillery lineman. One lineman to Advanced Brigade H.Q. for maintenance of forward lines. Lieut T.E.B. Young, O.C. No.4 Section evacuated sick.	
	8th		Work continued on new guards to BOOM RAVINE	
	9th		Party to consolidate forward lines from "Z" to BOOM RAVINE and bury where necessary. These lines were continually being broken by enemy shell fire, as much as 40yds being at one time completely destroyed. Owing to this it was decided to lay a pair of twisted D.V. round another route	

18th DIVL. SIGNAL CO., R.E.
Captain

WAR DIARY
INTELLIGENCE SUMMARY

18th DIVL. SIGNAL CO., R.E.

MAR 1917

Date	Hour	Summary of Events and Information	Remarks
9th Mar. (cont.)		D.V. Cable held throughout the operations. Party recovering cable at 23 Obtained. Div HQ THIRD STREET.	
10th		All lines from "Z" forward consolidated and completed. Recovery of 23 cables at THIRD STREET continued.	
11th		Investigation of old German buried system from MIRAUMONT to IRLES. No successful results.	
12th		All lines from "Z" to SM8 (Brigade HQ) overhauled and repaired. Party recovery 23 cables in back areas. Cpl. J. Burnham D.R. to England for commission in R.F.C.	
13th		Party of 1 N.C.O. and 6 men to "Z" Test Point to lead in all spares and make a new test point at A.11. d.o.w. Party from 2nd Division to lay a lateral line from Brigade on Right to this point. All spares from "Z" to R.C. to be overhauled and strengthened generally and to be buried where necessary. Lieut. T.E.A. Young rejoined No 1 Section from Hospital	
14th		2 Cable Carts with skeleton detachments to proceed to R.11. a.67 under command of 2/Lieut F.A. Henderson R.E. This party laid a twin field cable from R.11. a.67	

18th DIVL. SIGNAL CO., R.E.

Army Form C. 2118.

WAR DIARY
or
INTELLIGENCE SUMMARY
(Erase heading not required.)

18th DIVL. SIGNAL CO., R.E.

MAR 1917

Place	Date	Hour	Summary of Events and Information	Remarks and references to Appendices
	14th (contd)		A.5.a.5.5 and L.35.c.8.3 and thence along road to a position to be selected in IRLES. One Cable Cart (empty) and skeleton detachment to report to Lt Weston at MIRAUMONT at 9.0 a.m to complete in pairs poled Cable to IRLES.	
	15th		2nd Lieut J.L. Henderson R.E. joined for duty from "B" Corps Signal Company. Sgt. E.W. Beer to Signal Service Training Centre BLETCHLEY for commission. No. 3 Cable Cart and skeleton detachment to report to 2nd Lieut Riley R.E. at MIRAUMONT	
	16th		at 9.0 a.m. to lay a line (D.V. Cable) from PY's to Test Point at R.14.d.0.4. Party of 1 N.C.O and 5 O.R to rebuild to fair poled cable route from R.M. a.5.7. to IRLES, which has been partially destroyed by enemy shell fire during the night. 2nd Lt J.H. Turner R.E. joined for duty "X" Establishment.	
	17th		No. 3 Cable Cart and skeleton detachment to take 4 miles D.V. (route) and report to 2nd Lieut Riley R.E. at R.12.a.5.6. on E MIRAUMONT Road to Lay Artillery lines as necessary. No. 3 Detachment to move off at 7.0 a.m with 4 mile D.V. (route) and report to 2nd Lieut Riley to Lay F.A. lines as required.	
	18th		No. 1 Detachment to move off at 7.0 am with 4 miles D.V. (wires), poles etc	

Signed,
Captain R.E.
18th DIVL. SIGNAL CO., R.E.

WAR DIARY
INTELLIGENCE SUMMARY

18th DIVL. SIGNAL CO., R.E.

MAR 1917

(5)

Army Form C. 2118.

Place	Date	Hour	Summary of Events and Information	Remarks and references to Appendices
	18th (contd)		and report to Lieut. Weston at L35.d.4.5. Pair to be laid from end of existing 4-pair track, in L36, to G.27.B.7.9. on IRLES-GREVILLERS Road. Party consisting of 2 N.C.O's and 8 men to billet at L35.d to complete 4-pair route MIRAUMONT to IRLES. Lines to be poles from R.11.a.6.7. to L35.d.in.b. 2/Lieut Turner to take charge. Sergt F.W. Cornish to proceed to Fifth Army Wireless School HARPONVILLE for course of Instruction in Power Buzzzyrs.	
	19th		No. 3 Detachment to leave Camp at 6.0am and report to 2nd Lieut Riley at IRLES. Detachments to take 5 miles D.I wires and Bivouac at BIHUCOURT for work on Artillery lines as necessary.	
	20th		No. 2 Detachment to continue work on line laid yesterday to BIHUCOURT. To strengthen and improve line where necessary. Cpl Knights and party to continue work on 4-pair MIRAUMONT to IRLES. No. 1 and 4 Detachments to complete equipment of wagons and stand by ready to move off at short notice.	
	21st		No. 2 Detachment to salvage cable in forward area.	
	22nd		Orders received for move of Division by march route postponed. Division	

Army Form C. 2118.

WAR DIARY
or
INTELLIGENCE SUMMARY

18th DIVL. SIGNAL CO., R.E.

MAR 1917

Place	Date	Hour	Summary of Events and Information	Remarks and references to Appendices
	22nd (contd)		ordered to move by train, probably 2 days later. Advance party which has been sent to CONTAY (proposed 1st Halt) to open up Report Centre recalled.	
DURY. (AMIENS)	23rd	9.0 am	Company moved to DURY by march route. Moved off from BOUZINCOURT at 9.0 am and arrived at DURY 7.30 pm. Billeted one night at DURY.	
		1.0 pm	Advance party under Lieut. E.W. Benson moved off from WARWICK HUTS at 1.0 pm by lorry with 20-line exchange and necessary instruments. Instructed to proceed to STEENBECQUE — mess Divl. H.Q. — and open up Signal Office. Divnl. H.Q. closed at WARWICK HUTS at 12 noon and Report Centre opened at DURY at same hour.	
	24th		Sgt. Smith and 6 Despatch Riders to dispose of all work at R.C. Company moved by march route from DURY to SALEUX and entrained there for STEENBECQUE. Sgt. Smith and 6 D.R's left at DURY to maintain R.C. for 18th Divn. "Q".	
STEENBECQUE	25th		Company less 7 D.R's and small rear party arrived STEENBECQUE 5.30 pm Divl. H.Q. opened at STEENBECQUE.	
			BERGUETTE. — Communication through BERGUETTE Exchange to 4th Army	
	53rd Inf. Bde			
	54th "		THIENNES. — Pair already in existence from STEENBECQUE	
	55th "		BOESEGHEM. — Pair single line DX cable on 27th.	

Signed 18th DIVL. SIGNAL CO., R.E.

Army Form C. 2118.

WAR DIARY
or
INTELLIGENCE SUMMARY.
(Erase heading not required.)

18th DIVL. SIGNAL CO., R.E.

MAR 1917

(7.)

Instructions regarding War Diaries and Intelligence Summaries are contained in F. S. Regs., Part II. and the Staff Manual respectively. Title pages will be prepared in manuscript.

Place	Date	Hour	Summary of Events and Information	Remarks and references to Appendices
	26th		Division in G.H.Q. Reserve and programmes for training of all personnel issued. All lines laid in back area are to be considered practice lines and laid in accordance with instructions contained in Army Telegraphy and Telephony – Chapter 1.	
	27th		No. 3 Detachment to complete partly existing line to MORBECQUE for use of No. 3 Div. Supply Col. Capt. J. Castillo granted leave. Command assumed by Capt. C. Adlam R.E. No. 4 Detachment to lay single D.V. line to 55th Brigade at BOESEGHEM. "P" Cable Section attached for duty on and from to-day. Lieut. G.F. Chute transferred to "O" Corps Signal Coy; 2nd Lt. Henderson R.E. to be O.C. No. 4 Section.	
	28th			
	(26th)			
	29th to 31st		All Cable Carts, wagons, limbers etc. were thoroughly overhauled and painted and repairs where necessary. Equipment of all kinds inspected and all deficiencies made good. All available now employed on construction of horse standings and about 6 tons of clinker transported from STEENBECQUE Station for this purpose. Average strength of Company during month :- 6 officers 210 O.R. Horses 95.	
			Awards during month :- Lieut. G.F. Chute R.E. Military Cross	
			Sapper J. Dyer Military Medal	
			Pioneer W. Jones –do–	
			2nd Cpl. J. Clarkson Bar to Military Medal	

Enclosures (A) Diagram of Power Buzzer and "IT" Sets
(B) Diagram of Lines 10-3-17

[signature]
Capt. R.E.
18th DIVL. SIGNAL CO., R.E.

SECRET (A)

Scheme of Power Buzzers and "IT"s.

Map Ref. L35d 5.4.

Map Ref. Mic 85. [Boulder Redoubt]

Div. Station R116+3.

53rd Adv. Bde. H.Q. R11a 6.9.

Telephone

Corps Station. R.24 Central

53rd Rear Bde. H.Q.

To 18th Division

Telephone

Power Buzzer.

Listening Set.

NOTE:—
The Red Arrows indicate the directions in which messages can be sent from the various stations.

18th DIVL. SIGNAL CO., R.E.

Communications 18th Division.

(1) Scheme of ? ? & ?? ?
(2) Diagram of lines 10.3-17

Army Form C. 2118.

WAR DIARY
or
INTELLIGENCE SUMMARY.
(Erase heading not required.)

18th DIVL. SIGNAL CO., R.E.

APR 1917

Place	Date	Hour	Summary of Events and Information	Remarks and references to Appendices
STEENBECQUE	1st		From 1st to 25th the Division less Divisional Artillery were on G.H.Q. Reserve, II Corps, First Army. Divisional H.Q. at STEENBECQUE 53rd Inf. Bde. H.Q. " BERGUETTE 54th do. do. " THIENNES. 55th do. do. - BOESEGHEM. Lines to all these places were allotted on existing permanent line, cable, and airline routes.	
	3rd		Divisional Artillery joined the Division on 3rd April and Artillery H.Q. were established at HAZEBROUCK. Corps Signals were unable to allot a line and one of D.V. twisted cable was laid from STEENBECQUE to HAZEBROUCK on 4th April.	
	4th		A new line was also laid on 14th to 55th Bde. H.Q. at BOESEGHEM. During the period in Reserve much useful training was carried out and all cable carts, wagons, limbers etc were thoroughly overhauled, painted, and repaired where necessary. Technical stores, instruments etc were	

O.C. 18th DIVL. SIGNAL CO., R.E.

Army Form C. 2118.

WAR DIARY
or
INTELLIGENCE SUMMARY
(Erase heading not required.)

18th DIVL. SIGNAL CO., R.E.

APR 1917

(2)

Place	Date	Hour	Summary of Events and Information	Remarks and references to Appendices
			checks and deficiencies indents for. All lines which it was found necessary to erect were looked upon as practice lines and laid strictly in accordance with Instructions contained in Army Telegraphy and Telephony. In addition to this each Cable Detachment in its turn was sent out at short notice under its own Detachment Commander to lay and maintain tactical lines under conditions as near as possible to those which might reasonably be expected in moving warfare. Cable laying competitions between rival Detachments were held and encouraged, some very good results being obtained. Visual signalling by all methods was practised daily and all the latest devices experimented with. A Power Buzzer School was established and it is now for Infantry Battalion trainees in the use of these instruments which had proved very successful in previous operations. Twentyfour men per Infantry Brigade were trained in the working and care of pigeons. Moving off at short notice was also thoroughly practised and backs wagon allotted to definite loads. A Divisional Exercise was carried out on 9th April, communications being arranged in accordance with attached later marked "A". These arrangements	

O.C. 18th DIVL. SIGNAL CO., R.E.
Major R.E.

Army Form C. 2118.

(3)

WAR DIARY
or
INTELLIGENCE SUMMARY
(Erase heading not required.)

APR 1917

18th DIVL. SIGNAL CO., R.E.

Place	Date	Hour	Summary of Events and Information	Remarks and references to Appendices
PERNES.	26th		were entirely satisfactory. Division transferred from Gen H.Q. Reserve in II Corps to VII Corps, transfer to be completed by 12 Noon on 27th.	
			Company moved from STEENBECQUE to PERNES by march route arriving at the latter place at 5·30pm	
			Divisional H.Q. at PERNES	
			53rd Inf Bde H.Q. " NOEUX-LES-MINES	
			54th " H.Q. " PERNES area.	
			55th " H.Q. - BETHUNE	
			Communications with 53rd and 55th Infantry Brigades through Third Army and BETHUNE Exchanges and with 54th Infantry Brigade by D.R.	
HABARCQ	27th		Divisional H.Q. less "G" and "Q" Staff moves by march route from PERNES to HABARCQ	
NEUVILLE VITASSE (M.16.d.I.I.) (Sheet 51 B.)	28th		Advance party consisting of Signal Office Staff and known sent forward by lorry to new Divisional Headquarters with instructions to take over communications from 30th Div. Signal Coy. Four Runners to NEUVILLE VITASSE, 2 to "THE EGG"	

W. Wallis Major R.E.
O.C. 18th DIVL. SIGNAL CO., R.E.

Army Form C. 2118.

WAR DIARY
or
INTELLIGENCE SUMMARY.
(Erase heading not required.)

18th DIVL. SIGNAL CO., R.E.

APR 1917

Place	Date	Hour	Summary of Events and Information	Remarks and references to Appendices
	29th		Test Point and 2 to HENINEL for maintenance. One Signal office relief and 6 D.R's left at PERNES to maintain communications for "G" and "Q" Staffs. Company less Signal Office Staff and horsemen moved from HARARCQ to AGNY by march route arriving at the latter place at 1-35pm. Camped in large fires at M.8.b.7.8 Sheet 51.B. 8 reinforcements for road changes in Establishment joined from Corps Wing signals and were detailed to Cable Detachments; the 8 operators replaced being transferred to H.Q. Section. All communications at Advanced Div. H.a. M.18 & 11 Sheet 51.B taken over and a Subb Office established at AGNY for use of 18th Div. "Q" (Rear) D. A.D.V.S. and 18th Div. Train. "G" and "Q" offices closed at PERNES at 12 Noon and opened at new H.Q. at same hour. Considerable improvement ——— to all existing lines was necessary before superimposed counter working could be introduced. ———— A complete new system of Artillery lines was to be laid to	

Willis
Major R.E.
O.C. 18th DIVL. SIGNAL CO., R.E.

Army Form C. 2118.

WAR DIARY
or
INTELLIGENCE SUMMARY.

(Erase heading not required.)

18th DIVL. SIGNAL CO., R.E.

APR 1917

(5)

Place	Date	Hour	Summary of Events and Information	Remarks and references to Appendices
	30th		Provide the necessary communications for 18th Divisional Artillery. New D.V. pair laid from N.30.A.07 to Brigade H.Q. at N.28.C. central. Sub. Office moved from AGNY to ACHICOURT. Superseding counter from Advanced Div: H.Q. and a telephone Exchange with the following subscribers :— "A" Office; Signal Mess; S.S.O. and D.A.D.O.S.	
			Average strength of Company during month 6 Officers, 212 O.R., 95 horses	

ENCLOSURES
A. Communications for Divisional defence on 9th April 1917
B. Training Programme.

[signature] Major RE
O C 18th DIVL SIGNAL CO., R.E.

18th Divisional Signal Company R.E.

Ref. 1/40,000 map,
Sheet 36a Edition 6.

8th April, 1917.

ORDERS FOR SPECIAL EXERCISE.

Scheme.

Communication will be maintained between Division and Brigades as follows:-

1. Field Cable. (Telegraph vibrator and Telephone.)
2. Wireless.
3. Despatch Riders.

Communications existing on night April 8/9th.

1. (a). Field Cable to 54th Brigade at BOESEGHEM. (Existing)

   (b). No line will be laid to 55th Brigade, traffic to be disposed of by runners.

2. Wireless. - Reserved for move.

3. D.R's to be detailed as follows:-

   1 to report to 54th Brigade BOESEGHEM.

   1 "   "   " 55th   "   STEENBECQUE.

   2 "   " at Div.Signal Office STEENBECQUE.

N.B. These D.R's will actually report and be in position by 8.30a.m. on April 9th.

Communication on April 9th.

DETAILS.

1. (a). No.1 Detachment will report at H.Q., 55th Brigade STEENBECQUE (Signal Office) at 8.0a.m. April 9th. Feeds for horses and haversack rations for men.
Dress:- Marching order.
10 miles D.V. single to be carried. A Base (Vibrator) Office to be established in Signal Office and Detachment will stand by for orders.

No.3 Detachment to report as above as reserve, or for lateral communication if required.

No.4 Detachment R.E. Limber wagon will report as above for transport of Wireless Set when Brigade moves. Cpl. Knights to accompany this limber. (Mounted or bicycle)

2.

1. (b). No.2 Detachment will report at Signal Office 54th Bde., H.Q., BOESEGHEM at 8.0a.m.
Dress etc., as above. Detachment to carry 10 miles D.V. Cable and keep Brigade in touch with Division by extending existing line to 55th Brigade, or pick up 54th Brigade line if Brigade moves that way.

The limber of this Detachment will carry Wireless Set and "IT" when Brigade moves.

2. (a). Brigades will be kept in touch with Division by Wireless.
Personnel and Set for 55th Brigade H.Q. to be at Signal Office at 7.30a.m. Transport will be provided by No.4 Detachment
This transport will also carry "IT".

(b). Personnel and Set for 54th Brigade H.Q. to be in position by 8.0a.m. April 9th.
Corps Wireless Officer will arrange transport to 54th Brigade H.Q. Transport will be provided by No.2 Detachment if Brigade moves.

3. Sergeant Smith will detail D.R's as follows, to be in position by 8.30AM.

    1 for 54th Bde. H.Q. — BOESEGHEM.
    1 " 55th " " — STEENBECQUE.
    2 " Div. H.Q. — STEENBECQUE.

8th April, 1917.

Captain R.E.
O.C. Signals, 18th Division.

Copies to:-

1 O.C. Sigs.
2 Signal Office.
3 No.1 Detachment.
4 No.2 "
5 O.C. Wireless.
6 C.S.M.
7 ————

TRAINING OF SIGNAL PERSONNEL.

The following is submitted as an outline of arrangements made for training of Signal Personnel. Owing to billeting difficulties and varying requirements of units, the classes and schools have been decentralised.

SIGNAL COMPANY R.E.

Headquarters and No.1 Section.

6 hours per week.	Visual methods.	(Flag, Helio, Lamp - Day & Night.)
2 days per week.	Cable Drill.	
2 hours per week.	" " Fast.	
2 hours per week.	Infantry Drill.	
1 day per week.	Field Scheme.	(Moving Div. & Bde. H.Q's.

Periodical lectures on Horse Management; Harness fitting; Economy (care of equipment etc.); Map reading; Instruments; etc., etc.

A Riding School will be started at an early date.

BRIGADE SIGNAL SECTIONS.

2 days per week.	Field Line Drill.	
5 " " "	Visual methods.	(Flag, Helio, Lamps, Shutters
3 hours per week.	Infantry Drill.	
1 day per week.	Combined Field Line and Runner Scheme.	

Periodical lectures on Instruments; Economy (care of equipment etc.); Map reading; Aeroplane signalling.

R.F.A. BRIGADES.

Schools will be established and instructional personnel found by Divisional Signal Company and R.F.A. Brigades. Courses in the following for all signallers:-

    Flag Drill.   )
    Lamp signalling. (day & night.)   )
    Station work.   ) 5 hours per day.
    Buzzer practice.   )
    Cable laying.   )
    Lectures, etc.   )

An Officer has been detailed to supervise these schools.

INFANTRY BATTALIONS & R.E. SIGNALLERS.

Brigade Signal Officers will supervise training, and schools have been arranged for courses in:-

```
Flag Drill.                        )
Lamp signalling. (day & night.)    )   5 hours per day.
French shutters.                   )
Buzzer practice.                   )
```

Lectures on Instruments; Linemens' work; and Map reading.

Instructional staff will be found from Battalions and Brigade Signal Section.

A Power Buzzer course will start on April 3rd for 16 battalion signallers.
Instructional Staff for this course being found by Wireless Section. (vide 18/SXR/725.)

Arrangements are being made for training further battalion men in the care and use of pigeons.

Arrangements have also been made for a special course for battalion and R.F.A. signallers on a scale of 2 per battalion and R.F.A. brigade.
The course will last 6 weeks and will be under Corps instructional personnel.

8-4-17

Captain. RE.
O.C 18th Div. Signal Coy. RE.

Army Form C. 2118.

WAR DIARY
~~INTELLIGENCE SUMMARY~~
(Erase heading not required.)

18th DIVL. SIGNAL CO., R.E.

MAY 1917

Vol 18

Instructions regarding War Diaries and Intelligence Summaries are contained in F.S. Regs., Part II. and the Staff Manual respectively. Title pages will be prepared in manuscript.

Place	Date	Hour	Summary of Events and Information	Remarks and references to Appendices
NEUVILLE VITASSE. M (Sheet 51b)	1st May		Regulating and straightening lines round Camp.	
	2nd "		Reconstructing and labelling routes from Div. H.Q.	
	3rd "		Lieut. T.E.B. YOUNG, (3rd Yorks) Signal Officer 55th Inf. Bde. wounded. Active operations in conjunction with 14th and 21st Divisions. All communications held good throughout. No's 1 and 2 Detachments under 2nd Lieut CN Riley RE and 2nd Lieut J A Henderson RE. respectively standing by ready to lay forward lines if required.	
	5th "		Working parties to continue straightening up of lines and complete labelling. Poles D.V. line laid from BEAURAINES to AGNY Sub-office to replace existing faulty buried line.	
	8th "		Working party to complete poling line No. 102 and straighten line No. 101. No's 1 and 3 Detachments to build 2 pairs poles D.V. from N.33.b. central to 83rd Bde R.F.A.	
	10th "		Present 53rd Bde. H.Q. (N.22.d.5.4) and 1 pair poles D.V. from N.33.b. central to 83rd Bde R.F.A. Company Hars Signal Office Staffs at Advanced D.H.Q. and AGNY Sub-office.	

/Martin/ Major RE
OC 18th DIVL. SIGNAL CO., R.E.

WAR DIARY
INTELLIGENCE SUMMARY

18th DIVL. SIGNAL CO., R.E.

MAY 1917

Date	Hour	Summary of Events and Information
11th		to leave Camp at 10 a.m. and march to BOISLEUX ST. MARC, and bivouac near proposed new Divisional H.Q.
		Line (D.V. pair) run from new Camp BOISLEUX ST MARC to "Tee" into line from 18th Div Amm Col. to MERCATEL Exchange to provide temporary communication to Y.R.
		30th Div. Detachment to lay D.V. pair from proposed new Div H.Q. to pick up line to 118th and 149th Bdes R.F.A.
		No.3 Detachment to lay D.V. pair from end of P.L. at N.33.b. central to 281st Brigade R.F.A.
13th		Working party laying local lines and wiring up Signal Office at new D.H.Q.
		Two armoured grads laid from S.5.d.70. along HENIN-WANCOURT line to N.27.c.2.5., thence along 80 contour to Brigade in line N.22.d.4.4. Cables to be laid in above line so as to get mechanical protection.
		30th Div Detachment to continue building line from 149th Brigade R.F.A. to new Div. H.Q. and to build a line (D.III. pair) from new Div. H.Q. to 30th Div. Amm Col.
		Working parties from 281 A.T. Coy R.E. and Irish Labour Battalion to be

J. Walter
Major R.E.
O.C. 18th DIVL. SIGNAL CO., R.E.

Army Form C. 2118.

WAR DIARY
or
INTELLIGENCE SUMMARY
(Erase heading not required.)

18th DIVL. SIGNAL CO., R.E.

MAY 1917

Place	Date	Hour	Summary of Events and Information	Remarks and references to Appendices
	14th		Employed reeling up disused cables. All lines to new Div. H.Q. to be connected up and tested. Comic airline route from New Div. H.Q. to end of guards in WANCOURT LINE to be commenced forthwith. Four pairs armoured to Brigade in line to be completed and spur of 2 pairs armoured taken from about T.1.b.0.5. to Brigade in support at N.25.c.44. One pair on armoured quad route to be split at T.1.b.0.5. and looped into Brigade in support by means of above 2 pair spur to provide communication between Division and Brigade in support and between the latter and Brigade in line.	
BOISLEUX. ST. MARC. (S.17.a.8.4.) (Sheet 51B)	15th		Div. H.Q. closed at M.18.b. at 10.0am and reopen at New H.Q. at S.17.a.8.4. at same hour. New Lineman's Post to be established at ST. MARTIN and to be connected to New Div. H.Q. on No.3 pair on P.L. The "EGG" Lineman's Post to close and linemen to be established at	

[signature] Major R.E.
O.C. 18th DIVL. SIGNAL CO., R.E.

Army Form C. 2118.

WAR DIARY
or
INTELLIGENCE SUMMARY
(Erase heading not required.)

18th DIVL. SIGNAL CO., R.E.

MAY 1917

Place	Date	Hour	Summary of Events and Information	Remarks and references to Appendices
	16th		T.2.C. on permanent route. MERCATEL Exchange to close at 10.0am and 14gth Brigade to be put through to new Div. H.Q. at 10.0am. Airline party to complete airline route as follows:- 6 pairs Div. H.Q. to Camp and 4 pairs from Camp to S.S.d.7.0.	
	17th		WANCOURT LINE armoured route to be completed. 6-pair airline route to be regulated and strengthened. One pair Comic airline to be laid from Div. H.Q. to S.S.O. No.3 Detachment laid D.Y. pair from 14g Bde. RFA to pick up No.4 on P.L.	
	18th		7-pair lead covered cable to be laid in HINDENBURG TUNNEL from lower end of Tunnel to present British Front line. Cable to be fixed by tin clips to roof of Tunnel.	
	19th		Parties to continue laying 7-pair cable in HINDENBURG TUNNEL. Battalion Signalling Officers of 53rd and 55th Brigades instructed in use of Field Cypher.	

[signature]
Major R.E.
O.C. 18th DIVL. SIGNAL CO., R.E.

WAR DIARY
or
INTELLIGENCE SUMMARY

Army Form C. 2118.

MAY 1917 — **18th DIVL. SIGNAL CO., R.E.**

Place	Date	Hour	Summary of Events and Information	Remarks and references to Appendices
	20th		Work on 7 pair lead-covered cable in HINDENBURG Tunnel continued and 4 armoured quads laid from No. 8 Entrance to connect up with existing permanent route.	
	21st		7 pair lead covered cable to be continued as far as BROWN TRENCH and Test Box fitted at No. 8 Entrance. Battalion Signalling Officers of 54th Brigade instructed in Field Cypher. Two pair airline built from Div. H.Q. to D. A.D.O.S. at S.9.d Central, one pair to pick up existing D.A.C. line at S.10.d.	
	22nd		Quad route from HINDENBURG TUNNEL to permanent route NXO8 regulated and strengthened. No 3 Detachment laid D.V pair for lateral communication between 281st and 280th Field Artillery Brigades. Two pair airline to D. A.D.O.S. completed.	
	23rd 24th		7 pair lead covered cable completed as far as BROWN TRENCH. Fourth arm on comic airline route between Div H.Q. and S.12.C.3.6. Buzzer line to 83rd Field Artillery Brigade transferred to this route and	

M Mellor
Major R.E.
O.C. 18th DIVL. SIGNAL CO., R.E.

WAR DIARY
or
INTELLIGENCE SUMMARY

(Erase heading not required.)

18th DIVL. SIGNAL CO., R.E.

MAY 1917

Army Form C. 2118.

6

Place	Date	Hour	Summary of Events and Information	Remarks and references to Appendices
	24th (cont.) 25th		Fullerphone working instituted. About 60 yards of 7 pair lead covered cable in HINDENBURG TUNNEL destroyed by fire on night of 24th/25th. Repairs and through about 1-2pm. D.III pair pole Cable laid from 3rd Kite Balloon Wing Exchange at R 22. d. 29 to No 3 Divs Supply Col at WAILLY to give communication between Divs H.Q. and Supply Column.	
	27th		Comic G.S. pair built from S. 12. c. 3.6 to 83rd Field Artillery Brigade to replace existing cable line.	
	28th to 3rd		Clearing up and salvaging all disused lines in forward area. Under instructions from Signal Staff all earth return lines were cut and relies up except those on which Fullerphones were in use. This was rendered necessary owing to the fact that Amplifiers in the Divisional area were picking up many messages which might also have been overheard by the enemy and so might have conveyed useful information to him. After earth return lines were cut a big improvement was observed and very few communications of any tactical importance were picked up.	

[signature] Major R.E.
O.C. 18th DIVL. SIGNAL CO., R.E.

Army Form C. 2118.

WAR DIARY
or
INTELLIGENCE SUMMARY.
(Erase heading not required.)

18th DIVL. SIGNAL CO, R.E.

MAY 1917

Place	Date	Hour	Summary of Events and Information	Remarks and references to Appendices
			By our Amplifiers.	
			Honours & Awards during month:- Lieut. F E PELHAM-CLINTON RE - Awarded Military Cross	
			Lieut. (Acty/Captain) J A WESTON (1st S/Lancs) Mentioned in Dispatch dated 9th April 1917	
			No. 23338. A/2/Cpl. W. N. ELLOR R.E. Mentioned in Dispatch dated 9th April 1917	
			No. 24933. Lce/Cpl (Acty/Cpl) F.W.J. KNIGHT R.E. - do - - do -	
			Average Strength of Company during month:- Officers - 6	
			O.R. - 229	
			Horses - 95	
			Enclosures:-	
			"A" Arrangements for Communications on 3rd May 1917 - Operations against CHERISY.	
			"B" Route Diagram of Divisional Communications	
			"C" Straight-line Diagram of Lines	

Murphy
Major R.E.
O.C. 18th DIVL. SIGNAL CO., R.E.

War Diary.

"A"

1.

Arrangements made by 18th Divisional Signals for the forthcoming
Operations.
_____

Signal Communications for the forthcoming offensive will be dealt with under the following headings:-

(i) Telephone and Telegraph systems.
(ii) D.R.L.S. and Runners.
(iii) Pigeons.
(iv) Wireless and Power Buzzers.
(v) Visual
(vi) Aeroplane Contact Patrol.

(i). The Telephone system will consist of Exchanges at Rear Div. Headquarters, AGNY (M.9.a.7.4.); Advanced Divisional H.Q. at M.18.b.1.1 54th Inf. Bde. H.Q. at HENINEL (N.22.d.5.1.); and an Artillery Exchange at MERCATEL.
Of the H.Q. Offices, the Rear Divisional H.Q. Exchange at AGNY will serve S.S.O. and D.A.D.O.S.; the Advanced Divisional Exchange will serve "G", "A" & "Q", Divisional Artillery and C.R.E. These Exchanges will be connected by trunk lines. There will be direct lines from the Advanced Divisional Exchange to all 3 Infantry Brigades, to the 2 Artillery Brigades of the 18th Division, to VIIth Corps, to VIIth Corps C.R.A., to VIIth Corps Heavies, to the 14th Divnl. H.Q. on the Left at N.7.d.central (Sheet 51b.) and the 21st Divisional H.Q. on the Right at S.22.d.4.5. (Sheet 51b.), to the Forward Exchange at Brigade H.Q. near HENINEL, to the Corps Wireless Directing Station at NEUVILLE-VITASSE, to 18th D.A.C. and to MERCATEL Artillery Exchange.
On the Forward Exchange at Infantry Brigade H.Q. near HENINEL, there will be additional lines to the 2 Infantry Brigades in the line, to the 2 Artillery Brigades of the 18th Division (this giving duplicate lines from the Division), to the 280th and 281st Artillery Brigades of the 56th Divisional Artillery and to the Artillery Exchange at MERCATEL. From the MERCATEL Artillery Exchange there will be lines to the 148th and 149th F.A.B's of the 30th Divisional Artillery, to the 30th Divisional Ammunition Column and to the 73rd H.A.G. as well as the trunk lines to 18th Divisional Exchange, and 18th Advanced Exchange. There will also be lines from the 54th and 55th Brigade Exchanges to the Infantry Brigades on our Right and Left, belonging to the 21st and 14th Divisions respectively.

The Telegraph system will consist of Sounder lines from Advanced 18th Divisional H.Q. Signal Office to the 3 Infantry Brigades, to the Rear Divisional H.Q. Signal Office near AGNY, and one line to the 82nd and 83rd F.A.B's.

The above systems are all of poled or ground cables, with the exception of the lines to the Infantry and the 2 lines to the Artillery Brigades, which are of Permanent line. The general run of the forward lines is:-

       18th Advanced Divisional Headquarters.
       NEUVILLE-VITASSE Test Station.
       "The EGG"   Test Station.
       Infantry Brigade Headquarters near HENINEL.

There will be linemen at all the above points, and lines are laid as far as possible along different routes between Test points.

(ii). D.R.L.S. and Runners. There will be regular services of Motor Cyclist Despatch Riders between 18th Advanced Divisional H.Q., 18th Divisional Rear H.Q. and VIIth Corps, and also a regular service of Mounted Orderlies from 18th Advanced Divisional H.Q. and the Infantry and Artillery Brigades.

(ii) D.R.L.S. and Runners. (contd). D.R's will leave 18th Divisional Advanced H.Q. for 7th Corps at:-

        8.30 a.m.
        2.30 p.m.
        9.30 p.m.

D.R's will leave 18th Divisional Advanced H.Q. for 18th Div. Rear H.Q. at:-

        8.30 a.m.
        10.30 a.m.
        3.00 p.m.
        9.30 p.m.   arriving at 18th Advanced Div. H.Q. on their return journey about one hour later in each case.

Time Table for Mounted Orderlies is as follows:-

Leave 18th Div. Advd. H.Q.	8.30am.	10.30am.	3.00pm	9.30pm
Arrive Brigade H.Q.	9.30am.	11.30am.	4.00pm	10.30pm
Leave Brigade H.Q.	7.00am.	12.Noon.	4.30pm	8.00pm
Arrive 18th Div. Advd. H.Q.	8.00am.	1.00pm.	5.30pm	9.00pm

Mounted Orderlies will be stationed at 18th Advd. Div. H.Q. and also at Brigade H.Q. (in the Line.)

(iii). Pigeons. The VIIth Corps Pigeon Loft is at SIMENCOURT, which is in telephonic communication with VIIth Corps. There are 40 birds available for use of 18th Division, which will give an allotment of 10 birds per Infantry Brigade per day. These birds are brought up by a Corps Despatch Rider to 18th Advd. Div. H.Q. at 9.30 each morning and will be sent on to the Brigades by Divisional Orderly. They will be allotted by Brigades to their Battalions according to tactical requirements. It is recommended that these pigeons be sent forward with Company Headquarters, and if the birds are not required they should be released 24 hours after delivery.

Average time of flight of pigeon from front line to Pigeon Loft is about 20 minutes.

(iv). Wireless and Power Buzzers. The VIIth Corps Wireless Directing Station will be at NEUVILLE-VITASSE, which will be in telephonic communication with 18th Advd. Div. H.Q. Two Trench Wireless Sets, two Power Buzzers and one Amplifier have been allotted to 18th Division. One Trench Wireless Set working back to the Corps Directing Station and also the Amplifier will be set up at N.29.a.10.4. The Amplifier will receive messages from the 2 Power Buzzers which will be stationed at Battalion H.Q. at O.25.d.6.5. and O.31.b.0.5. respectively. The Second Trench Wireless Set will be held in readiness at N.30.c.1.6. to move forward after objectives have been obtained, and will be set up under orders of Divisional Signals. All messages sent by Power Buzzer before Zero hour must be in B.A.B. Code. An Officer should be detailed by each Brigade to act as "encoder" of messages at each battalion H.Q. After Zero hour, however, messages may be sent in clear by order of an Officer.

(v). Visual. A Divisional Visual Station has been established near NEUVILLE-VITASSE at N.20.a.2.4., and a Brigade Visual Station at N.22.c.4.5. Messages can be sent between these stations in either direction by Daylight Signalling Lamps.

Battalion Visual Stations have been established as follows:-

   (a). O.31.b.1.3. working to N.22.d. central. Messages can only be sent from front to rear.

   (b). O.25.d.6.5. working to the Quarry at M.30.b.6.2.

(vi) <u>Aeroplane Contact Patrol.</u>   No signalling to aeroplanes will be attempted.

Aeroplane Contact Patrol in VIIth Corps area is distinguished by one black band under starboard lower plane.   Dropping grounds will be at VIIth Corps H.Q. and 18th Advd. Divisional H.Q.

1st May, 1917.

J. C. WILLIS   Captain R.E.
O.C. Signals, 18th Division.

SCHEME FOR DIVISIONAL SIGNALLING SCHOOL.
18th DIVISION.

1. **OBJECTS OF THE SCHOOL.**

    (a). To train Signallers of the Infantry and Artillery. The students who are nominated for this course must know the Morse Code and must be able to read and write.

    (b). To train Battalion Signalling Officers in Fullerphone, Power Buzzer, Pigeons and any other recent development of Signalling.

2. **NUMBERS OF STUDENTS.**

    (a). Each Battalion will furnish - 4 men.
    (b). Each Battery will furnish   - 2 men.
    (c). The D.A.C. will furnish   - 4 men.
    (d). Signal Company will furnish - 5 men.
    (e). M.G. Companies will furnish - 1 man.

                              TOTAL.   86 men.

3. **INSTRUCTORS.**

    1 Commandant.
    6 N.C.O. Instructors.

    N.B. The above will be permanently attached for duty with the School. The Signal Company will provide 1 Officer to act as Commandant, also 1 N.C.O.
    The remaining 5 N.C.O. Instructors will be found by the 3 Infantry Brigades and the Artillery of the Division.

    Also:-
        1 N.C.O. for Lectures on Instruments.
        1   "   "   "   " Power Buzzers.
        1   "   "   "   " Pigeons.
    N.B. These will be found by the Signal Company.

4. **ACCOMMODATION.**

    The following will be required:-

        2 Marquees.
        6 Bell Tents.
    N.B. It will be absolutely necessary to have Marquee Tents for lecturing to the School in wet weather.

5. Each student will bring with him:- 1 Large white flag and 1 Small blue and 1 Small white flag.

6. The School will be held at BOISLEUX ST.MARC and will open on June 1st.

7. The Course of Instruction will last 6 weeks and will be so arranged that each week will be a short course in itself; i.e., that a certain amount of instruction will be given in all forms of Signalling. Each successive week, therefore, the students will undergo a more advanced course than the last, untill finally after the last week they will have the whole. Thus, if the Division were moved from this area and the Signalling

2.

School were forced to disband, the portion of the course would be more or less complete in itself and would be anyhow of some use to the students.

8. Arrangements will be made for each Battalion Signalling Officer of the Division to undergo a short "Refresher" course of 1 week with the Divisional School, i.e., 2 Battalion Signalling Officers would be at the School at the same time. These Officers could be spared by the Battalion in Rest.

9. Any student who does not make satisfactory progress at the School will be sent straight back to his Battery or Battalion.

10. The course will include instruction in the following:-

    (a). Flag Drill.
         Flag and Disc: reading and sending.
         Buzzer: " " "
         Lamp: " " "
         Helio: " " "
         Station work connected with the above.

    (b). Theory of Telephony.
         Telephone D.Mk.III.
                " Trench 100.
         Fullerphone, 3 patterns.
         Buzzer Exchange.
         Magneto Exchange.
         The Lucas Lamp.
         The French Lamp.
         The Heliograph.
         The Telescope and Binoculars.

    (c). Signalling to Aeroplanes by Lamp and Ground Shutter.

    (d). Lectures on Office Work connected with Signalling.

    (e). Care of Cables in the Field and in Trench Warfare.

    (f). Power Buzzers and Amplifiers.

    (g). Pigeons.

11. Examinations will be held at the end of every fortnight.

26th May, 1917.   Major R.E.,
                                O.C. Signals, 18th Division.

Communications — 18th Division

(1.) Army Form C. 2118.

WAR DIARY
INTELLIGENCE SUMMARY

(Erase heading not required.)

18th DIVL. SIGNAL CO., R.E.

JUN 1917

Vol 19

Place	Date	Hour	Summary of Events and Information	Remarks and references to Appendices
BOISLEUX-ST. MARC. (S.17.a 8.4) (Sheet 51b)	1st		Four pairs armoured quad laid from forward termination of P.L. to join up with quads feeding HINDENBURG TUNNEL Route. Old cable line to 83rd Bde. R.F.A. reeled up.	
	2nd		All D.V. cables running from terminal pole on permanent route to Brigade in line poles.	
	3rd		Armoured quad laid from end of HINDENBURG TUNNEL route along BROWN TRENCH for communication to proposed Battalion H.Q. at N.36.d.00. Armoured quad laid from junction of CABLE and BROWN TRENCHES at T.6.a.8.9 to proposed Battalion H.Q. in CONCRETE TRENCH at N.36.c.67.	
	4th		D.v. pair poled cable laid from terminal pole on permanent route to 280th Bde. R.F.A. Old line to 54th D.A.C. reeled up and relaid to new H.Q. of same unit. Parties clearing up all badly laid lines in HINDENBURG TUNNEL, BROWN TRENCH and HINDENBURG SUPPORT. All earth return lines reeled up unless many telephone	
	5th		Signal School for infantry and artillery signallers opened at BOISLEUX ST MARC. Clearing up of all lines in forward area continued. Test strips erected on HINDENBURG TUNNEL Route at No 4 Entrance and lines bridged through at No.3 Entrance.	Appendix "A"

[signature] Capt. R.E.

18th DIVL. SIGNAL CO., R.E.

(2) Army Form C. 2118.

WAR DIARY
or
INTELLIGENCE SUMMARY
(Erase heading not required.)

18th DIVL. SIGNAL CO., R.E.

JUN 1917

Instructions regarding War Diaries and Intelligence
Summaries are contained in F. S. Regs., Part II.
and the Staff Manual respectively. Title pages
will be prepared in manuscript.

Place	Date	Hour	Summary of Events and Information	Remarks and references to Appendices
	8th		Forward portion of P.L. badly damaged by hostile shell fire on night of 7/8th. Communications very slightly interrupted as in most cases alternative routes were employed. All forward lines through and working by 3:0pm. D.V. pair laid from N.26.d.53 to N.32.d.2.r. Owing to changes in F.A.B's the following changes in existing lines and new lines were necessary:-	
	9th		280th F.A.B. connected up by means of existing lateral to 281st F.A.B. Old 280th F.A.B. line reeled up as far as its 281st F.A.B. position and relaid to 250th F.A.B. at N.27.B.6.7. New pair D.Y. laid from old 281st F.A.B. position to 46th F.A.B. at N.27.8.4.6. Old 83rd F.A.B. liaison line at present out of use, diverted to 250th F.A.B. and put through on Brigade in Lines Exchange. D.Y. pair laid from 46th F.A.B. at N.27.C.4.6 to Bde in line D.Y. pair laid from Brigade in Lines to "A" Test point at N.22.d.4.7 to be joined up to B.C. as for superimposed line to Right Brigade of 114th Division. Comi airline built from 55th D.A.C. position to 18th D.A.C.	
	10th		New D.Y. pair laid from terminal pole on permanent line to new H.Q. of 82nd F.A.B. at N.27.C.35. New D.Y. pair laid from H.Q. 82nd F.A.B. to Brigade in Lines.	

J. Mullo Major R.E.

18th DIVL. SIGNAL CO., R.E.

Army Form C. 2118.
(5)

WAR DIARY
or
~~INTELLIGENCE SUMMARY.~~
(Erase heading not required.)

18th DIVL. SIGNAL CO., R.E.

JUN 1917

Instructions regarding War Diaries and Intelligence Summaries are contained in F. S. Regs., Part II. and the Staff Manual respectively. Title pages will be prepared in manuscript.

Place	Date	Hour	Summary of Events and Information	Remarks and references to Appendices
			Average Strength of Company during month:-	
			Officers. 7	
			O.R. 242	
			Horses. 100.	
			Awards during month:-	
			No. 17424 Sapper F.G. MORRIS. MILITARY MEDAL	
			No. 64962 " G. WILLY. do.	
			Enclosures:-	
			"A" Training Programme	
			"B" Scheme for Divisional Signalling School.	
			"C" Diagram of Communications	
			"D" Route Diagram of Lines in HINDENBURG TUNNEL.	

J.W. Willis
Major R.E.
18th DIVL. SIGNAL CO., R.E.

"A"

SCHEME OF TRAINING TO BE CARRIED OUT BY 18th DIVISIONAL SIGNAL COMPANY R.E. WHILE THE DIVISION IS IN REST.

1. For purposes of Training the Divisional Signal Company will be divided up as follows:-

    (a) Headquarters of Company.

        (i) Signallers and Despatch Riders.
        (ii) Motor Cyclist D.R's.
       (iii) Wireless Sub-Section and Operators.

    (b) No.1 Section.

        A and B Cable Sections.

    (c) Infantry Brigade Sections.

    (d) Artillery Signal Company.

        (i) R.A., Headquarters Detachment.
       (ii) Field Artillery Brigade Sub-Sections.

2. It is hoped that it will be possible for each Infantry Brigade Section and Field Artillery Brigade Sub-Section to be withdrawn for one week from its Brigade Headquarters for training with the Headquarters of the Signal Company.

3. Training will be carried out as follows:-

| (a) Headquarters of Company. | (b) No.1 Section. | (d) R.A. Signal Company. |

1st Week. Infantry Drill, Driving Drill, Riding School, Cable Drill for N.C.O's and Detachment Commanders, Airline Drill and Construction for N.C.O's and Map Reading.

Parades. - Drill Order, Marching Order, Mounted, Harness Inspection, Wagon Inspections, Wagon Stores Inspection, Kit Inspection, Inspection of Motor Cycles, Inspection of Bicycles, Inspection of Lorries.

2nd Week. Infantry Drill, Driving Drill, Riding School, Cable Drill for Cable Detachments, Map Reading, Instruction in Permanent Line for N.C.O's, Musketry and Revolver Practice, Instruction in Instruments for N.C.O's., Airline Drill for detachments.

Parades. - Drill Order, Marching Order, Inspection of Motor Cycles, Inspection of Bicycles.

3rd Week. Infantry Drill, Driving Drill, Riding School, Cable Drill, Airline Drill, Map Reading, Permanent Line - Design and Construction, Divisional Signalling Scheme.

Parades. - Drill Order, Marching Order, Inspection of Motor Cycles, Harness Inspection, Wagon Stores Inspection, Kit Inspection.
Parade of whole Signal Company.

Training. (continued)

	(a)	(b)	(d)
	Headquarters of Company.	No.1 Section.	R.A. Signal Company.

4th Week.   Infantry Drill, Driving Drill, Riding School, Cable Drill, Schemes, Divisional Scheme, Visual Signalling Scheme.

Parades. - Drill Order, Marching Order, Inspection of Motor Cycles, Inspection of Bicycles, Wagon Inspections, Wagon Stores Inspection, Kit Inspection, Inspection of Lorries.

4.   The Wireless Sub-Section will be trained independently of the rest of the company, in Wireless, Power Buzzers and Amplifiers.   They will, however, do all Drills with the Company.

5.   Training of Brigade Sections will be carried out under Brigade Signalling Officers.   When each Brigade Section is attached to the Headquarters of the Company, it will of course do the same training as the Headquarters and No.1 Section.

Training of Brigade Sections will include the following:-

    Infantry Drill.
    Flag Drill.
    Reading and Sending by Lamp.
        "   "   "   " Shutter.
        "   "   "   " Disc.
        "   "   "   " Flag.
        "   "   "   " Helio.
    Signalling Schemes with Battalions.
    Instruments.
    Power Buzzers and Amplifiers.
    Wireless.
    Map Reading.

All Stores and Equipment will be overhauled, Deficiencies will be checked and made up and all unserviceable equipment replaced.

21st June, 1917.

J. Challis.
Major R.E.,
O.C. Signals, 18th Division.

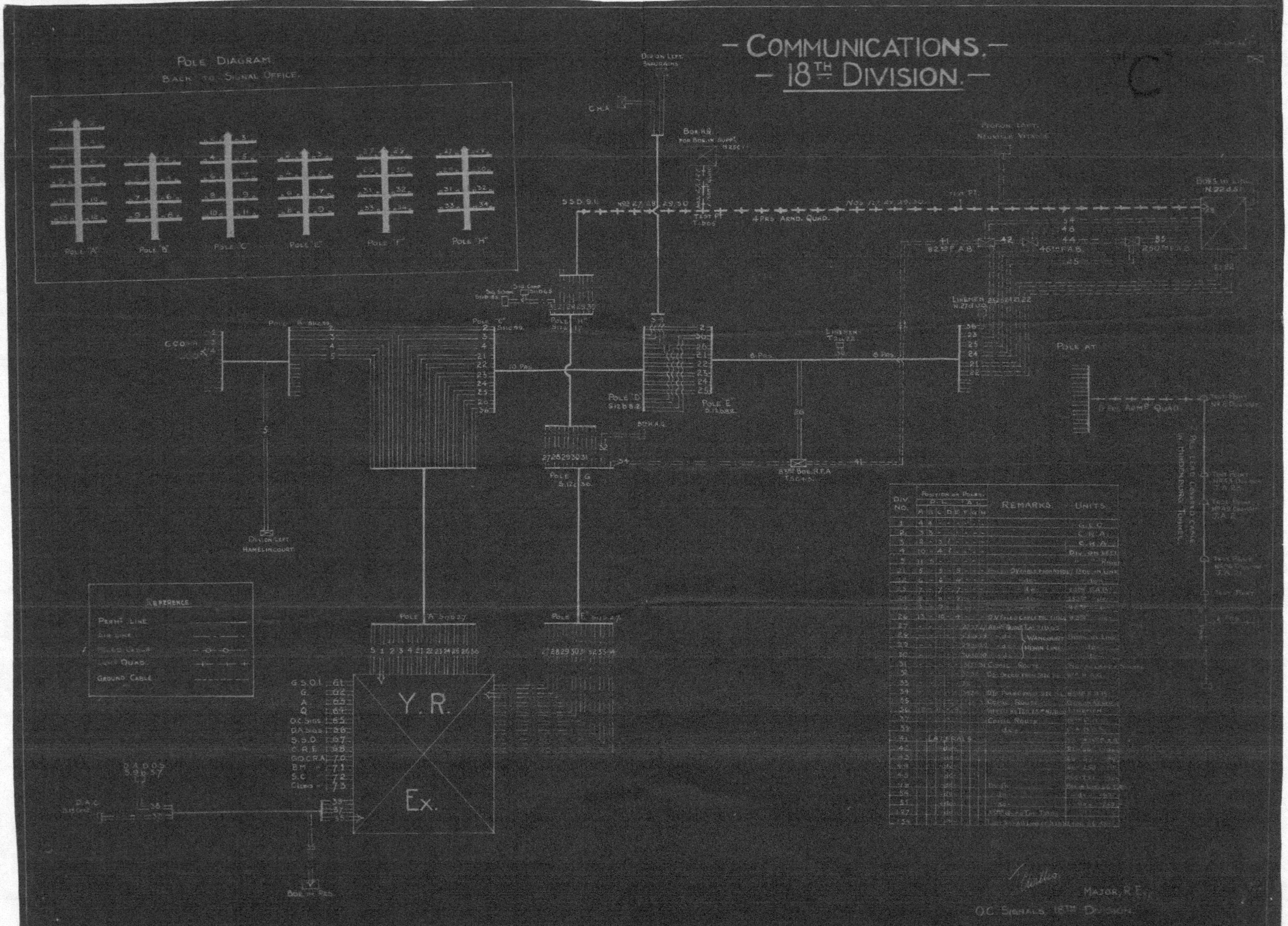

- COMMUNICATIONS. -
- 18TH DIVISION. -
POLE DIAGRAM
BACK TO SIGNAL OFFICE.
POLE "A"
POLE "B"
POLE "C"
POLE "E"
POLE "F"
POLE "H"
C.H.A.
4 PRS. ARMD. QUAD.
POLE "D"
POLE "E"
POLE "G"
POLE "A"
POLE "F"
POLE AT
REFERENCE
PERMT. LINE
GROUND CABLE
DIVISION LEFT
HAMELINCOURT
Y.R.
Ex.
G.S.O.1
G.
A.
Q.
O.C. SIGS.
D.A. SIGS.
S.S.O.
C.R.E.
G.O.C.R.A.
B.M.
S.C.
CLERKS
D.A.C.
DIV. NO.
REMARKS
UNITS
LATERALS
PB. LEAD COVERED CABLE
IN HINDENBURG TUNNEL.
MAJOR, R.E.
O.C. SIGNALS. 18TH DIVISION.

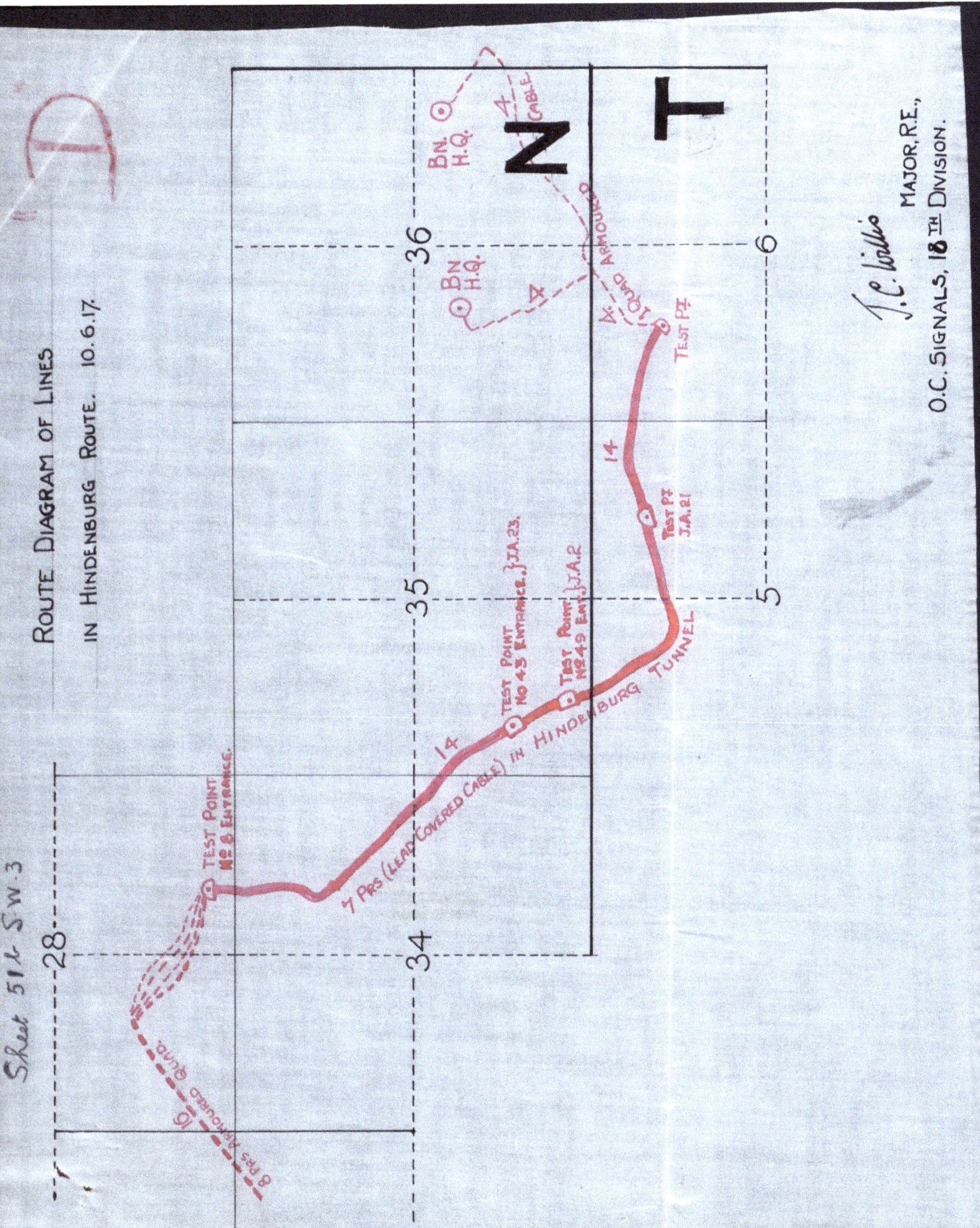

Army Form C. 2118.

WAR DIARY

INTELLIGENCE SUMMARY

18th DIVL. SIGNAL CO., R.E.

JULY 1917

Place	Date	Hour	Summary of Events and Information	Remarks and references to Appendices
COUIN	July 1917. 1st		Rest area	Vol 20
	2nd		Preparations for move of Division to STEENVOORDE began. Electric Light lorry with Advance party of one complete Signal Office relief sent forward by road with instructions to open up Signal Office at STEENVOORDE at 10.0am on 3rd.	
	3rd		Company less one Signal Office relief marches to DOULLENS for entrainment. Left COUIN at 2.0pm and bivouaced at DOULLENS for night. Divisional H.Q. closed at COUIN at 10.0am and opened at STEENVOORDE	
STEENVOORDE			at same hour. Lorry with second Signal Office relief left COUIN at 11.30am and proceeded direct to STEENVOORDE by road.	
	4th		Entrained at DOULLENS Nth Station at 3.19am and left at 6.19am for GODEWAERSVELDE. Detrained at GODEWAERSVELDE at 12.35pm and proceeded by march route to STEENVOORDE. Accommodated in Camp just outside town. Necessary lines allotted by II Corps.	
	5th		Nos 1 and 2 Detachments complete m left Camp at 9.0am for RENINGHELST – proposed new Divisional Headquarters. Six linesmen sent forward by lorry at 10.0am to learn and take over all lines of 30th Division	

O.C. 18th DIVL. SIGNAL CO., R.E.

Army Form C. 2118.

(2.)

WAR DIARY
or
~~INTELLIGENCE SUMMARY~~
(Erase heading not required.)

18th DIVL. SIGNAL CO., R.E.

JUL 1917

Place	Date	Hour	Summary of Events and Information	Remarks and references to Appendices
	5th	—	Test panels, exchanges, etc to be installed ready for taking over on 7th. Lorries to Brigades etc allotted by Corps. Two Wireless Sets, 1 Amplifier and 3 Power Buzzers with personnel complete sent forward by lorry to relieve stations of 30th Division. One Wireless Set to be installed at DORMY HOUSE (I.23.a.9.4.) and one at BEDFORD HOUSE (I.26.a.9.9.)	
	6th.		Both these Sets worked to II Corps Directing Station at H.22.w.07. Power Buzzers installed at :— Company H.Qrs at I.24.b.2.8.; Company H.Q. of Right Bn at I.24.b.4.9. and Right Bn H.Q. I.24.d.73. All these to work to an Amplifier installed at Bn H.Q. DORMY HOUSE. This Amplifier also had to receive from Power Buzzer of 8th Division at Railway Wood (I.11.b.). Owing to the extreme difficulty of keeping lines through in forward area, Wireless and Power Buzzers proved invaluable. One Signal Office relief complete sent to RENINGHELST and arrange to take over from 30th Divl Signals.	
RENINGHELST.	7th		Divl S.O. closed at STEENVOORDE at 10.0am and opened at RENINGHELST at same hour.	

2353 Wt. W2544/1454 700,000 5/15 D. D. & L. A.D.S.S. Forms/C. 2118.

[signed] W..... Major R.E.
O C 18th DIVL. SIGNAL CO., R.E.

Army Form C. 2118.

(3)

WAR DIARY
or
INTELLIGENCE SUMMARY
(Erase heading not required.)

18th DIVL. SIGNAL CO., R.E.

JUL 1917

Place	Date	Hour	Summary of Events and Information	Remarks and references to Appendices
	7th (Contd)		Company moved to BENINGHELST by march route and took over Camp at G.3b.c.6.6. Renewing Signal office tent forward by lorry. Started work on forward bury and clearing up all leads in to Signal Office. Stray single cables to be replaced by multicore.	
	10th		Two additional buzzers sent to E.N.1. (H.21.B.83) for maintenance.	
	12/8.		Cables from BEDFORD HOUSE to DORMY HOUSE to be junct'd and tested. Lines laid from E.N.1. to 18th D.A.C. and put on to Exchange at E.N.1. 12-pair buried cables led on to BEDFORD HOUSE and brought on to Test Strips. Each 7-pair cable put on to a separate strip ptk so as to be easily accessible.	
	13th			
	14th		Party under 2/Lieut C.V. Riley R.E. to fit up Advanced Exchange at DORMY HOUSE, Wireless, Amplifier and Power Buzzer Stations inspected.	
	15th		Two pair D.V. cable laid from Advanced Divl. H.Q. at H.27 & 3.7 to Test Point at H.27.d.1.1.	
	17th & 18th		Interior wiring of Signal Office at Adv'd. Div. H.Q commenced. Fitting up Signal Office and laying local lines at Advanced S.O.	

J.W. Miller Major R.E.
O.C. 18th DIVL. SIGNAL CO., R.E.

Army Form C. 2118.

WAR DIARY
or
INTELLIGENCE SUMMARY
(Erase heading not required.)

18th DIVL. SIGNAL CO., R.E.

JUL 1917

Place	Date	Hour	Summary of Events and Information	Remarks and references to Appendices
	19th 21st		Two new DV pair poles cable laid from EN.20 to FR Test Point. All lines and cables leading in to DORMY HOUSE to be cleared up and led on to Test strips.	
	22nd		Two 7-pair cables laid from Artillery Group HQ to DORMY HOUSE Wireless Station at DORMY HOUSE relaid.	
	24th		Two pair DV cable laid in ZILLEBEKE Lake from "D" Test Point to "HC" Test Point. Unable to complete owing to hostile fire. New DV pair laid from Div. AHQ to 18th DAC at H.31.d.5.0. and 2 new poles in.	
	26th		Two pairs DV cable in ZILLEBEKE Lake completed. Lines at 03rd BH.Q tested and local lines run for D.A., C.R.E., G.S.O.I., G and O Chipolo. A 5-line ringing exchange installed at Pioneer H.Q. near CHATEAU SEGARD, and 2 pair twisted DV cable laid from OB~F Route.	
	27th		7-pair cable laid from Advanced Infantry Brigade HQ at I.17.c.9.2 (RIDGE STREET) along trench via RITZ STREET to DORMY HOUSE. 32 Horses Killed and 35 wounded by enemy bombs	

[signature] Major R.E.
O.C. 18th DIVL. SIGNAL CO., R.E.

Army Form C. 2118.

(5)

WAR DIARY
or
~~INTELLIGENCE SUMMARY~~
(Erase heading not required.)

18th DIVL. SIGNAL CO., R.E.

JUL 1917

Place	Date	Hour	Summary of Events and Information	Remarks and references to Appendices
	28th		7-pair cable from RIDGE STREET to DORMY HOUSE completed.	
	29th		Lines on loop from "I" to "G" tested and regulated and No. 1 to 10 pairs labelled for use of 18th Division.	
H.27.8.5.7.	30/31st		Advanced S.H.Q. opened at E.N.20 at 12:00 midnight for active operations on 31st.	
	31st		Cable laying party, Runner party and Wireless party to move off at 2:00 a.m. and take up instructions at YEOMANRY POST.	Appendices C.D.

Awards during month:-

    Captain C. Bellam R.E.   MILITARY CROSS

13868   Sgt (A/C.S.M)   G.A. Wills   DISTINGUISHED CONDUCT MEDAL

53223   Sapper   S.H. Forsyth   MILITARY MEDAL

4084   Sapper   J.H. Smith   MILITARY MEDAL

Average strength of Company during month: 7 Officers, 256 O.R. and 127 Horses.

ENCLOSURES
"A" System of Communications for operations on 31st July.
"D" Orders for Cable laying "E" "B" Signal Tank "C" Runner Service
"F" Buried Cable Route "E" Buried Cable Route BEDFORD HOUSE to DORMY HOUSE

J. Moulton, Major R.E.
O.C., 18th DIVL. SIGNAL CO., R.E.

SECRET.   APPENDIX..........

~~PROPOSED~~ SYSTEM OF COMMUNICATIONS

for

FORTHCOMING OFFENSIVE OPERATIONS.

General Scheme.

On "Z" day, the 30th Division will, in conjunction with Divisions on Right and Left, attack and capture the 1st and 2nd objectives shewn on attached map. After the 2nd objective has been secured, the 53rd Brigade of the 18th Division will advance from vicinity of RITZ Trench, move up over territory conquered by 30th Division, and will pass through Left Brigade of 30th Division to the assault of the 3rd objective, i.e., the "Green Line". The attacking brigade will be supported by a second brigade of the 18th Division, the 54th Brigade, which will be ready to move forward from the vicinity of CHATEAU SEGARD at Zero plus 4 hours.

After the "Green Line" has been taken, the "Rod Line" will be captured by the 53rd Brigade on the same day if the opposition is not too serious.

In the event of the opposition proving to be too serious, the 54th Brigade will assault and take the "Rod Line" on Z plus 1 day.

General Principles of Communications.

i. As the forthcoming operations will be essentially an Artillery Battle, every assistance possible will be rendered to the Artillery by the Divisional Signal Company with regard to forward lines.

ii. The fullest possible use will be made of Wireless, Amplifiers and Power Buzzers, Pigeons and Visual Signalling for maintaining communication between Brigade H.Q. and advancing battalions.

Carrying parties for Wireless Stations will have to be supplied from battalions, and these men should be detailed at least one week before actual operations, in order that they may be trained in erecting aerials and setting up stations.

iii. Cables will be run together after the advancing troops along a well defined route which will follow the Divisional Track. This will be marked by pickets and white tape. The cable route will, however, be about 50 yards off the track to the North, and at intervals along this route there will be combined Runners' and Linemens' Posts. These posts will be indicated by small blue and white signalling flags with the letter "R" printed on the white portion of the flag.

iv. All personnel required from infantry battalions and R.A. for forward communications during the battle will be withdrawn from their units 4 days before Zero for training and rehearsals under arrangements to be made by O.C. Signals.

v. A Divisional Information Bureau will be established on the Divisional Track at J.13.a.20.15. This will be marked "A.T.N. Intelligence Office". Captain PRICE D.S.O. - attached "G" Branch, 18th Divisional H.Q. - will be in charge of this post.

The object of this office is to provide a centre where information can be received and disseminated, and the latest information given to troops or individuals passing to the front.

2.

~~Communications in detail~~ will be dealt with prior to the attack and ~~after~~ the attack under the following headings:-

       (a). Telephonic and Telegraphic.
       (b). Runners and D.R.L.S.
       (c). Wireless and Earth Induction.
       (d). Pigeons.
       (e). Visual.
       (f). Contact Patrol.

(a). i. **Prior to the Attack.**

A complete system of lines will be established in addition of 30th Divisional Signals, connecting up all the H.Q's in the Divisions. Lines from Divisional Report Centre at H.27.b.   to Brigade H.Q., and from Brigade H.Q. to Battalions will be a buried system.
Similarly, lines connecting Divisional R.A., H.Q. and F.A.B's, F.A.B's and Batteries, also Batteries and O.P's will be on buried system as far as possible.
Points nearest present front to which there are buried cables are:- I.24.a.8.4. and I.24.d.7.4. These points will be known in future as Cable Heads.

ii. **After the Attack.**

Cables will be run forward from heads of buried systems behind the attacking troops. All these cables will be concentrated on one route for ease in maintenance and laying, and one route per Brigade will be run out. These routes will consist of five pairs of D.V. cable, each pair being marked with different coloured tape every 5 Yards.
These lines will be utilised as follows:- 2 pairs for Divisional Artillery and 2 pairs for Infantry Brigade. The Divisional Information Bureau will be "teed" in on one of the latter lines, so that it will be in direct communication with Infantry Brigade H.Q. The remaining pair will be for linemen.
    The route which these lines will follow is shewn on attached diagram; also the cable routes of the 30th Division, the Northern route of which will subsequently be taken over by the 18th Divn.
    Every 400 yards there will be a post manned by 2 linemen. These Men will have a telephone "teed" in on Linemens' line, and will maintain in both directions from their posts.
    The cable routes will terminate at the battalion H.Q. situated on or near the Divisional Track in each case, but the lines can be extended from these points by Artillery and Battalion signallers as may be required. As regards lateral communication between battalions, the onus of laying and maintaining the lateral line will always rest with the battalion on the Right, which will always lay its line to the battalion on the Left. This line will then be joined through to Brigade on one of the five pairs.

(b). **Runners and D.R.L.S.**

    Prior to the attack, all despatches to Brigades will be carried by Despatch Rider. Despatches will be carried forward from Bde., H.Q. to battalions by a Runner Service which will be arranged by Brigade Signals.
    After the attack and after the infantry have advanced to the 2nd objective, i.e., the "Black Line", with Battalion H.Q. at J.8.c.4.0 and J.14.a.5.9 approximately, a series of Runners' Posts will be established at intervals of 400 yards along the line of the Divisional Track. These Runners' Posts will be marked with a small blue and white signalling flag with the letter "R" printed on the white portion of the flag.

3.

They will each consist of 2 runners and will be within easy reach of telephonic communication with either Brigade of Battn., H.Q. By means of this service of runners, despatches will be carried between Brigade H.Q's, The Divisional Information Bureau, and the H.Q's of the Battalion situated near the Divisional Track.

Despatches for the battalion on the Right will, however, be carried from Left Battalion H.Q. by runners of the Right Battalion attached for the purpose. Each Battalion Commander should ensure that he has a sufficient number of orderlies for this "lateral service", and to replace casualties in the "Runner System" back to Brigade if required.

When Advanced Brigade H.Q. moves up to J.8.c.4.0, the existing runner service will be utilised for carrying despatches between Division and Brigade. The line of Runners' Posts will also be extended up the Divisional Track to Battalion H.Q.

The number of runners required for this service is 30.

(c). Wireless and Earth Induction.

Prior to the attack, the II Corps Wireless Sub Directing Station will be installed at DORMY HOUSE - J.23.a.6.5. This Set will send and receive all messages for 53rd Brigade, and will work back to the II Corps Directing Station at H.22.c.5.8. The latter station is on the Corps Area Telephone Exchange at EN 1.

Two combined stations, each consisting of an Amplifier and Power Buzzer with shelters complete, will also be sent up to EQ 23, i.e., Company H.Q. at I.24.b.2.5. One of these stations will be installed at this point the moment the Amplifier Station of the 30th Division stationed there has moved forward. The other station will be sent up with Captain PRICE D.S.O. to the Divisional Information Bureau at J.13.a.20.15. This station will be installed here and will work back to the station at EQ 23.

After the 2nd objective has been taken, and while battalions of the 53rd Brigade are forming up to assault the "Green Line", a combined station consisting of 2 Trench Sets complete with shelter, 1 Amplifier with shelter and 1 Power Buzzer will be sent forward from Brigade H.Q. One Wireless Set will be left and installed at the Divisional Information Bureau at J.13.a.20.15. This set will work back to the 2nd Corps Wireless Sub Directing Station at DORMY HOUSE. The remaining Wireless Set, the Amplifier and Power Buzzer will be taken up to Battalion H.Q. at J.8.c.4.0. The Power Buzzer and Amplifier will be installed and will work back. either to the station at the Divisional Information Bureau at J.13.a.20.15 or to the station at EQ 23, i.e., I.24.b.2.5. The Wireless Set will work back to the II Corps Sub Directing Station at DORMY HOUSE.

Arrangements will be made with 30th Division for their Amplifier and Power Buzzer Stations at J.18.d.1.7 and DORMY HOUSE to cease working after the 53rd Brigade has taken over from the Left Brigade of the 30th Division. This is to avoid "jamming", and will occur at approximately Zero plus 5 hours 46 minutes.

After the 3rd objective has been taken, the Amplifier and Power Buzzer at the Divisional Information Bureau will be dismantled and sent up to and installed at Battalion H.Q. at J.9.a. This will work back to station at J.8.c.4.0, while the latter station will transmit messages by Wireless to Corps Sub Directing Station at DORMY HOUSE.

In the event of the 4th objective being taken and Battalion H.Q moving to vicinity of J.4.c., the Amplifier and Power Buzzer Station at EQ 23 will be dismantled and sent up to Battalion H.Q. at J.4.c. Two schemes of Wireless communications for 18th Div. are shewn, the first (a) being before the capture of the 3rd objective, the second (b) being after the capture of the 4th objective.

4.

(a).

W.   ⊕ A.   Battalion H.Q. - J.8.c.4.0
             (1200 yards)
W.   ⊕ A.   Divisional Information Bureau - J.13.a.20.15
             (1000 yards)
     ⊕ A.   EQ 23 - I.24.b.2.5
             (On the Telephone)

W.   II Corps Sub Directing Station DORMY HOUSE.
             (On the Telephone)

(b).

     A ⊕   Battalion H.Q. - J.4.c.
            (1200 yards)
     A ⊕   Station at - J.9.a.
            (1300 yards)
W.   A ⊕   Brigade H.Q. at - J.8.c.4.0
            (1200 yards)
     W   Divisional Information Bureau - J.13.a.20.15
            (2000 yards)
     W   II Corps Sub Directing Station DORMY HOUSE.

REFERENCE.

⊕ = Power Buzzer.   A = Amplifier.

     W = Wireless Set.

~~~~~~ = Route between Wireless Stations.

-·-·-·- = Route between Power Buzzer and Amplifier Stations.

As a general rule all messages sent by Power Buzzer after Zero will be sent in clear by order of an officer. All messages sent by Power Buzzer before Zero will be sent in Field Cipher, and all messages sent by Wireless, whether before or after Zero, will be sent in Field Cipher.

Combined Power Buzzer and Amplifier Stations of 30th Division will be established before Zero at:-

        EQ 23   -   I.24.b.2.5
        EQ 45   -   I.24.d.9.3
        DORMY HOUSE.   I.23.a.60.45

There will be an officer with each Wireless Station for encoding and decoding messages.

(d). <u>Pigeons</u>.

Twenty pigeons have been allotted by II Corps to 18th Division for "Z" day and the 53rd Brigade will receive all of these. On "Z plus 1 day", thirty birds will be available and these will be given to 54th Brigade. Pigeons will be re-allotted by Brigades (according to tactical requirements) to attacking battalions.

Brigades will submit to General Staff, 18th Division a report shewing the allotment of pigeons they wish to make to battalions, giving the uses they intend to make of them, bearing in mind that the majority will be required on the Right flank, the communications existing on the Left being more assured.

(e). <u>Visual</u>.

Brigades will make the fullest possible use of visual during the advance. The 53rd and 54th Brigades will submit to General Staff, 18th Division a report giving their suggestions as to what visual they intend to use.

(f). <u>Contact Aeroplane Patrol</u>.

There will be a "Dropping Ground" for messages from Aeroplanes at Advanced Divisional H.Q. at H.26.b.central. Arrangements will be made with 4th Squadron R.F.C. as to methods of acknowledging the receipt of messages.

<u>ACKNOWLEDGE</u>.

20th July, 1917.

SCHEME for TANK detailed for DIVISIONAL SIGNALS.

I. The following stores will be loaded on the Tank before it proceeds to its assembly position :-

       1 Wireless Set complete.
       1 R.F.C. Signalling Lamp.
       1 Helio.
      10 Pigeons.
       4 Miles twisted D.V cable, (Wound on 1/4 mile drums).
       8 Miles D.III cable.
       8 Miles D.II cable.
      10 Miles Armoured Twin.
      10 Rockets.

II. If possible, a mast for the Wireless aerial should be erected on top of the Tank before the start of operations. If this is not possible, a mast will be carried and erected only when it is desired to use the Wireless. The Tank will have a distinguishing mark painted on it, - a Blue and White Flag.

III. The uses of the Tank will be as follows :-

(a). To take up stores of cable to a Forward Cable Dump.

(b). To take up one Wireless Set and 10 pigeons to new forward area.

(c). To act as a Mobile Signal Office. Any messages handed in by anyone to the Tank will at once be sent off by Wireless or Pigeon.

(d). To signal by means of a Helio and R.F.C. Signalling Lamp to Kite Balloon detailed in II Corps G.T.2742.

(e). To lay an experimental line of D.V or armoured cable from Cable Head to forward positions of Brigade and Battalion H.Q's at J.8.c.4.0 and J.9.a.central.

IV. The following personnel will accompany the Tank :-

      2 Wireless men.
      1 Visual Signaller.
      1 Cableman.

N.B. The Tank Commander will let off any pigeons.

V. In the event of poor dug-out accommodation at Battalion H.Q's at J.9.a.central, it is proposed to use the Tank as a Wireless, Amplifier and Power Buzzer Station. The Tank would be run into POLYGONE - DE - ZONNEBEKE Wood and camouflaged.

(sgd). J.C. WILLIS, Major, R.E.,
O.C. Signals, 18th Division.

26th July, 1917.

SECRET.

ORDERS.
for
RUNNER SERVICE, 18th DIVISION.

I. The Runner Service will work between the H.Q's at I.17.c.9.2, (occupied at Zero by the 53rd Brigade), and the H.Q's of Brigades and Battalions as they advance. All messages, whether from R.A. units, Battalions, or units of the 30th Divn., will be carried by this Service down to I.17.c.9.2, whence they will be sent on by D.R. if necessary.

II. The Runners will wear Blue and White Armbands, and will invariably carry their despatches in their top, right-hand pockets.

III. In the event of the "Red Line" being taken, the Runner Service will consist of 13 posts, each manned by two Runners. These posts are the same as the Linemans' Posts, consequently there will be 4 men in each post. These posts will be marked by a Blue and White signalling flag with an "R" painted on it, and will be on the telephone.

IV. The Runners are not to be employed in any other duties except the carrying of messages.

V. Lieut. Pelham-Clinton, R.E., O.C., Signals, 53rd Brigade will be the officer responsible for having the Runners posted in their correct positions during the advance. The posts are to be 400 yards apart, and are to be on the Divisional Track.

VI. The Service ought to be complete and in running order as far up as the Battalion H.Q's on or near the Divisional Track. That is to say, Runners ought to advance with Battalion H.Q's, and be posted by the Battalion Signalling Officer if possible. The Runners may alter the positions of their posts afterwards if it is found that their first positions are not on the Divisional Track.

VII. Runners will not carry messages further than the post next to their own.

VIII. If it is found that there is an insufficient number of Runners to cope with the messages, Lieut. Pelham-Clinton will make arrangements to increase the number of Runners from Battalions.

IX. It is hoped that it will be possible to equip each Runners' Post with a certain number of message rockets.

26th July, 1917.

Major, R.E.,
O.C. Signals, 18th Division.

O R D E R S

for

CABLE LAYING ON "Z" DAY.

I. Working party will consist of :-

    2nd Lieut. Riley, R.E.
    Sergt. Coulter.
    6 Sappers.
    20 Linemen, (R.E., R.A., and Infantry)
    5 Drivers, R.E.

    2nd Lieut. Beaver, R.E.
    Corpl. McNeill.
    5 Sappers.

II. The above working party will parade in fatigue order without arms but with 2 days rations.

The 20 linemen will carry 10 D.Mk.III telephones, jointing stores, tape and solutions, mattocks, labels, small kits and 2 days rations.

As the cables are being laid, two linemen will be posted on the cable route at each Lineman's Post, i.e., at the end of each 400 yard length of cable. These Linemans' Posts are numbered 1 - 13, and will be at the same places as the Runners' Posts, which will be marked with a Blue and White Signalling Flag with an "R" painted on it in black. As the linemen are posted, they will at once "tee in" with a short length of D.V cable on to the Linemans' Line (marked with white tape), and will lead "tee" into dug-out or shelter if one is available. They will immediately put their D.III telephone on to the line and will get into touch with DORMY HOUSE and the other Linemans' Posts.

III. Throughout the day and night one lineman will sit in the post with the receiver of the D.III strapped to his ear. The only occasion when it may be necessary for 2 linemen to go out is when the cables get broken in two places, the second lineman will then, of course, leave his post to go out and repair the second fault. The lineman before leaving, however, will detail one of the Runners to attend to the telephone until his return.

IV. All cable will be dumped near YEOMANRY POST in 3 or 4 small dumps before Zero, and a storeman will be left in charge. Cable and stores dumped at YEOMANRY POST will be as follows:-

    5 miles twisted D.V cable on 5 drums.
    Cradle and spindle for taking same.
    50 small drums, each containing 1/4 mile twisted D.V cable.
    3 coils of 7-pair brass-sheathed cable.
    5 miles twisted D.III cable on small drums.
    3 spare D.Mk.III telephones.
    Jointing stores, tape and solution.
    Two days rations for 50 men.

V. During the advance work will be started (at about 2½ hours after Zero) on laying cables, by Lieut. Rileys party. The first mile of cable will be pulled off D.V drums on cradle at YEOMANRY POST. This will take the cables up to Divisional Information Bureau at J.13.a.2.2 (IGNORANCE LANE). While the party are pulling out the cables, 5 pack horses will advance behind them along Divnl. Track, each carrying 4 small drums of cable, i.e., 4 lengths. This will take the cables up to Battn. H.Q., with 5 drums for next stretch. The pack horses will then return to dump for one more load of 4 small drums each, which will be brought up to Battn. H.Q. Work will then be started (sometime after Zero plus 6 hours) extending the cables up to position of Battn.H.Q. at J.9.a.central.

The

2.

V. contd. The cable carried up will be sufficient to complete 5 cable lines up to No.12 Post. The pack horses will then return to the dump and the final load cable will be sent up when required.

VI. All of the 5 cables will be laid with plenty of slack which should be left in coils after every 1/4 mile length. A rear party consisting of 1 Lce/Cpl. R.E. and 2 Sappers will make the cables safe after they have been laid. The cables will be tied together with spun yarn every 20 yards, and will be buried under track crossings, and poled over trench crossings. Linemans' Posts will be manned as follows:-

```
YP      - - - -  2 18th Division linemen.
No.1 )
No.2 )  - - - -  6 Sappers "O.B." Cable Section.
No.3 )
Nos.4 - 13 - - - 20 Linemen supplied by Division.
```

VII. In the event of casualties to linemen, application will be made over Linemans' Line to DORMY HOUSE.

VIII. Distances are as follows :-

YP — Divisional Information Bureau = 1600 yds.
Divl. Information Bureau — Battn. and 53rd Bde.H.Q's = 1300 yds.
53rd Brigade H.Q's — Battn. and 54th Bde.H.Q's = 1300 yds.
54th Brigade H.Q's — Battn. H.Q's of 54th Bde. = 1800 yds.

Total distance cable has to be laid = 6000 yds or $3^{1}/3$ miles

IX. A Tank will be available for carrying up cable. This tank will advance along Tank Track as shewn in Map. Separate instructions will be issued about this.

X. Officer responsible for laying and maintenance of Cable Route is 2nd Lieut. C.V. Riley, R.E.

24th July, 1917.

Major, R.E.,
O.C. Signals, 18th Division.

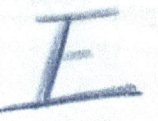

ACCOUNT of BURIED CABLE ROUTE from BEDFORD HOUSE TO DORMY HOUSE.

The length of this route is about 4500 yards, and when taken over from the 30th Division about 500 yards had been completed and the cable laid. Accordingly, work was started by 18th Division Signals on night of 8th/9th July with a working party of 15 R.E's and 750 Infantry. Great difficulty was experienced on account of the trench filling up with water as fast as it was dug out.

Work was continued every night for five nights and good progress made although the cable trench was continuously kept under heavy hostile artillery fire.

At last, however, on night of 14th/15th, the shelling became so bad, (5·9 hows., 4·2's and gas shell), that it was considered impossible to continue by night.

Work was therefore continued in the early morning, the working party being reduced to 200 men, and starting work at 3-30 a.m. at dawn.

Much better progress was made and the Bury was finally completed on morning of 19th, 31 pairs being put through from BEDFORD HOUSE to DORMY HOUSE.

This Buried Cable trench cost the following casualties:-

R.E.
  3 killed.
  18 wounded.

Infantry.
  2 Officers killed.
  2 Officers wounded.
  10 men killed.
  50 men wounded.

10th August, 1917.

Major, R.E.,
Commanding Signals, 18th Division.

MAP SHEWING BURIED CABLE

YPRES

REFERENCE
WORK FINISHED ————
  "   UNDER CONSTRUCTION ━━━

Scale 1:10,000

J. C. Walker
Major R.E.
O.C. Signals, 18th Division

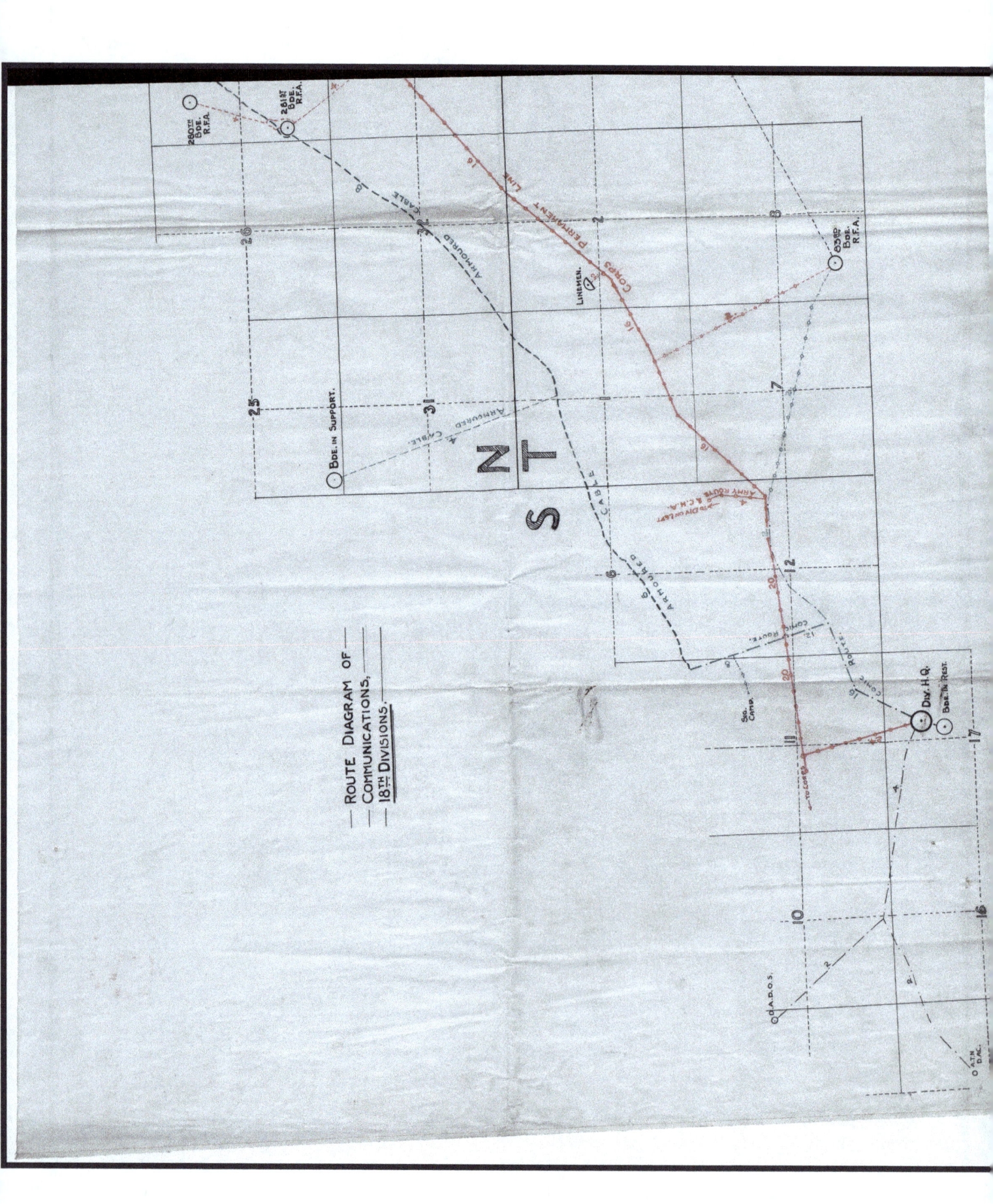

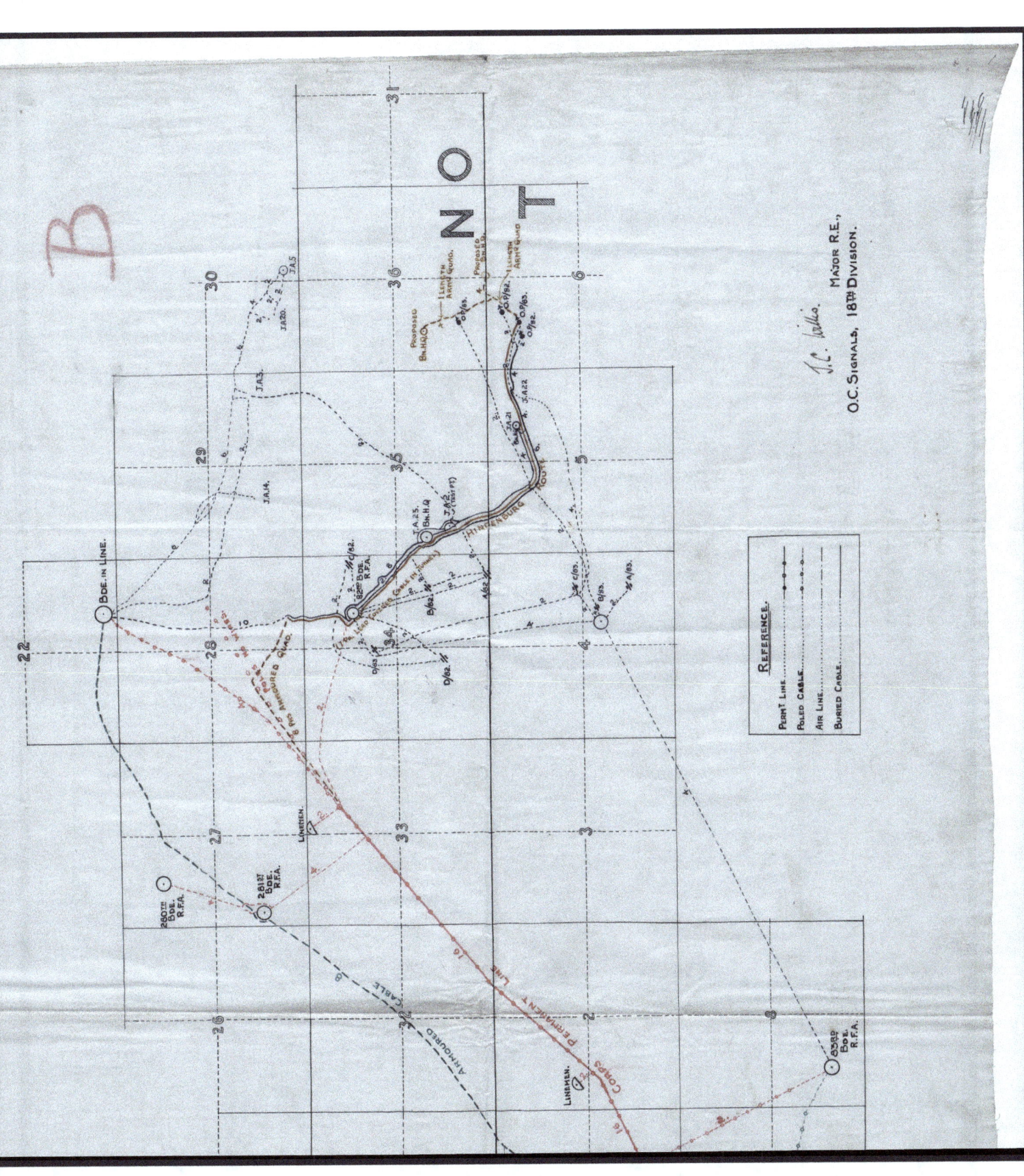

Army Form C. 2118.

WAR DIARY
or
INTELLIGENCE SUMMARY
(Erase heading not required.)

18th DIVL. SIGNAL CO., R.E.

AUG 1917

Vol 21

Place	Date	Hour	Summary of Events and Information	Remarks and references to Appendices
	August 1917			
RENINGHELST	1st		Divisional Headquarters closed at EN 20 (H 27 b 5.6) at near DICKEBUSH at 3.0 pm and opened at RENINGHELST at same hour	
	2nd		Runner, Cable laying and Wireless parties re-organised and equipped ready to move forward again at short notice.	
	3rd		One Signal Office relief and linesmen sent forward to EN 20 to learn and take over lines from 30th Div Signals in anticipation of relief at 6.0am on 4th.	
H.27 R.5.6 (Sheet 28) 1/40000	4th		Divisional Headquarters closed at RENINGHELST at 6.0am and re-opened at EN 20 (near DICKEBUSH) at same hour. Forward communications in very bad condition and immediate re-organisation necessary. Artillery communications taken over at same hour. Four linesmen sent forward to DORMY HOUSE (I 23 d 33) for maintenance of forward lines.	
	5th		One new pair D.V. cable laid from "D" Test Point to "HC" Test Point through ZILLEBEKE Lake and one existing pair repaired and put through. Local lines at DORMY R regulated and strengthened	
	6th		Buried route "G"—"UR"—"RY"—"M"—"WS" (see diagram for July) thoroughly surveyed by party under 2/Sergt C.V. Riley R.E. and 5 pair put through to cable head	

Nepier
O.C. 18th DIVL. SIGNAL CO., R.E.

WAR DIARY
INTELLIGENCE SUMMARY
AUG 1917 — 18th DIVL. SIGNAL CO., R.E.

Date	Hour	Summary of Events and Information	Remarks
6th (contd)		Buried route G-YP-DO similarly surveyed by party under Lieut Jepson R.E. and 5 pairs put through to cable head. Both these routes were frequently shelled, each receiving many direct hits, and it was only through the greatest perseverance and unitiring efforts on the part of officers and men that a few lines on each route were kept through.	
7th		Parties as yesterday continued work on Northern buried route from DORMY HOUSE to cable head DO. After many hours hard work under most difficult and trying circumstances, both parties being frequently exposed to enemy shell fire, eight pairs were put through. One pair twisted DV laid from DO to Power Buzzer and Amplifier Station at VINCE STREET. Four pairs twisted DY cable laid from RY to WINNEPEG STREET and joined through or bury at RY to DORMY HOUSE. Two Antenna posted at RY to maintain these lines up to Advanced Brigade Report Centre WINNEPEG STREET. An Amplifier and Power Buzzer was also established at this Report Centre.	
8th		Work on Northern bury between YP and DO completed. Fifteen pairs put through and a strong test point built at DM. Two pairs DY twisted and	

O.C. 18th DIVL. SIGNAL CO. R.E.

WAR DIARY or INTELLIGENCE SUMMARY

18th DIVL. SIGNAL CO, R.E.

AUG 1917

Army Form C. 2118.

(3)

Place	Date	Hour	Summary of Events and Information	Remarks and references to Appendices
	8th (contd)		from DM to VINCE STREET - Brigade HQ and one pair put through to 55th Bde and one to 55th Bde. Four good pairs put through on bury from BEDFORD HOUSE to DORMY HOUSE. Ground lines of armoured twin were laid between points where bury was not found fair.	
	9th		One cable detachment complete and two special breakdown parties each with an R.E. limber held in readiness to lay or repair lines during expected active operations.	
	10th		Operations postponed owing to heavy rainfall and above parties were kept ready to move off at short notice. Company transport lines moved from RENINGHELST to new camp at H.27.b.56 near Divisional Headquarters.	
	11th		Four D.Y. pairs in ZILLEBEKE Lake overhauled and repaired where necessary. Four armoured twins from "I" Test Point to I.22.c.6.2 overhauled and all joints remade. One D.Y. pair laid as spare for above.	
	12th		Division to be relieved by 56th Division on 13th. No. 4 Detachment moved to RENINGHELST and took over camp vacated by 56th Divl Signals there. One	

One *Willie*
Major R.E.
OC 18th DIVL. SIGNAL CO., R.E.

Army Form C. 2118.

(A)

WAR DIARY
or
INTELLIGENCE SUMMARY
(Erase heading not required.)

18th DIVL. SIGNAL CO., R.E.

AUG 1917

Instructions regarding War Diaries and Intelligence Summaries are contained in F. S. Regs., Part II. and the Staff Manual respectively. Title pages will be prepared in manuscript.

Place	Date	Hour	Summary of Events and Information	Remarks and references to Appendices
	12th (contd)		Signal Office relief and two linesmen sent to RENINGHELST to take over 51st Divl Signal Office at 9.0 am on 13th. Test panels and one 20-line exchange exchanged with 51st Divsn.	
RENINGHELST/13th			Relieved by 51st Division. Divisional H.Q. closed at H.27.b.5.b at 10.0am and reopened at RENINGHELST at same hour. Artillery remaining in line with H.Q. at H.27.b.5.b. All linesmen at various test points on buried routes relieved by linesmen of 51st Division and Power Buzzer, Amplifier and Wireless stations taken over. Company marched to RENINGHELST via ST HUBERTUSHOEK and OUDERDOM at 10:00am to camp vacated by relieving division.	
	14th		Division ordered into Rest. Advanced party under Lieut Sn'Benson with necessary technical stores sent to LEDERZEELE — proposed Rest area. Arrangements made to take over necessary communications from VIII Corps and to open up signal office at LEDERZEELE at 10.0am on 15th.	
LEDERZEELE/15th			Divisional Headquarters closed at RENINGHELST at 10.0am and opened at LEDERZEELE at same hour, coming under jurisdiction of VIII Corps. Company marched to LEDERZEELE, via STEENVOORDE - OUDEZEELE - HARDIFORT.	

O.C. 18th DIVL. SIGNAL CO., R.E.

WAR DIARY
INTELLIGENCE SUMMARY

AUG 1917 — 18th DIVL. SIGNAL CO., R.E.

Date	Hour	Summary of Events and Information	Remarks
15th (contd)		WAEMERS CAPPEL, leaving Camp at 6.30am. Arrived LEDERZEELE 4.30pm and Camped on CASSEL-WATTEN Road outside LEDERZEELE. 53rd Brigade at RUBROUCK — Communication through VIIIth Corps ESQUELBECQ. 54th Brigade at BUYSCHEURE — Direct line to BUYSCHEURE. 55th Brigade at ERINGHEM — Through ZEGGERS CAPPEL Exchange. Necessary lines allotted by VIII Corps Signals.	
16th to 31st		Division in Rest. Preparations were made for training early and all wagons and stores were overhauled and checked. Deficiencies noted and indented for and all technical equipment brought thoroughly up to date. A further course of training for Wireless Section was arranged at VIII Corps Signal School ESQUELBECQ. It was proposed to withdraw each Brigade Section in turn from its Brigade for training with the Headquarters of the Company but owing to various causes this was found impracticable. Subsequently however, a Signal School was formed and as many as possible of the personnel of each Brigade Section were passed through the School. In addition to this one specially N.C.O. was sent from each [?]	

O.C. 18th DIVL. SIGNAL CO., R.E.

Army Form C. 2118.

(b.)

WAR DIARY
or
INTELLIGENCE SUMMARY
(Erase heading not required.)

18th DIVL. SIGNAL CO., R.E.

AUG 1917

Place	Date	Hour	Summary of Events and Information	Remarks and references to Appendices
			Battalions and with a view to instructing other battalion signallers on their return, they were given thorough instruction in the practical use of Power Buzzers, Amplifiers, Wireless and Lucas Daylight Signalling Lamps. In addition to this frequent lectures were given on various types of instruments and after 10 days an examination which showed excellent results was held. All Brigade Section personnel went through similar courses, particular attention being paid to visual.	

Enclosures :- "A" Training Programme

Average Strength of Company during month :- 9 Officers 269 O.R. 133 horses.

Awards during month :- Captain C. Bolton R.E. - MILITARY CROSS

13868 Sergt (A/C/M) G.A. Wills - DISTINGUISHED CONDUCT MEDAL

MILITARY MEDAL

53223	Sapper J.H. Smith	471727	Sapper S.E. Stokes
40612	" S.H. Forsyth	64944	" W.H. Sparkes
97870	- A.G. Austin	64775	Corpl F.R.W. Archer
197907	L/Cpl G/R.A. Williams	47063	Sapper W. Worrall

[signature]
Major R.E.
O.C. 18th DIVL. SIGNAL CO., R.E.

SCHEME OF TRAINING TO BE CARRIED OUT BY 18th DIVISIONAL SIGNAL COMPANY R.E. WHILE THE DIVISION IS IN REST.

1. For the purposes of Training the Divisional Signal Company will be divided up as follows :-

   (a). Headquarters of Company.

      (i) Signallers and Despatch Riders.
     (ii) Motor Cyclist D.R's.
    (iii) Wireless Sub-Section and Operators.

   (b). No.1 Section.

      A and B Cable Sections.

   (c). Infantry Brigade Sections.

   (d). Artillery Signal Company.

      (i) R.A., Headquarters Detachment.
     (ii) Field Artillery Brigade Sub-Sections.

2. It is hoped that it will be possible for each Infantry Brigade Section and Field Artillery Brigade Sub-Section to be withdrawn for 10 days from its Brigade Headquarters for training with the Headquarters of the Signal Company.

3. The Signallers and Despatch Riders, i.e., 1 (a)(i), will join the Divisional Signalling School on the 21st inst., and will receive a thorough training in all methods of visual signalling. They will do the drills and parades with the remainder of the Company.

4. The Wireless Sub-Section of the Signal Company, i.e., 1 (a)(iii), has joined the 8th Corps Wireless School at ESQUELBECQ; it will be trained in the use of Amplifiers, Power Buzzers, Trench Wireless, "C.W." Sets, and Ground Antennae Sets.

5. Training for the remainder of the Company will be carried out as follows :-

(a)	(b).	(d).
Headquarters of Company.	No.1 Section.	R.A. Signal Company.

1st Week. Infantry Drill, Driving Drill, Riding School, Cable Drill for N.C.O's and Detachment Commanders, Airline Drill and Construction for N.C.O's, and Map Reading.

Parades. - Drill Order, Marching Order Mounted, Harness Inspection, Wagon Inspection, Wagon Stores Inspection, Kit Inspection, Inspection of Motor Cycles, Inspection of Bicycles, Inspection of Lorries, and Route March.

2nd Week. Infantry Drill, Driving Drill, Riding School, Cable Drill for Cable Detachments, Map Reading, Instruction in Permanent Line for N.C.O's, Musketry, and Revolver Practice, Instruction in Instruments for N.C.O's, Airline Drill for Detachments.

Parades. - Drill Order, Marching Order, Inspection of Motor Cycles, Inspection of Bicycles, Route March.

Training. (continued).

	(a).	(b).	(d).
	Headquarters of Company.	No.1 Section.	R.A. Signal Company.

3rd Week. Infantry Drill, Driving Drill, Riding School, Cable Drill, Airline Drill, Map Reading, Permanent Line - Design and Construction, Divisional Signalling Scheme.

Parades. - Drill Order, Marching Order, Inspection of Motor Cycles, Harness Inspection, Wagon Stores Inspection, Kit Inspection, Parade of whole Signal Company, with Brigade and R.F.A. Sub-Sections.

4th Week. Infantry Drill, Driving Drill, Riding School, Cable Drill, Schemes, Divisional Scheme, Visual Signalling Scheme.

Parades. - Drill Order, Marching Order, Inspection of Motor Cycles, Inspection of Bicycles, Wagon Inspections, Wagon Stores Inspection, Kit Inspection, Inspection of Lorries.

8. Training for Brigade Sections will be carried out under Brigade Signalling Officers. When each Brigade Section is attached to the Headquarters of the Company, it will join the Divisional Signalling School for training, but will do all Drills and Parades with the remainder of the Company.

Training of Brigade Sections will include the following:-

Infantry Drill.
Flag Drill.
Reading and Sending by Lamp.
"   "   "   " " Shutter.
"   "   "   " " Disc.
"   "   "   " " Flag.
"   "   "   " " Helio.
Signalling Schemes with Battalions.
Instruments.
Map Reading.
Instruction in use of Message Rockets.

All Stores and Equipment will be overhauled, Deficiencies will be checked and made up, and all unserviceable equipment replaced.

19th August, 1917.

Major, R.E.,
O.C. Signals, 18th Division.

Army Form C. 2118.

WAR DIARY
or
INTELLIGENCE SUMMARY.
(Erase heading not required.)

18th DIVL. SIGNAL CO., R.E.

SEP 1917

Place	Date	Hour	Summary of Events and Information	Remarks and references to Appendices
LEDERZEELE	2nd		Division ordered to move to ESQUELBECQ. One Signal Office relief and a linesmen sent forward by lorry to take over Signal Office and lines from VIII Corps Signals.	
ESQUELBECQ	3rd		Divisional H.Q. closed at LEDERZEELE at 10:30am and reopened at ESQUELBECQ at same hour.	
	4th to 21st		Company proceeded by march route at 7.0am via BROXEELE and RUBROUCK. From the 1st to 21st the programme of training commenced on 19th August was resumed and all sections and detachments were given thorough courses in their respective branches. Particular attention was paid to fast cable laying, and each cable detachment was in turn thoroughly instructed in this work. Classes of instruction in cable jointing were held and linesmen instructed in the correct methods of jointing all kinds of cable. Schemes were arranged for the training of the Wireless Sections, and Amplifier, Power Buzzer and Wireless Stations were erected and worked under conditions approaching as near as possible those actually found in the line. The Divisional Signal School which was dispersed owing to the move	

O.C 18th DIVL. SIGNAL CO., R.E.
[signature] Major R.E.

Army Form C. 2118.

(2)

WAR DIARY
~~INTELLIGENCE SUMMARY~~
(Erase heading not required.)

18th DIVL. SIGNAL CO., R.E.

SEP 1917

Place	Date	Hour	Summary of Events and Information	Remarks and references to Appendices
			was reopened on 3rd instant and part of the personnel of each Brigade Section was attached to the School for courses in visual signalling and Linesmen's duties. Particular attention was paid to the Fullerphone and this instrument was thoroughly explained to all students. Numerous experiments with Message Carrying Rockets were made all of which were attended by the students of the school. Results varied considerably but some useful data was obtained). The "Signallers and Despatch Riders" of the H.Q. Section were trained in all methods of visual signalling and despatch riding work. Two message dogs were trained in message carrying from various outlying signal stations and some good times were recorded over distances of from 1 to 2 miles. No actual experience of these animals for message carrying on the line has been obtained but judging from results recorded during training it is considered that some useful work may be done by them when the keeping up of communications by other means is a difficult matter. Classes in cable jointing were held and Linesmen instructed in the correct method for jointing all types of cable.	

J.M.M. Major R.E.
O.C. 18th DIVL. SIGNAL CO., R.E.

Army Form C. 2118.

WAR DIARY
or
INTELLIGENCE SUMMARY
(Erase heading not required.)

18th DIVL. SIGNAL CO. R.E.

SEP 1917

(3)

Place	Date	Hour	Summary of Events and Information	Remarks and references to Appendices
	22nd		Preparations for move to POPERINGHE put in hand and the lorry sent forward with 1 Signalmaster, 3 Linemen and the necessary technical stores, etc., in charge of Lieut. Ensberoom.	
	23rd		Lorry sent forward with load of C.Q.M.S. stores, etc., and one Signal Office relief.	
POPERINGHE	24th		Division places in XVIII Corps Reserve. Divisional H.Q. Signal Office closed at ESQUELBECQ at 10.30am and reopened at Town Hall, POPERINGHE at same hour. Company under Lieut J.S. Holmes R.E. moved by march route via WORMHOUDT – HERZEELE – HOUTKERQUE – ST JAN TER BIEZEN. Remaining Signal Office personnel proceeded by lorry at 10.30am. 53rd Inf Bde at ST JAN TER BIEZEN. 54th " " TUNNELLING CAMP (F.27.a+c) – Sheet 27 55th " " SCHOOL CAMP (L.3.) " " 27.	
	25th		Lines to above allotted by XVIII Corps on permanent routes. Local lines at TOWN HALL overhauled and reported.	

[signature] Major R.E.
O.C. 18th DIVL. SIGNAL CO. R.E.

WAR DIARY or INTELLIGENCE SUMMARY

Army Form C. 2118.

18th DIVL. SIGNAL CO., R.E.

SEP 1917

Place	Date	Hour	Summary of Events and Information	Remarks and references to Appendices
	25th to 30th		From 25th to 30th training was continued and the overhauling and repainting of aragora completed. All technical stores and equipment brought thoroughly up to date and finally checked and inspected. Six infantry signallers were sent to XVIII Corps Signal School for course of instruction in wireless. On the night of the 29th the town was violently bombed by hostile aircraft. Several of the local lines were broken but these were all put through again in a very short time. 2nd Lieut W.A. LANE, 55th Aux Signals and one O.R. wounded. Mule attached to Maltese Cart belonging to No 4 Section bolted and has not yet been recovered. Awards during month:— No 312385 Sergeant J. GRINYER The D.C.M. MILITARY MEDAL No 451412 Sergeant W.S. SMITH No 443398 L/Cpl W.E. MOULAND " 64807 Sapper R. DAVIES " 97926 Sapper H. JENKINS " 249102 2nd Corpl R. MENDOZA " 551149 " C.W. BRAY No 444100 Actg/Sergt F. RISELEY	

O.C. 18th DIVL. SIGNAL CO., R.E.

Army Form C. 2118.

WAR DIARY
or
INTELLIGENCE SUMMARY

(Erase heading not required.)

18th DIVL. SIGNAL CO., R.E.

SEP 1917

Instructions regarding War Diaries and Intelligence Summaries are contained in F. S. Regs., Part II. and the Staff Manual respectively. Title pages will be prepared in manuscript.

Place	Date	Hour	Summary of Events and Information	Remarks and references to Appendices
			Average strength of company during month:-	
			Officers — 9	
			Other Ranks — 277	
			Horses — 129	
			Enclosure:-	
			A — Diagram of lines.	

J.Muller Major R.E.
O.C. 18th DIVL. SIGNAL CO., R.E.

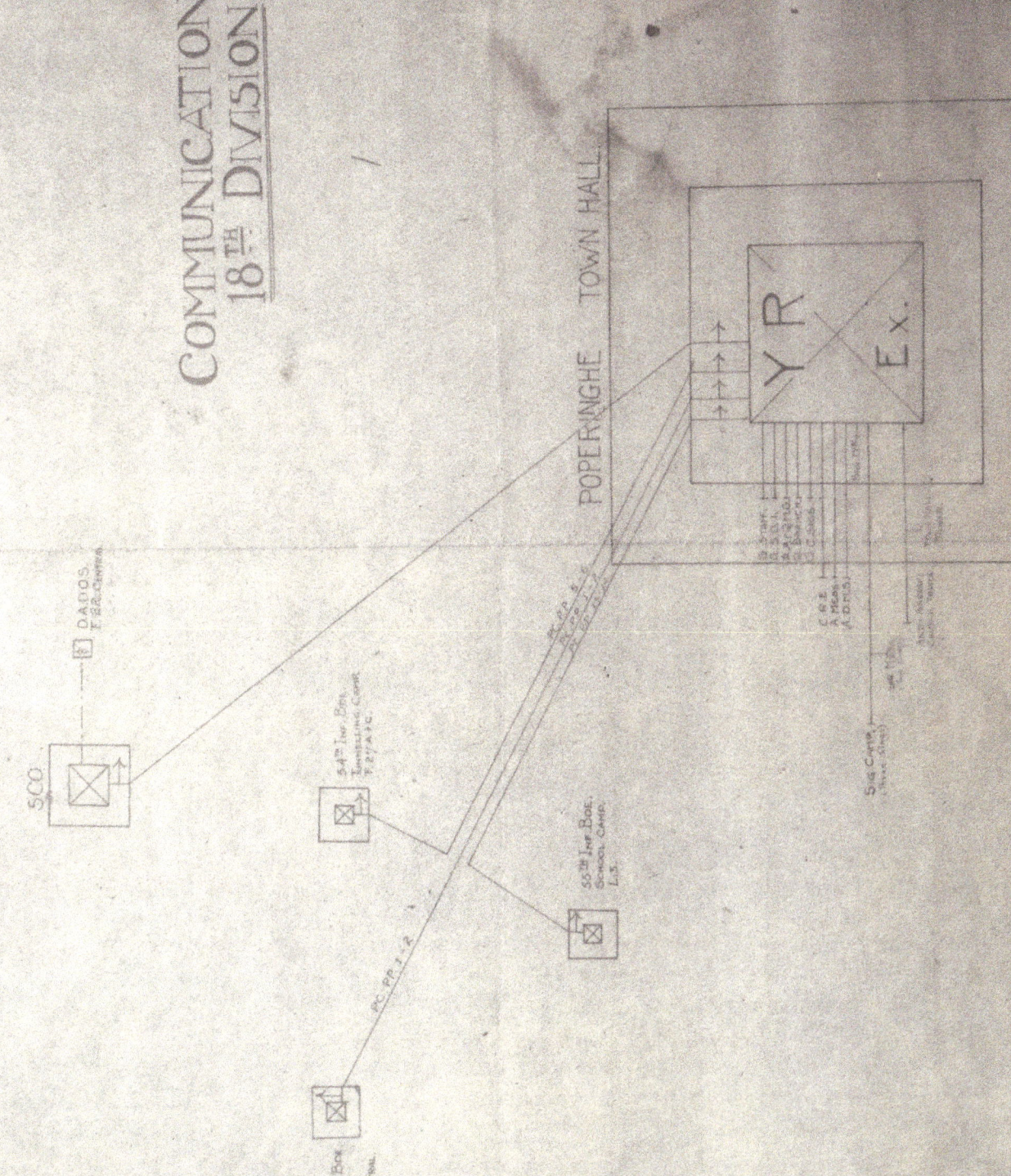

Army Form C.2118.

WAR DIARY
or
INTELLIGENCE SUMMARY
(Erase heading not required.)

18th DIVL. SIGNAL CO., R.E.

OCT 1917

Place	Date	Hour	Summary of Events and Information	Remarks and references to Appendices
POPERINGHE	1st		During the period 1st to 10th October training was continued, particular attention being paid to the instruction of specialists. All cable detachment linemen were thoroughly instructed in localising faults and the care and maintenance of buried cable routes. All kinds of cables were dealt with and the men shown the correct method of jointing these. The Wireless Section with its stores was brought thoroughly up to date and practical experiments were carried out daily, particular stress being laid on the value of Power Buzzers and Amplifiers during active operations when the maintenance of the ordinary means of communication becomes an extremely difficult matter.	
	2nd		Lieut E.W. Benson, 7th Bedfords, took over command of N°. 1 Section vice 2/Lieut W.A. LANE, 8th East Surreys wounded.	
	6th		Captain C. Bellam M.C., R.E. proceeded to Kake over command of 2nd Divl Signal Co. RE	
	7th		Preparations for forward move and relief of 11th Division put in hand. Four N.C.O's and 13 men sent forward by lorry at 10:00am to learn and take over lines and test points on buried system opposite POELCAPELLE, from CANAD[?]	

O.C. 18th DIVL. SIGNAL CO., R.E.

WAR DIARY
INTELLIGENCE SUMMARY

OCT 1917

Army Form C.2118.

18th DIVL. SIGNAL CO., R.E.

Place	Date	Hour	Summary of Events and Information	Remarks and references to Appendices
BANK to SNIPE HOUSE.	7th (contd)		N.C.O's went round all test joints and inspected buries system generally. Thirty infantry signallers attached as extra linemen and wireless carrying parties for forthcoming operations. Eight of these were attached to the Wireless Section for training in Power Buzzer and Amplifier so that they should be available to man additional Power Buzzer stations and replace casualties as required. Remainder were thoroughly instructed in jointing all classes of cable and will eventually be posted to test points to assist the Signal personnel in maintaining lines.	
	9th		Winter Time came into force at 1:0 a.m. Captain N.S. Regnart, 8th Hussars assumed duties of 2nd in Command vice Captain C Bilton.	
CANAL BANK C.19.c.2a. (Sheet 28 NW)	10th		Two H.Q. linemen and all necessary instruments and stores sent forward to take over from 11th Divl Signals. All Wireless, Power Buzzer and Amplifier personnel and instruments sent forward to take over stations from 11th Division. One Signal office relief out forward to BORDER CAMP to be prepared.	[signature] Major R.E. O.C. 18th DIVL. SIGNAL CO., R.E.

Army Form C. 2118.

WAR DIARY
or
INTELLIGENCE SUMMARY
(Erase heading not required.)

18th DIVL. SIGNAL CO., R.E.

OCT 1917

(3)

Place	Date	Hour	Summary of Events and Information	Remarks and references to Appendices
	10th (contd)		to take over Rear Divn HQ Signal Office from 11th Division. One Signal Office relief sent forward to Advanced Divn H.Q. (CANAL BANK) to be prepared to take over communications at Advanced DvnHQ 11th Division. Breakdown party consisting of 1 N.C.O. and 10 men under Lieut Lepper detailed for maintenance of forward lines.	
CANAL BANK (C.19.c.2.6 - 11b/L Sheet 28 NW)			No 1x Detachment complete sent forward to CANAL BANK. Advd DvnH.Q closed at POPERINGHE at 10.0am and opened at CANAL BANK at same hour. Rear DvnH.Q. closed at POPERINGHE at 12 Noon and opened at BORDER CAMP at same hour. Company proceeded by march route at 9.30am to BORDER CAMP, taking over billets and horse lines occupied by 11th DivlSignal Co. Lines laid from BORDER CAMP Exchange to 18th DivnTrain.	
	12th		Local lines run from Advanced Exchange to C.R.E. and A.P.M. Four pairs cable on Trestle Route from Y.R. to B.N. thoroughly overhauled and repaired and 2 new pairs laid from BN to LD, thus providing 6 pairs from YR to LD. Seven pairs armoured cable laid in ditch from RD to MON BULGARE	

J. Walker Major R.E.
O.C. 18th DIVL. SIGNAL CO., R.E.

WAR DIARY
INTELLIGENCE SUMMARY

Army Form C. 2118.

18th DIVL. SIGNAL CO., R.E.

OCT 1917

Place	Date	Hour	Summary of Events and Information	Remarks and references to Appendices
	13th		Work on Trestle Route completed. Two pairs armoured cable laid in shallow trench from L.D. to MINTY FARM.	
	14th		Overland armoured quad from GOURNIER FARM to L.D. reeled up and laid close alongside duckboard track for the better protection of lines.	
	15th		Armoured quad between R.C. and L.D. repaired and retapped. Suoi parties, each consisting of 1 N.C.O. and 3 men, under supervision of Lieuts Leffler Watson and Coe detailed to thoroughly overhaul Divisional Lines between L.F. and M.W. and effect any necessary repairs to Test Points.	
	16th		Work on overhaul of Buried Cable System complete, with very satisfactory results. Owing to intense shelling of practically the whole forward area it was found very difficult to maintain the buried cables and repairs were necessary daily. Many alternative lines had to be laid out over ground and some of these proved safer and more useful than the buried routes.	
	17th		Seven pairs armoured twin laid in ditch between G.N. and L.H. Top arm of Permanent Route from Y.R.R. to BRITANNIA FARM removed and routes into R.C. Test Point.	

O.C. 18th DIVL. SIGNAL CO., R.E.
Major R.E.

Army Form C. 2118.

(5).

WAR DIARY
or
INTELLIGENCE SUMMARY
(Erase heading not required.)

18th DIVL. SIGNAL CO., R.E.

OCT 1917

Place	Date	Hour	Summary of Events and Information	Remarks and references to Appendices
	18th/19th		Ditched cables between SNIPE HOUSE and PHEASANT FARM overhauled and repaired, also ditched cables between LT and SNIPE HOUSE.	
	20th		One pair D.V. twisted cable laid overground from LH to AU BON GITE for use of 54th Bde. Armoured grass cable laid along duckboard track from PHEASANT FARM to Jeff'm Ho.	
	21st		Poles cable route of 2 pairs constructed from MINTY FARM to VARNA FARM to act as emergency lines. Three pairs of D8 cable laid along duckboard track from LH to LT to replace action of ditches cables almost completely destroyed between these two points.	
	22nd		Trestle and permanent routes which were broken by shell fire yesterday repaired and put through at 6:30am. Division attacked in front of POELCAPPELLE. Communications held good throughout the battle. Some very useful work done by Wireless, Power Buzzer and Amplifier Stations and trigons.	
	23rd		Poles cable route between RC and GN and Trestle route from YRR to LD repaired and overhauled. Section of buried cable between IN and KN relaid.	
	24th		Buried cable route extended from SNIPE HOUSE to PHEASANT FARM.	

J. Collins Major R.E.
O.C. 18th DIVL. SIGNAL CO., R.E.

Army Form C. 2118.

WAR DIARY
or
INTELLIGENCE SUMMARY
(Erase heading not required.)

18th DIVL. SIGNAL CO., R.E.

OCT 1917

Place	Date	Hour	Summary of Events and Information	Remarks and references to Appendices
	24th (contd)		200 infantry details for digging trench and the work was completed and cables laid with very little interruption between 6.0am and 3.0pm. Work on section of bury between IN and KN completed. Preparations for relief by 58th Division commenced. All known relies and instruments replaced by those of incoming Division. One Signal Office relief sent to POPERINGHE to be prepared to take over communications at Town Hall at 8.0am on 25th. This relief was replaced at CANAL BANK by a similar relief of 58th Division.	
POPERINGHE	25th		18th Division relieved by 58th Division. Advanced and Rear HQ closed at CANAL BANK and BORDER CAMP respectively at 10.0am and 8am at Town Hall POPERINGHE at same hour. Company moved from BORDER CAMP to POPERINGHE by march route at 8.0am.	
	26/27/17		All wagons harness and equipment overhauled and cleaned. All technical stores and instruments overhauled and checked and deficiencies indented for. All infantry personnel temporarily attached to Signal Company for duty returned to their respective units on 26th.	
	27th		Division orders to move to PROVEN. Advanced detachment and one Signal	

Magarth
[signature]
O.C. 18th DIVL. SIGNAL CO., R.E.

Army Form C. 2118.

WAR DIARY
or
INTELLIGENCE SUMMARY.

(Erase heading not required.)

18th DIVL. SIGNAL CO., R.E.

(7)

OCT 1917

Place	Date	Hour	Summary of Events and Information	Remarks and references to Appendices
	29th (Contd)		Offr. relief sent forward to take over Camp and Signal Office respectively.	
PROVEN.	30th		Divisional H.Q. closed at POPERINGHE at 11.0.am and opened at PROVEN at same hour. Company proceeded by march route at 9.0.am.	

Awards during month:-

MILITARY MEDAL

No 62234 2/Cpl. A.C. L.H. Bulmer   No 74952 Sapper E. & C. Smedler   No. 103961 Sapper E.M. Hartley

Average strength of Company during month:-
9 Officers   268 O.R.   116 Horses.

Enclosures:-

A. Diagram of lines

B. Route diagram "A"

C. Route diagram "B"

D. System of Communications during operations

J.C.Willis
O.C. 18th DIVL. SIGNAL CO., R.E.
Nupot/18.

S E C R E T.

System of Communications of 18th Division for forthcoming offensive operations - October, 1917.

The system of communications of the 18th Division for the forthcoming operations will be dealt with in detail under the following headings:-

    (a) Telegraphic and Telephonic.
    (b) D.R.L.S., Runners, Mounted men and D.R's.
    (c) Wireless and Earth Induction.
    (d) Pigeons.
    (e) Visual Signalling.
    (f) Rockets.
    (g) Messenger Dogs.
    (h) Contact Aeroplane Patrol.

(a) Telegraphic and Telephonic.

Prior to the attack there is to be no telephonic communication forward of Brigade Headquarters. Brigades and battalions are now complete as regards their establishments of Fullerphones, and sufficient personnel have been thoroughly trained to use them; consequently, Fullerphones only are to be used before 'Zero' hour.

There is one Buried Cable Route running from CANAL BANK (Advanced Divisional Headquarters) up to SNIPE HOUSE. This is duplicated by poled and 'ditched' cables. Forward of SNIPE HOUSE all lines are either 'ditched' or ground lines, and cannot be absolutely relied on. Ditched lines will be run up to Battalion H.Q's, time permitting. After each successive advance the 'ditched' cable routes will be extended by Divisional Signals.

(b) D.R.L.S.

Usual system of D.R.L.S. between Corps, Rear Divisional H.Q's and Brigade in Reserve, up to Advanced Divisional H.Q's on CANAL BANK.
Forward of the Canal to Brigade Headquarters in Line, despatches will be carried by mounted orderlies (Troopers of K.E.H.). Distribution of these mounted orderlies is as follows:-

    2 at Brigade H.Q. (VARNA FARM)
    4 at Intermediate Post at GOURNIER FARM. (C.9.d.3.8)
    4 at Advanced Divisional Headquarters.

As the advance is continued the Intermediate Post will be moved up nearer the line.

Each Brigade and Battalion will organise its own Runner Service on the lines laid down in S.S.148 - Forward Inter-Communication in Battle - Runner Posts being established along definite main routes every 400 yards or so. Brigade and Battalion Runner Schemes to be forwarded to Divisional H.Q.

(c) **Wireless and Earth Induction.**

Corps Wireless Directing Station at C.25.b.0.2. This is in direct telephonic communication with Advanced Divisional H.Q.

Trench Wireless Set at Brigade H.Q. VARNA FARM. (C.4.a.5.2)

Trench Wireless Set at PHEASANT FARM. (U.30.b.2.7)

N.B. - Both these stations will work back to Corps Directing Station and are complete with encoding officers.

Power Buzzer and Amplifier Station at PHEASANT FARM (U.30.b.2.7), working to:-

  (i) Power Buzzer and Amplifier Station at Left Battalion H.Q. (V.19.a.7.3)

  (ii) Power Buzzer and Amplifier Station at Right Battalion H.Q., GLOUCESTER FARM. (V.20.c.4.3)

N.B. - These last two stations will only be installed if sufficient accommodation can be found.

(d) **Pigeons.**

70 Pigeons are available for operations. These have been allotted as follows:-

```
Tanks attached 18th Division      -   20.
R.A. covering 18th Division Front -   20.
55th Infantry Brigade             -   16.
53rd    "         "               -   14.
```

Pigeon Lofts used by the 18th Division are:-

```
No. 4 Mobile Loft.  (40 birds)  at  A.28.b.
 "  38 Mobile Loft. (50 birds)   "  A.28.b.
    WATOU Loft.     (50 birds)
```

No's. 4 and 38 Lofts are connected to 18th Divisional Rear Headquarters Exchange, and the WATOU Loft is connected to XVIII Corps Exchange.

Pigeons will be brought up each day to HURST PARK by motor cyclist, at which place they will be issued to Pigeoneers.

No pigeons will on any account be kept out longer than 48 hours.

(e) **Visual Signalling.**

The fullest possible use of visual signalling is to be made by Brigade and Battalion signallers.

(f) **Rockets.**

40 Rockets will be issued for operations; 20 to the 55th Infantry Brigade and 20 to the 53rd Infantry Brigade

(3)

Five foot angle irons for use as troughs will also be issued. Method of use is as follows:-

Drive angle iron into ground at about angle of 70°, then pull over to required angle (50°) and anchor down to pegs driven into the ground.

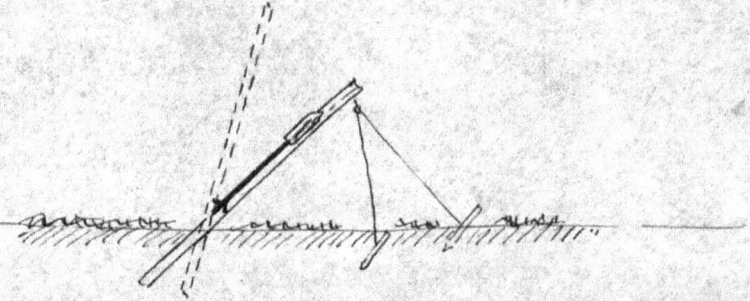

Rockets will be re-allotted by Brigades to Battalions according to tactical requirements.

(g) <u>Messenger Dogs</u>.

Two dogs will be allotted to the 53rd Brigade for "Z" day. Brigade H.Q. will re-allot these dogs to either Battalion or Company H.Q. according to tactical requirements.

It is suggested that as these dogs can carry as much as two or three sheets of paper, they would be extremely useful to a Brigade Forward Observing Officer, who could thus send back a moderately long despatch. Messenger dogs must be taken forward on a chain from their keeper, who will remain at Brigade H.Q. They will 'home' thus to Brigade H.Q. There is practically no limit to the distance they will travel and they 'home' at the rate of about 25 m.p.h. All ranks should be warned that they are on no no account to interfere with these dogs while on a journey. The only occasion when anyone is justified in interfering with them is when the dogs have been killed or wounded, in which case the despatch should be taken out from the pouch on the dog's collar and handed in to the nearest Signal Office.

(h) <u>Contact Aeroplane Patrol</u>.

Message Dropping Ground at C.19.c.1.4, near Advanced 18th Divisional H.Q. on CANAL BANK.

This will be marked with an 'X', receipt of messages being acknowledged by means of Ground Signalling Shutter.

(Sgd) Wallace Wright
Lieut. Colonel,
10th October, 1917.   General Staff, 18th Division.

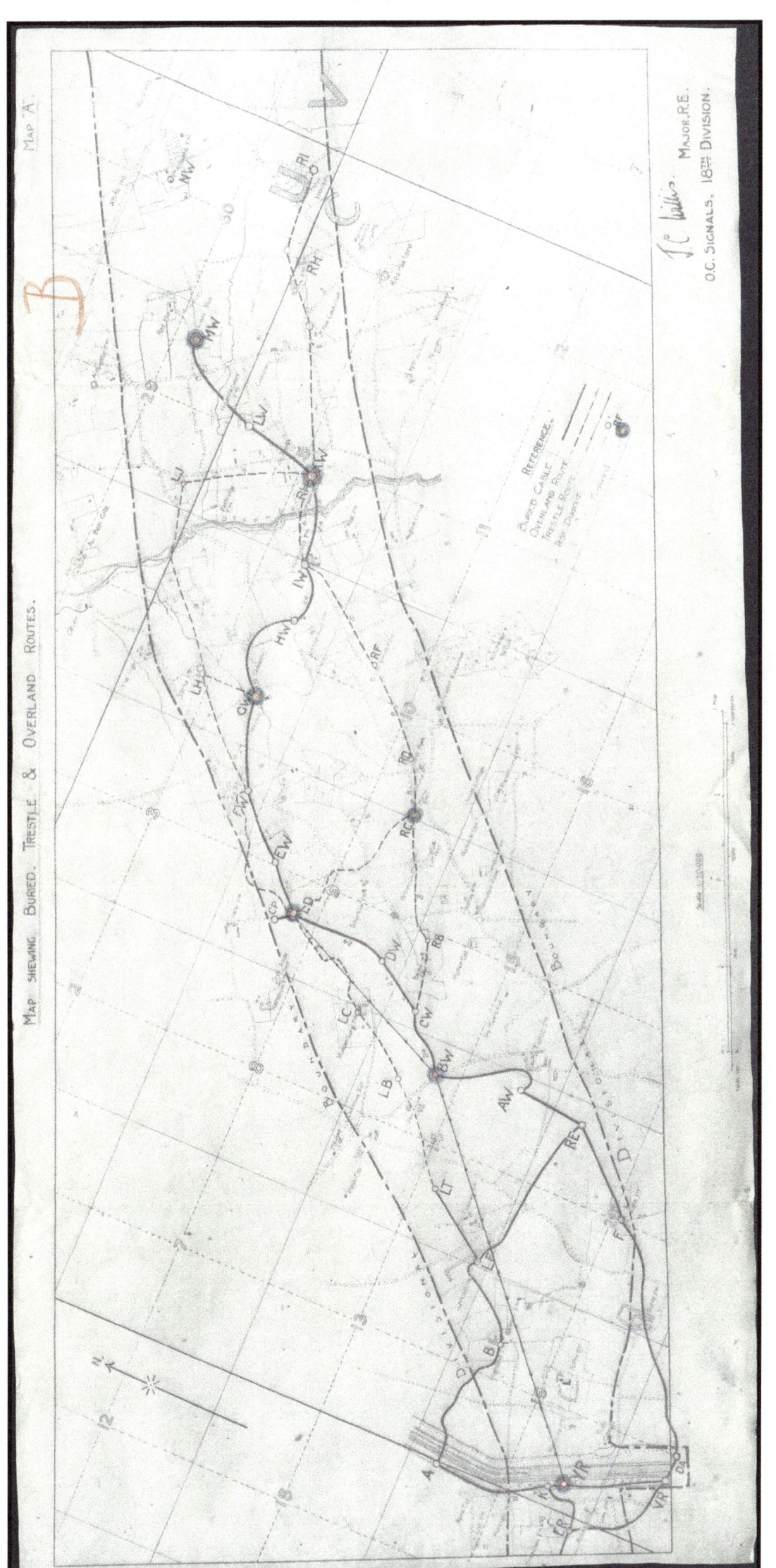

Map A

B

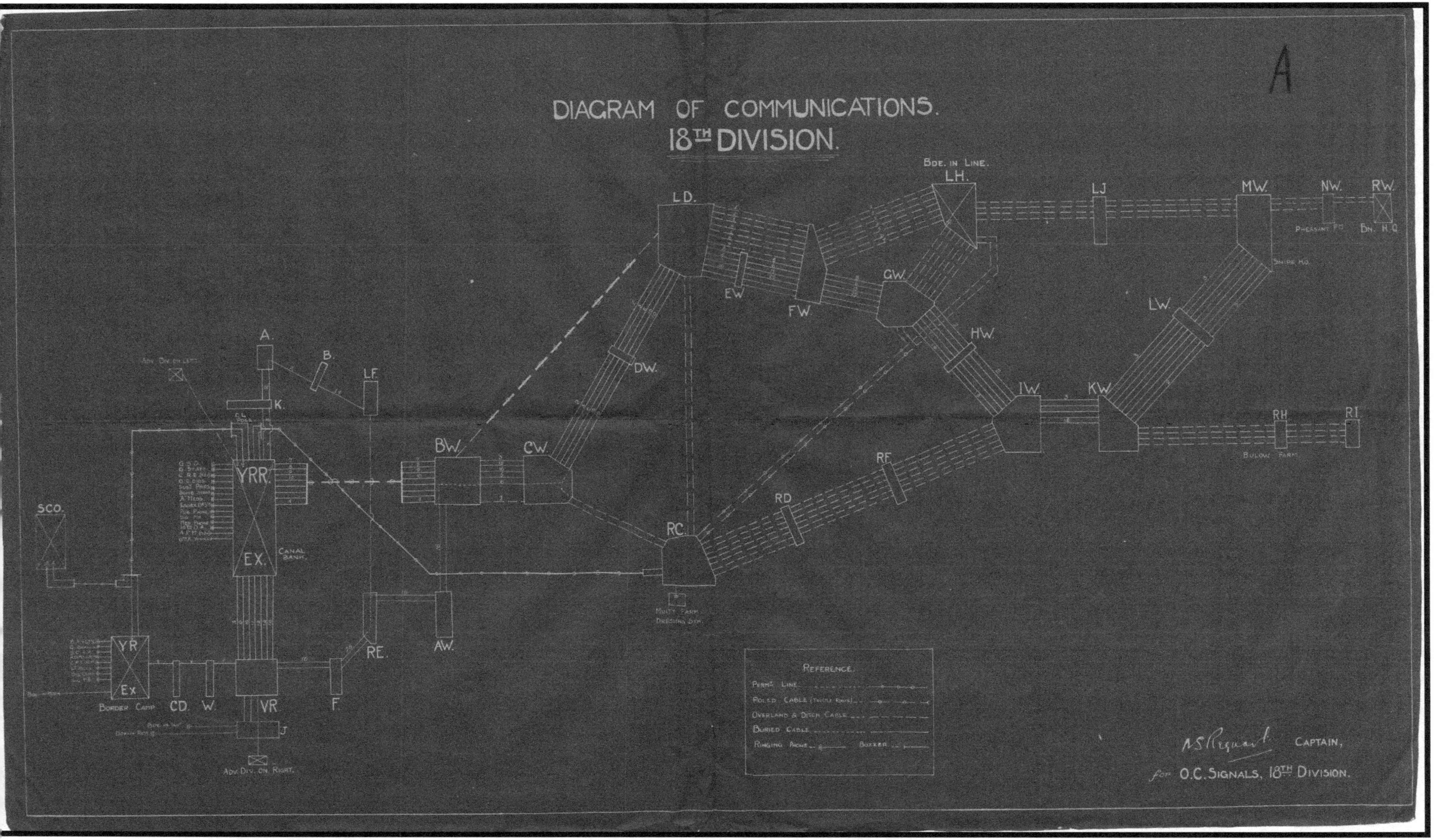

A
DIAGRAM OF COMMUNICATIONS.
18TH DIVISION.
BDE. IN LINE.
LH.
LD.
LJ
MW.
NW.
RW.
BN. H.Q.
EW
FW.
GW.
HW.
LW.
IW.
KW.
RH
RI
BULOW FARM
RF
RD
RC.
DW.
CW.
BW.
A.
B.
LF.
K.
YRR.
EX.
CANAL BANK.
SCO.
YR
Ex
BORDER CAMP
CD.
W.
VR
J
F.
RE.
AW.
ADV. DIV. ON RIGHT.
REFERENCE.
PERMT. LINE
POLED CABLE
OVERLAND & DITCH CABLE
BURIED CABLE
RINGING PHONE
BUZZER
CAPTAIN,
for O.C. SIGNALS, 18TH DIVISION.

WAR DIARY
INTELLIGENCE SUMMARY

18th DIVL. SIGNAL CO., R.E.

NOV. 1917

Place	Date	Hour	Summary of Events and Information	Remarks and references to Appendices
PROVEN	1st/2nd/3rd		Division in rest at PROVEN. Preparations for taking over from 35th Division put in hand. Eight Linesmen sent forward to take up duty at various Test Points and make themselves generally acquainted with lines and arrangements for maintenance of same.	
	4th		One Signal Office relief complete sent forward to "J" Camp (A.8.b.1.5 Sheet 28 N.E. 1/20,000) Proposé Duriska to take over from 35th Division. One Cable Section to J. Camp to take over horse lines and billets. Linesmen posted to Brigade H.Q. in line (WOOD 15); WOOD HOUSE and St Test Points.	
J. Camp 5th (A.8.b.1.5 Sheet 28 N.E.)			Divisional H.Q. closed at PROVEN at 10.0 a.m. and opened at J. Camp at same hour. Advanced Signal Office opened at ZONNEBLOOM. Company moved by march route from PROVEN to J. Camp. Remainder of Signal Office personnel and Wireless Section with instruments and stores moved to ZONNEBLOOM.	
	6th		Two pairs armoured twin laid from B.F. Test Point to Brigade H.Q. in line (WOOD 15). One pair D2 cable laid from Brigade H.Q. to WH Test Point. Three pairs D8 cable (air) along permanent route from ZONNEBLOOM to "O" Test Point via ELVERDINGHE.	

W. Raynor. Captain
18th DIVL. SIGNAL CO. R.E.

Army Form C. 2118.

(2)

WAR DIARY

INTELLIGENCE SUMMARY.

NOV 1917 (Erase heading not required.)

18th DIVL. SIGNAL CO., R.E.

Instructions regarding War Diaries and Intelligence Summaries are contained in F. S. Regs., Part II. and the Staff Manual respectively. Title pages will be prepared in manuscript.

Place	Date	Hour	Summary of Events and Information	Remarks and references to Appendices
	7th		Three pairs paper D.E. cable from ZOMMERBROOM to "O" Test Point completed.	
	8th		Three pairs armoured twin from "ZB" to "O" overhauled and regulated. Line from C.F. Test Point to Div. Bomb Store overhauled and put through. Two 7-pair armour-sheathed cables laid from ZB to Signal Office at ELVERDINGHE Chateau.	
	9th		Spare cables running from ZOMMERBROOM office which were replaced by armoured twin and 7-pair cables yesterday rolled up. Preparations for taking over Signal Office at ELVERDINGHE Chateau from 50th Division put in hand. Two H.Q. linesmen to make a general survey of lines at the Chateau.	
	10th		Advanced Div.Signal office closed at ZOMMERBROOM at 4pm and opened at ELVERDINGHE Chateau at same hour.	
ELVERDINGHE Chateau	11th		Div H.Q. closed at J Camp at 11am and opened at ELVERDINGHE Chateau at same hour. Local lines to all Div H.Q. Offices in Chateau grounds laid and electric light installed. Started replacing all single and multicore cables leading from terminal pole in front of Chateau to Signal Office by lead covered cables laid under roadway. Signal Office at J Camp closed at 11am and all lines with exception of D.A.D.O.S. stripped through to ELVERDINGHE.	

W Reynolds, Captain
18th DIVL. SIGNAL CO., R.E.

Army Form C. 2118.

WAR DIARY
INTELLIGENCE SUMMARY
18th DIVL. SIGNAL CO., R.E.

NOV 1917

(3)

Place	Date	Hour	Summary of Events and Information	Remarks and references to Appendices
Chateau D.20.01	11th (contd)			
	12th		Work on leading in from terminal pole and internal wiring of Signal Office continued. 5-line Magneto Exchange at S.O. closed and lines put through to Divisional Exchange.	
			Two miles lead covered cable moved forward for proposed extension of bury.	
	13th		Two cables on permanent pole from Z.3 to O reeled up. Proposed route of bury between WOOD HOUSE and SIGNAL FARM traced out and marked.	
	14th		One pair D.8 cable laid from CF to Div Bomb Store at GOUVY FARM with extension to 19th Northumberland Pioneers at B.11.c.6.6.	
	15th		Work started on extension of buried cable system from WOOD HOUSE to SIGNAL FARM, two Companies of 7th R.W.Kents being detailed to dig trench. Owing to the very wet nature of the ground it was found impossible to dig deeper than 3ft bins without meeting with serious interference from water and to counter-balance this a bank 3ft high was built up overground, this being camouflaged to render it less conspicuous from the air. 7pair lead sheathed cable was used and this was laid from specially contructed "cradles". 7pair armoured cable was	

L Raymond Captain
18th DIVL. SIGNAL CO., R.E.

WAR DIARY
INTELLIGENCE SUMMARY
NOV 1917

Army Form C. 2118.
18th DIVL. SIGNAL CO., R.E.

Place	Date	Hour	Summary of Events and Information	Remarks and references to Appendices
	15th (contd)		used for the crossing of the STEENBEEK where it was impossible to obtain sufficient protection for lead-sheathed cables. Particular attention was paid to jointing and all joints were treated with No.5 compound, covered with lead sleeves and soldered. Party of 300 men started work at 6:00am and 400 yards of trench were dug, 28 pair cable laid and the trench filled in to ground level by 12 Noon.	
	16th		Work on buy continued. Party of 180 infantry started work at 7am and built up bank of earth 3ft high along 400 yards of trench completed yesterday. 28 pair tested, all through and a Test box was installed at ANCHOR FARM. In order to improve the existing D.R.L.S. between Division and Brigade an lyre a Runner Post was established in a sandbagged elephant shelter at BOESINGHE. Telephonic communication was established with this post which was manned by 2 motor cyclist DRs, 4 cyclists and 2 runners, the former to work between Runners Post and Divisional H.Q. and the latter to work forward to Brigade H.Q. on lyre via CLARGES STREET.	
	17th		15th on buy forward of ANCHOR FARM continues. Party of 180 infantry started work at 7am and a further 400 yards of trench were dug to an average	

W. Percival Copson
18th DIVL. SIGNAL CO./R.E.

WAR DIARY

INTELLIGENCE SUMMARY

NOV 1917 — 18th DIVL. SIGNAL CO. R.E.

Place	Date	Hour	Summary of Events and Information	Remarks and references to Appendices
	17th (contd)		depth of 3 feet, 25 pairs cable laid and trench filled in by 11-30am. Six pairs of cable on the EL-ZB. route replaced by 60 lb G I wire and cable rods in. Earth banked up to a height of 3' 6" on the 100 yards of cable trench completed yesterday and the 28 pair cable taken and led into Test Box at end of bury to date.	
	18th			
	19th		Work on bury continued and a further 300 yards of trench dug to an average depth of 3'6". Cables laid and trench filled in. Trench now completed and cables throughout up to VULCAN CROSSING – FOURCHE FARM Road. EL-ZB route re-strained and regulated and 7-pair twin sheathed cable between these two points recovered.	
	20th		Cable trench up to VULCAN CROSSING – FOURCHE FARM Road banked up to a height of 3 feet and camouflaged. One pair D.V. twists built on permanent poles between WOOD 15 and BOESINGHE Road. Permanent route along ELVERDINGHE – BOESINGHE Road restrained and regulated.	
	21st		Bury completed up to within 100 yards of SIGNAL FARM and all cables testing through to this point	

M. Renard, Captain
18th DIVL. SIGNAL CO., R.E.

Army Form C. 2118.

(6)

WAR DIARY
or
INTELLIGENCE SUMMARY
(Erase heading not required.)

NOV 1917

18th DIVL. SIGNAL CO., R.E.

Place	Date	Hour	Summary of Events and Information	Remarks and references to Appendices
	22nd		Cable trench completed up to SIGNAL FARM. Twentyeight pairs through from WOOD HOUSE to SIGNAL FARM and ringing and speaking excellent.	
	23rd		Completed portion of buzz between ANCHOR FARM and SIGNAL FARM was given an extra banking of earth in all weak places, particular attention being paid to that portion nearest SIGNAL FARM which is likely to be subjected to heavy shelling.	
	24th		Cable trench dug from SIGNAL FARM to a point just across the STEENBEEK. Average depth 4 feet. Cable across STEENBEEK laid between upon girders and sandbagged for better protection. Test box erected at end of buzz and all lines tested through to that point. Four top pairs on BF-GF Route re-wired and allotted as follows:- 1 pair to Div. Bomb Store (GOUVY FARM). 1 pair to Pioneers Post, BOESINGHE and 1 pair connected up to pole's cable to Brigade in fusee.	
	25th		Trench between SIGNAL FARM and the STEENBEEK brought up to an average height of 3½ feet and cable brought up for laying tomorrow.	
	26th		Cable trench dug between the STEENBEEK and WIDJENDRIFT, cables laid and trench filled in. Test points at SIGNAL FARM and WIDJENDRIFT wired and	

[signature]
18th DIVL. SIGNAL CO./R.E.

WAR DIARY

INTELLIGENCE SUMMARY

NOV 1917

18th DIVL. SIGNAL CO., R.E.

Date	Hour	Summary of Events and Information	Remarks
26th (contd)		All cables tested OK between these points.	
27th		Got 200 yards of cable trench up to WIDIENDRIFT banked up and all Test boxes sandbagged. Crossing over the STEENBEEK was also protected by 3 further layers of sandbags. Route from E1 to GF regulated and cleared of all derelict lines.	
29th		A further 300 yards of trench was dug in direction of MONTMIRAIL FARM, cables laid and trench filled in.	
30th		Portion of trench completed yesterday banked up and cable taken up for continuation of burying. Up to date only one casualty to working parties has been reported.	

Army Form C. 2118.

WAR DIARY
INTELLIGENCE SUMMARY.
(Erase heading not required.)

18th DIVL. SIGNAL CO., R.E.

NOV 1917

(8)

Place	Date	Hour	Summary of Events and Information	Remarks and references to Appendices
			Awards during month :-	
			<u>MILITARY CROSS</u>	
			Lieut L.W. Bird – 10th Essex Regt – Attached 18th Divl Signal Coy R.E.	
			<u>MILITARY MEDAL</u>	
			No 62234 2nd/Cpl A.C.L.H. Bulmer No 103961 Spr F.M. Hartley	
			" 74952 Sapper F.J. Chandler " 45858 Sergt. J Whitehead	
			No 161461 A/2/Cpl L.G. Martin	
			Average strength of company during month :- 10 Officers 281 OR 116 Horses	
			Enclosures :-	
			"A" Signal Communications – Defence Scheme	
			"B" Report on Power Buzzer and Amplifier Working	
			"C" Line Diagram	
			"D" Route Diagram	

W Raymond Captain
18th DIVL. S——L CO., R.E.

SECRET

SYSTEM OF COMMUNICATIONS
18TH DIVISIONAL DEFENCE SCHEME.

"A"

The system of communications in the Divisional Area will be dealt with in detail under the following headings :-

    (i)   System of Lines.
    (ii)   Wireless and Earth Induction.
    (iii)   D.R.L.S. and Runner Systems.
    (iv)   Visual System.
    (v)   Pigeons.
    (vi)   Rockets.

(i)   System of Lines.

There are three main routes forward of 18th Divisional Headquarters at ELVERDINGHE CHATEAU to Brigade Headquarters in Line.

These routes are :-

(a)   Permanent line to BOESINGHE and poled cable on to Brigade with alternate lines in buried cable route starting at LUNAVILLE FARM and going via WOOD HOUSE also to Brigade.

(b)   Permanent line to ZOMMERBLOOM (ZB) and ground armoured cables on to Brigade, passing through LUNAVILLE FARM, BOESINGHE and BOIS FARM.

(c)   Permanent line to ZOMMERBLOOM and buried cable forward to Brigade also via LUNAVILLE FARM and WOOD HOUSE.

The Brigade Headquarters at ZOMMERBLOOM and BENSON'S FARM are connected to Divisional Headquarters by permanent line, and there is also direct telephonic communication with units at "J" Camp, e.g., D.A.D.O.S. and Divisional Train.

Forward of Brigade Headquarters in Line, there will be two main routes forward, which when complete, will be as follows:-

(a)   Buried cable route of 28 pairs from WOOD HOUSE - ANCHOR FARM - SIGNAL FARM - WIJDENDRIFT - POINT U.16.c.1.9., crossing the BROENBEEK by Light Railway Bridge - New Brigade H.Q. - KOEKUIT - OBTUSE BEND - LES 5 CHEMINS. Pairs on this route will be allotted to Brigade in Line, Divisional and Corps Artilleries.

(b)   Ground Cable from BOIS FARM - SAULES FARM - SIGNAL FARM - RUISSEAU FARM - DESAIN FARM - CANNES FARM - NEW BRIGADE HQRS. - along HUNTER STREET to VEE BEND - across to GLANGES STREET and along CLARGES STREET to near CINQ CHEMINS.

In the rear area this route will consist of steel armoured cable; forward of new Brigade Headquarters it will consist of field cable for ease in repairing.

Linesmens' stations, manned by Divisional, Brigade and Artillery Linemen, will be placed at regular intervals along this route.

Telephone Exchanges.

> 18th Divisional Hqrs.) ELVERDINGHE CHATEAU.
> 38th Div. Arty. Hqrs.)
> Sub-exchange at WOOD HOUSE, C.2.a.2.8.
> Sub-exchange at BOESINGHE, B.12.c.9.9.
> Exchanges at all Artillery and Infantry
> Brigade Headquarters.

(ii) **Wireless and Earth Induction.**

System of communication will be as in diagram :-

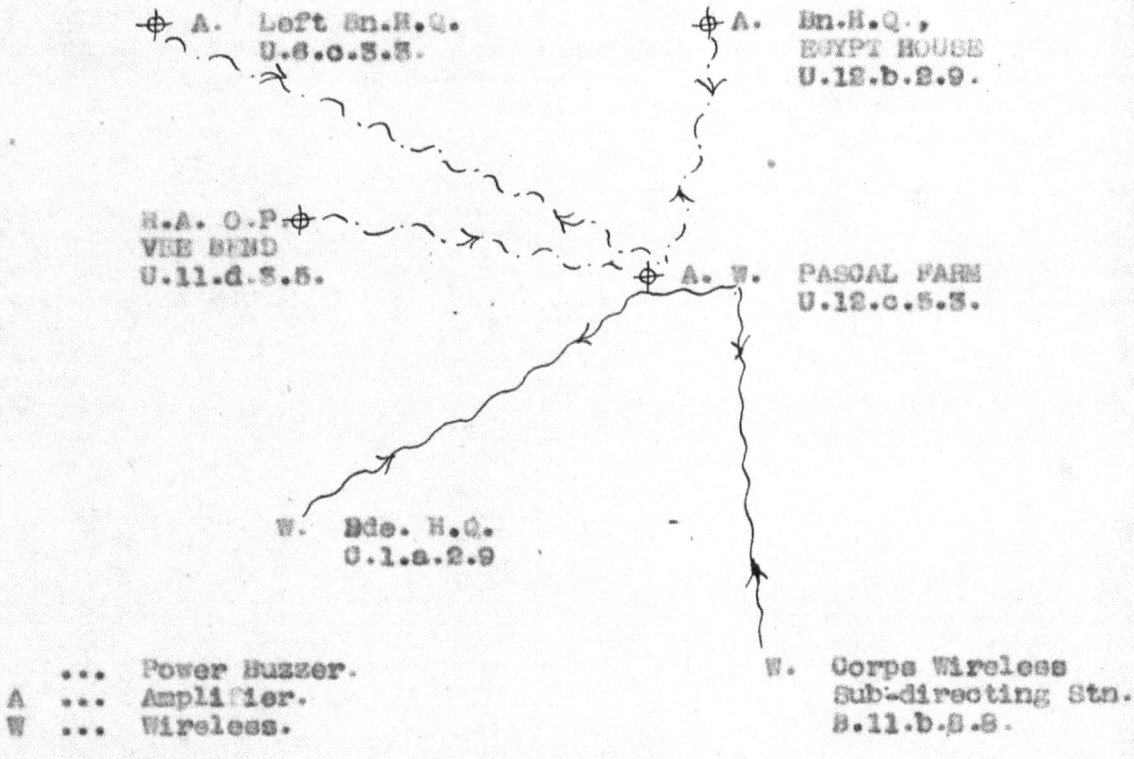

```
...   Power Buzzer.
A ...   Amplifier.
W ...   Wireless.
```

W. Corps Wireless
Sub-directing Stn.
B.11.b.8.8.

(iii) **D.R.L.S. and Runner Systems.**

Motor cyclist D.R's will carry despatches to all units from Divisional Headquarters except Brigade in line; for Brigade in Line they will take despatches to Runners Post, BOESINGHE, B.12.c.9.9. They will be carried on from this point to Brigade Headquarters by Runner. There are three motor cyclist D.R's and six runners at this post, which is on the telephone.

Brigade in Line will organise and maintain its own Runner Service up to Battalion Headquarters.

(iv) **Visual.**

Visual Signalling (Lucas Lamp) will be established forward of Brigade Headquarters to Battalions. Brigade in Line will report the positions of all visual stations in forward area.

(v) Pigeons.

Owing to the misty weather it has been found to be useless to release pigeons. In the event of better weather, 4 pigeons per Infantry Brigade in Line and 2 pigeons per Divisional Artillery will be drawn each day from the Pigeon Loft at ZOMMERBLOOM.

(vi) Rockets.

A system of sending messages by Message Rocket is to be established by Brigade in Line between Brigade and Battalion Headquarters. Troughs at Battalion Headquarters will be sited to drop rockets at a forward receiving station, say GRUYTERSZALE. From this point messages could be sent back to a second receiving station, say WIJDENDRIFT. Brigade will furnish a report giving positions of stations.

J. Challis

Major, R.E.,
O.C. Signals, 18th Division.

23rd November 1917.

"B"

Report on Forward W/T and P.B. and A. Station.

BASES.   The cable issued for bases for P.B. and A. stations in Forward Areas is found to be very little use, owing to its poor insulation and tendency to get broken both by concussion and by parties walking over it. In practice, we have found D.V. cable quite satisfactory.

From the four months experience we have had in BELGIUM with Forward Power Buzzer Stations, we have come to the conclusion that this form of communication is not reliable over distances of more than 1,000 to 1,200 yards. This is due to the fact that the ground is absolutely saturated by the water which remains just below and on the surface and also owing to the fact that the soil has been so thoroughly loosened by heavy and continuous shell fire.

To obtain best results we consider that all bases should be about 200 yards in length to provide sufficient resistance between the earths of the same base.

Apart from the above suggestions, the methods adopted by G.H.Q. have proved fairly satisfactory.

J.C. WILLIS
Major, R.E.,
13th November 1917.   O.C. Signals, 18th Division.

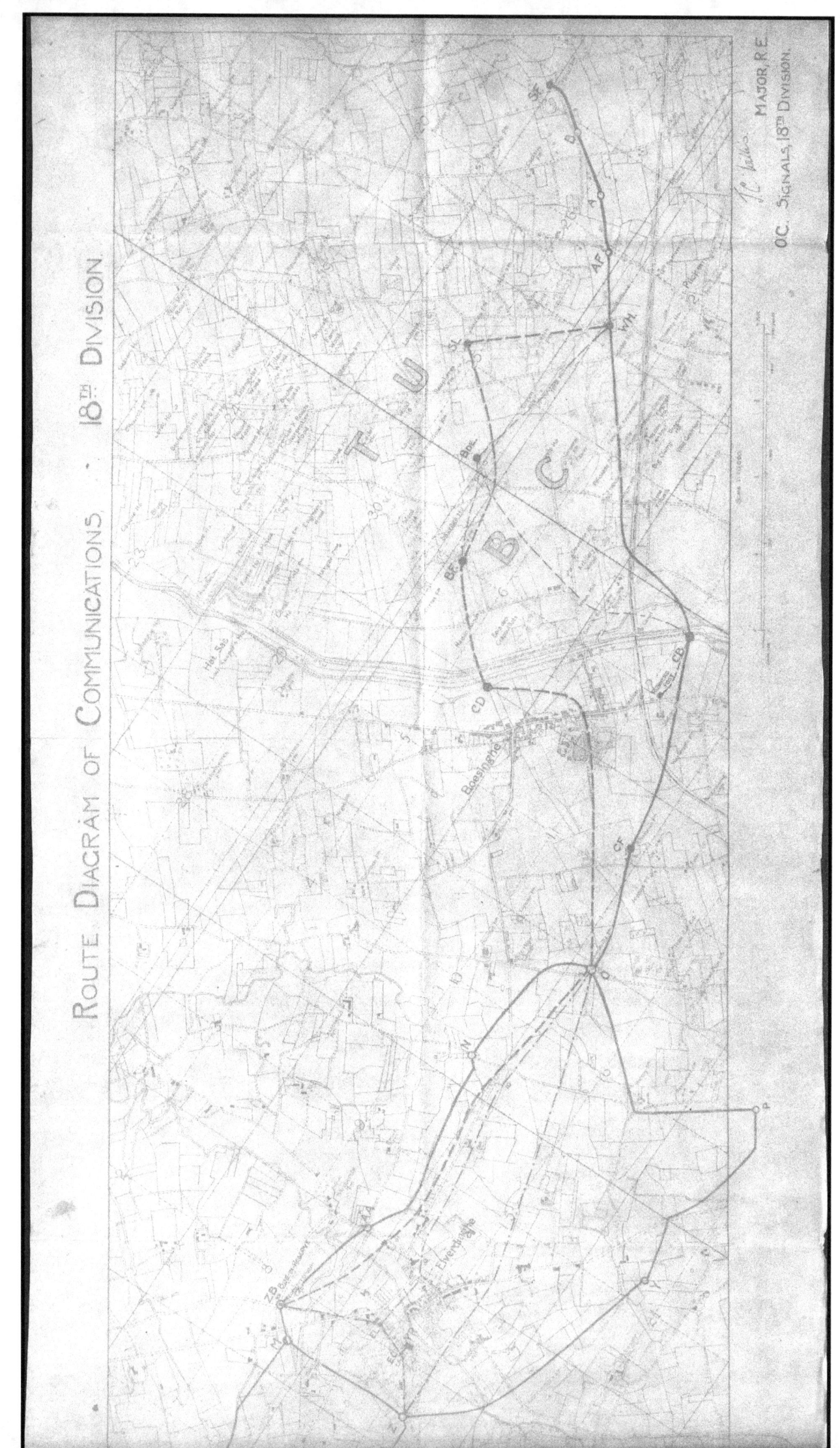

18 D Lemal
Pl 24

Army Form C. 2118.

WAR DIARY
or
INTELLIGENCE SUMMARY.
(Erase heading not required.)

18th DIVL. SIGNAL CO., R.E.

DEC 1917

Place	Date	Hour	Summary of Events and Information	Remarks and references to Appendices
ELVERDINGHE	1st/12		On 30th November the buried cable system (28 pair) was completed as far as WIJDENDRIFT, the cables being buried at depths varying from 6 feet to 2 feet the average being 3 feet 6 inches. To give the cables more protection from hostile artillery a bank of 3 feet of earth was built up along the route. During the week the route was extended as far as a point 150 yards east of CRAONNE FARM and 400 yards S.W. of the Light Railway Crossing over the BROOMBEEK, 28 pair being through to this point. Since 30th ulto. 4 direct hits, assumed to be 5.9a, were made on the trench, but beyond blowing away the overground bonding no damage was caused as all cables tested clear. Experiments were carried out by 53rd Infantry Brigade signals with message rockets between NEY CROSS ROADS and SIGNAL FARM. Results were satisfactory as it was found that occasional rockets fired at same range with same elevation varied in range as much as 300 yards in their range.	
	5th/12		Buried cable system completed up to the BROOMBEEK (U.4.c.1.0) and a junction box erected at cable zone's permanent and semi-permanent routes	

O.C. 18th DIVL. SIGNAL CO., R.E.

WAR DIARY
or
INTELLIGENCE SUMMARY.
(Erase heading not required.)

Army Form C. 2118.

18th DIVL. SIGNAL CO., R.E.

(2)

Place	Date	Hour	Summary of Events and Information	Remarks and references to Appendices
	DEC 1917		west of the YSER Canal have been regulated and taken into use, replacing lines on the bray from ELVERDINGHE forward.	
			Communication from Brigade in Joie (WOOD 15) to its Right and Left Battalions is provided by 2 overland routes, one via SIGNAL FARM and one direct. From YEE BEND two pairs of overland cables go out direct to each Battalion H.Q., one at EGYPT HOUSE and one at 5 CHEMINS, and a third pair to EGYPT HOUSE is diverted by way of PASCAL FARM.	
			Further experiments were made with Message Rockets between NEY CROSS ROADS and SIGNAL FARM and these shewed that no great amount of reliance can be placed on this means of communication. Four rockets were fired, the first of which made a direct hit, the other three going two or three hundred yards either right or left of the target. In every rockets got observers usual) have to be fired near the objective and if this is done messages should be marked with a fair amount of certainty.	
			A chain of visual stations was established forward of Brigade H.Q. (WOOD 15) to Battalions, the Lucas Lamb being the chief transmitting medium.	

O.C. 18th DIVL. SIGNAL CO., R.E.

WAR DIARY
or
INTELLIGENCE SUMMARY.
(Erase heading not required.)

18th DIVL. SIGNAL CO., R.E.

DEC 1917

Army Form C. 2118.

(3)

Place	Date	Hour	Summary of Events and Information	Remarks and references to Appendices
	12th		Lieut G E PELHAM-CLINTON, M.C., R.E transferred to 21st Divisional Signal Co. R.E. as 2nd in Command.	
	15th		Preparations for relief by 57th Division put in hand. Wireless Section relieved by personnel of 57th Division, and 57th Division Linesmen posted to the various Test Points. Lieut S.H. Lepper R.E. assumed command of No.2 Section vice Lieut G.E. Pelham-Clinton	
	17th		One Signal Office relief complete sent forward to ROUSEBRUGGE and were relieved at ELVERDINGHE CHATEAU by a similar relief of 57th Division. "A" Cable Section moved to ROUSEBRUGGE.	
ROUSEBRUGGE 18th			Divisional H.Q closed at ELVERDINGHE CHATEAU at 10.0am and opened at same hour at ROUSEBRUGGE. Remainder of company moved to ROUSEBRUGGE by march route.	
	18th to 31st		From 18th to 31st December the Division was in XIV Corps Reserve in the ROUSEBRUGGE area. Orders to Corps and Brigades were issued by Cos. Signals, Brigades being supposed as follows:-	

A. Multi[?]

O.C. 18th DIVL. SIGNAL CO., R.E.

Army Form C. 2118.

WAR DIARY
or
INTELLIGENCE SUMMARY.
(Erase heading not required.)

18th DIVL. SIGNAL CO., R.E.

DEC. 1917

Instructions regarding War Diaries and Intelligence Summaries are contained in F. S. Regs., Part II. and the Staff Manual respectively. Title pages will be prepared in manuscript.

Place	Date	Hour	Summary of Events and Information	Remarks and references to Appendices
			53rd Bde at HERZEELE, 54th Brigade at HARINGE, 55th Brigade at NORDAUSSQUES.	
			All cable cart wagons etc, were thoroughly overhauled and all deficiencies in technical stores made good. Reinforcements fitted to cable sections to fill vacancies. Company made up to strength except for motor cyclist despatch riders, reinforcements of this class not being available at Base. Some signal courses were held and trigon instruction was given to selected infantry personnel from each Brigade.	
			Average strength of Company during month:- 10 Officers, 280 O.R. and 118 horses.	
			Enclosures:-	
			"A" Route diagram	
			"B" Diagram of Lionel Stations	
			"C" Diagram of Power Buzzer Stations	

[signature] Major
O.C. 18th DIVL. SIGNAL CO., R.E.

Army Form C. 2118.

WAR DIARY
INTELLIGENCE SUMMARY.
(Erase heading not required.)

18th DIVL. SIGNAL CO., R.E.

Vol 26

Place	Date	Hour	Summary of Events and Information	Remarks and references to Appendices
January 1918. ROUSEBRUGGE	1st		Preparations for relieving 57th Division but in hand and twelve Linesmen were sent forward to take over test points on buried cable system.	Map ref: Sheet 27 1/40,000
	2nd		One Signal Office relief complete sent forward to take up duty at 8-0am tomorrow. Telephones, instruments, etc, to replace those of 57th Division were also taken forward as well as all wireless stores. Runners Post BOESINGHE taken over by personnel of 18th Division	
ELVERDINGHE Chateau	3rd		Divisional Headquarters closed at ROUSEBRUGGE at 10-0am and opened at same hour at ELVERDINGHE CHATEAU. Remaining Signal Office personnel and NCO's and men for work in forward area sent forward by lorry at 7-30am. Company Hrs Stores and transport to "J" Camp near INTERNATIONAL CORNER ( ) by march route via CROMBEKE. The following through connections were made in the ROUSEBRUGGE Signal Office at 10-0am :- 38 C.C.S. to PROVEN Ex.; 51st of Bde to XIX Corps Ex.; Pumping Station ROUSEBRUGGE to Area Commandant CROMBEKE	Map ref: Sheet 28 1/40,000
	4th		2nd Lieut S H Maddox RE i/c of a party of 4 sappers opens out all shell holes on line between CM Test Point and BB Test Point and investigates	[signature] Major

18th DIVL. SIGNAL CO., R.E.

WAR DIARY
or
INTELLIGENCE SUMMARY.

(Erase heading not required.)

JAN 1918

Army Form C. 2118.

18th DIVL. SIGNAL CO., R.E.

Place	Date	Hour	Summary of Events and Information	Remarks and references to Appendices
	4th (contd)		and repaired any damage to cables.	
	5th		Permanent joints made on all leading in cables outside W.T. Test Point and the cables sandbagged.	
	6th		All leads in bury forward of "BB" Test Point tested out and jointed and test frame at W.T. completed.	
	7th		Four pairs on permanent route between BF and GF repaired and put through and faults on line pairs between GF and Runner Post BOESINGHE cleared.	
	8th		A Divisional Signal School for the training of Artillery and Infantry signalling instructors was opened today, vacancies being allotted as follows: 2 per Battalion and 6 for Divisional Artillery. Course to last 6 weeks and all N.C.O's and men attending to be given thorough instruction in all methods of signalling with a view to their being able to instruct a reserve of signallers in their units on returning thereto. Pigeon Courses, each to last 2 days, and to take 12 Officers and 2 n C.O's per infantry brigade, were started at ZOMMERBLOOM Pigeon Loft. Lectures on the	

18th DIVL. SIGNAL CO., R.E.

Army Form C. 2118.

(3)

WAR DIARY
or
INTELLIGENCE SUMMARY.
(Erase heading not required.)

18th DIVL. SIGNAL CO., R.E.

JAN 1918

Instructions regarding War Diaries and Intelligence Summaries are contained in F. S. Regs., Part II. and the Staff Manual respectively. Title pages will be prepared in manuscript.

Place	Date	Hour	Summary of Events and Information	Remarks and references to Appendices
	8th (contd)		handling and care of birds were delivered on the first day of each course by the N.C.O. i/c Pigeon Lofts, and the second day was devoted to a practical scheme illustrating the value of pigeons as a means of communication.	
	12th		Work was commenced on a new permanent route between Runner Post BOESINGHE and WOOD HOUSE. The section of the old buried route between those two posts has constantly been giving trouble principally through earth leakages and the construction of a new route of a permanent or semi-permanent nature was necessary to ensure reliable communications from the end of the present route at CANAL BANK forward to WOOD HOUSE. The route was finished and four wires through when the Division was relieved on 30th January.	
	17th 21st 24th		Six pair pole cable route between WOOD HOUSE and WOOD 15 completely rebuilt.	

J. Mullio
Major R.E.
18th DIVL. SIGNAL CO., R.E.

WAR DIARY
INTELLIGENCE SUMMARY
(Erase heading not required.)

18th DIVL. SIGNAL CO., R.E.

JAN 1918

Army Form C. 2118.

(1)

Place	Date	Hour	Summary of Events and Information	Remarks and references to Appendices
	27th		Preparations for relief by 32nd Division put in hand and Liaison Officers of the incoming Division were posted to the various Test Points to learn and take over lines. Part of technical stores moved to ROUSEBRUGGE — proposed new Divl. H.Q.	
	28th		Liaison sent forward to ROUSEBRUGGE to pick up lines to :— CROMBEKE (for 54th Bde.), HERZEELE (for 55th Bde.), HARINGE (for 53rd Bde.), PROVEN and XIX Corps. Twenty line exchange, sounders and test panels installed in Signal Office at ROUSEBRUGGE.	
	29th		Signal School moved to ROUSEBRUGGE. One office relief sent forward at 2.0pm to be prepared to open up Signal Office at 8.0am tomorrow. Runners Post BOESINGHE closed and delivery to units in that neighbourhood being effected by D.R. on routine runs to WORD 15 (ASM F3)	
ROUSEBRUGGE	30th		Divisional H.Q. closed at ELVERDINGHE Chateau at 10.30am and opened at ROUSEBRUGGE at noon hour. Company moved by march route via ELKHOEK and CROMBEKE and took over billets and horse lines previously occupied. The Signal Office at ELVERDINGHE Chateau	

[signature] Major R.E.
18th DIVL. SIGNAL CO., R.E.

WAR DIARY
INTELLIGENCE SUMMARY.
(Erase heading not required.)

18th DIVL. SIGNAL CO., R.E.
JAN 1918

Army Form C. 2118.

(5)

Place	Date	Hour	Summary of Events and Information	Remarks and references to Appendices
	30th (contd)		was not taken over by the incoming division and all circuits as was with the exception of locals were put through on multicore cable to WELSH FARM (3rd Divn. H.Q.)	
	31st		Division in rest at ROUSEBRUGGE	

Awards during month:-

MILITARY CROSS:- Lieut. E.W. BENSON, 7th Bedfords A/O.C. No 4 Section.

DISTINGUISHED CONDUCT MEDAL:- No 23133 Sgt. (A/C.S.M) H.P. ASHTON R.E.

Average Strength of Company during month:- Officers 10 O.R. 280 Horses 116.

Enclosures:- A. Route Diagram of Communications
 B.   "   "   "   "

J. Munro
Major R.E.
18th DIVL. SIGNAL CO., R.E.

18 D Sitzung
Ja 27

Army Form C. 2118.

WAR DIARY
or
INTELLIGENCE SUMMARY.

(Erase heading not required.)

18th DIVL. SIGNAL CO., R.E.

FEB 1918

Place	Date	Hour	Summary of Events and Information	Remarks and references to Appendices
ROUSEBRUGGE	1st to		Division in rest in the ROUSEBRUGGE area.	
	4th		Training commenced.	
	5th		Divisional Headquarters closed at ROUSEBRUGGE at 12 Noon and moved by tactical trains to NOYON, Headquarters being established at SALENCY. Transport from XIV Corps, Fourth Army to III Corps, Fifth Army. A lorry was despatched by road on 6th instant with a skeleton Signal Office relay and the necessary instruments to form an Advanced Divisional Report Centre at SALENCY at 12 Noon on 8th. Company moved by tactical train from PROVEN at midnight on 7th, detraining at NOYON at 7am on 8th and moving by march route to SALENCY. Communication with temporarily detached units was maintained by motor cyclist DRs up to time of entrainment. Telephonic communication with 54th Infantry Brigade and 18th Divisional Artillery who had not moved from old area till 8th was maintained through XIX Corps Division came under administration of III Corps on 7th and lines to respective Brigade and Artillery Headquarters were allotted in SALENCY area by Aulnoye III Corps it being only necessary therefore to lay local circuits to the	

W Aylward Captain
p.o.C. 18th DIVL. SIGNAL CO., R.E.

WAR DIARY
or
INTELLIGENCE SUMMARY.
(Erase heading not required.)

FEB 1918

18th DIVL. SIGNAL CO., R.E.

Army Form C. 2118.

Place	Date	Hour	Summary of Events and Information	Remarks and references to Appendices
SALENCY (On'ze)	8th		Various Headquarter Offices Divisional H.Q. established at PONTOISE	
	9th		Local lines laid to C.R.E. and Divisional Train	
	13th		Four G.9 semi-permanent lines built along French permanent route from MAREST DAMPCOURT to CAILLOUEL for use of Brigade at latter place	
	15th		French permanent route from the main NOYON-CHAUNY route to BABOEUF repaired and one additional pair added for use of Division en route to BABOEUF. Six also laid to "G" and "A/Q" Branch office buildings and a trestle route of 6 bairs was built from main NOYON-CHAUNY route to proposed Signal Office at BABOEUF.	
	16th		Local telephone lines laid to D.A.D.O.S and 18th Div Train	
BABOEUF (On'ze)	17th		Divisional H.Q. closed at SALENCY at 11:00am and opened up at same hour at BABOEUF. All cables used for local lines at SALENCY were rolled up for re-issue.	

W Raymond Captain
for O.C. 18th DIVL. SIGNAL CO., R.E.

WAR DIARY
INTELLIGENCE SUMMARY
(Erase heading not required.)

Army Form C. 2118.

18th DIVL. SIGNAL CO., R.E.

FEB 1918

(3)

Place	Date	Hour	Summary of Events and Information	Remarks and references to Appendices
	19th		One pair picked up on L.O. trunk route to APPILLY and one pair to MONTESCOURT for use of No. 2 Ammunition Sub-Park and 18th Machine Gun Battalion respectively.	
	24th		Preparations put in hand for relief of 58th Division (HQ ROUEZ CAMP - S.21.b.9.3 - Sheet 66.C. 1/20000) and the necessary personnel and instruments sent forward to effect exchange in Signal Office. One Cable Section complete sent forward to ROUEZ to take over Signal Camp from Signals 58th Division.	
ROUEZ	27th		Divisional HQ closed at BABOEUF at 10am and opened at ROUEZ at noon. Company moved by march route via CHAUNY-VIRY NOREUIL Signal School remaining at BABOEUF. On arrival in the ROUEZ area it was found that all communications forward (with the exception of two short metallic buried cable routes, one from GIBERCOURT to BENNAY and one from LIEZ to FORT de VENDEUIL) consisted of permanent line and ground cables and these were not only very circuitous but routed too in the event of any	

W.H. Mort Capt.
for O.C. 18th DIVL. SIGNAL CO., R.E.

Army Form C. 2118.

WAR DIARY
or
INTELLIGENCE SUMMARY.
(Erase heading not required.)

18th DIVL. SIGNAL CO., R.E.

FEB. 1918

Place	Date	Hour	Summary of Events and Information	Remarks and references to Appendices
			shelling at bombing very unreliable. It was considered that some further buried cable routes should be constructed so as to provide reliable communications forward to Brigades and important tactical points. This was agreed to by the General Staff and a working party of two infantry was promised for work on 1st March. Work commenced on the building of a hop pole route from LIEZ to RÉMIGNY and the adding of an extra arm to the forward route ROUEZ – QUESSY.	
	28th		During the month no active operations were undertaken by the Division and the opportunity was availed of to thoroughly overhaul all stores and to complete technical equipment of all units as far as possible. A programme of training for open warfare was got out and all cable detachments were given a "refresher" course of cable drill and were thoroughly practiced as independent units in the laying of all kinds of cables, and in the building and maintaining of open	

W Raymont
Capt
ot 18th DIVL. SIGNAL CO., R.E.

WAR DIARY
or
INTELLIGENCE SUMMARY.
(Erase heading not required.)

FEB 1918
18th DIVL. SIGNAL CO., R.E.

(5.)

Army Form C. 2118.

Place	Date	Hour	Summary of Events and Information	Remarks and references to Appendices
			routes. Particular attention was paid to the training of the Infantry and Artillery signallers and Brigade and Divisional Signal Classes were maintained as far as the tactical situation permitted, the former to act as elementary classes and the latter to turn out a number of N.C.O's capable of acting as instructors in their own units for the training of reinforcements.	
			Average strength of company during month:-	
			10 officers 283 other ranks horses 117.	
			Enclosures:-	
			"A" System of communications	
			"B" Proposals for buried cable systems	
			"C" Diagram of communications	
			"D" Diagram of visual communication	

W Flynn Captain
p/ O.C. 18th DIVL. SIGNAL CO., R.E.

SECRET.

SYSTEM OF COMMUNICATIONS — 18th DIVISION.

The system of communications in the Divisional Area will be dealt with in detail under the following headings:-

    (i) System of Lines, both Telegraph and Telephone.
   (ii) Wireless and Earth Induction.
  (iii) D.R.L.S., Mounted Orderlies and Runner Systems.
   (iv) Visual System.
    (v) Pigeons.
   (vi) Message Rockets.

(i) System of Lines.

The system of lines will be described :-
    (a) As it exists at present.
    (b) As it will exist.

(a) There are two main routes of lines forward of Divisional Headquarters, ROUEZ Camp (S.27.a.1.2), the first to the Left Infantry and Artillery Brigade Headquarters, ADOLPHE QUARRY (H.33.d.central) via VILLEQUIER-AUMONT - FAILLOUEL - JUSSY (with alternative lines along the railway) to LIZEROLLES. At this point this route goes into a French buried cable route running just north of GIBERCOURT, to a Test Point 400 yards N. of LY-FONTAINE. This bury turns at this point and runs due N. to BENAY, but inter Divisional and Brigade lines are all taken off at Test Point N. of LY-FONTAINE, and run in to the Brigade H.Q's on ground cables.

The second main route forward of Divisional H.Q. runs to QUESSY passing just north of the BUTTE de VOUEL, and from QUESSY along the right side of the canal up to Right Infantry and Artillery Brigade H.Q's, LIEZ (T.31.b.7.3). There is a lateral line of cable between Left and Right Brigade H.Q's.

All the above lines, with the exception of the Brigade lateral, are open wires (Permanent Line) of French construction and of course in the event of shelling or bombing could not be relied upon.

Forward of Brigades, in the Left Brigade sector, all lines to battalions and batteries are ground lines and are unreliable. In the Right Brigade sector there is a French buried cable route of 12 pairs running from LIEZ to FORT de VENDEUIL. Lines to battalions and batteries are all put through on this route.

(b) The system of communications as it will exist when completed is as follows. Forward of Divisional Headquarters there will be 3 main routes to Brigades; the first 2 will be from ROUEZ to the sand pit 600 yards N.E. of the BUTTE de VOUEL along different routes. At this place there will be a mined Test Point, and lines will be put through to Brigade H.Q's,

LIEZ on a 6 ft. 6 ins deep buried cable route now in course of construction. From this Test Point forward to Brigade H.Q. LIEZ there will be three alternative routes; the first buried cable, the second airline to LIEZ and the third French permanent line viâ QUESSY to LIEZ. From LIEZ forward to Left Brigade H.Q. there will be three alternative routes also. The first a 6 ft. 6 ins deep buried cable route now in course of construction, running from LIEZ (N.13.a.4.3) due west of RUMIGNY (N.31.c.central) and thence viâ French buried cable to Brigade H.Q., ADOLPHE QUARRY. The second a route of open wires (semi-permanent line) running parallel to the LIEZ - ESSIGNY Road and about 50 yards off it, to a point 500 yards east of MONTESCOURT, and thence along old German permanent line viâ GIBERCOURT and LY-FONTAINE to Brigade H.Q. The third a poled cable line from LIEZ to RUMIGNY Exchange (N.14.a.2.4) and thence viâ buried cable forward spur from RUMIGNY to point 500 yards south of LY-FONTAINE and on to Brigade H.Q. as a ground line.

The third main route forward of Divisional H.Q. to Brigades will be the same as that described in para (i), sup-para (a), i.e., ROUEZ viâ VILLEQUIER-AUMONT - FAILLOUEL - JUSSY - LIEZROLLES viâ French buried cable to Brigade H.Q. The line to Brigade in Reserve runs viâ VILLEQUIER-AUMONT to CAILLOUEL.

Forward of Brigade H.Q. in the Left sector there will be a "forward spur" 6 ft. 6 ins. deep from the French buried cable route starting from Test box 400 yards north of LY-FONTAINE, to battalion headquarters. In the Right sector there will be two buried routes forward of LIEZ, one to FORT de VENDEUIL (12 pairs completed), and the second to FORT de LIEZ (14 pairs, 6 ft. 6 ins. deep) now under construction.

In all cases the lines will be so arranged that each line will serve the Headquarters of a Unit in its present position and its Battle Zone position. All lines must be buried into all H.Q's of Division and Brigades in Line (Infantry and Artillery), and all Telephone Exchanges are to be in dug-outs.

(ii)   Wireless and Earth Induction System.

This is as shewn in attached diagram.

(iii)   D.R.L.S.

All despatches are carried forward of Divisional H.Q. to Brigades in Line by motor cyclist D.R. Route as follows:- ROUEZ - VOUEL - LIEZ - RUMIGNY - GIBERCOURT - LY-FONTAINE.
In cases of urgency a D.R. can do the journey between Divisional H.Q. and the furthest away Brigade (Left Brigade) in 35 minutes. Brigades will organise their own D.R.L.S. systems, the Left Brigade by runners and the Right Brigade by mounted orderly.

3.

(iv) **Visual.**

The visual systems of both Brigades in Line are at present in process of being altered. The approximate visual scheme is as follows:-

[Diagram showing visual stations:
Left Bn, Support Co. H.24.b.88
Z.E.C. M.33.d.88
55th Bde. H.33.d.6.8
Co. of CAPONNE F.M. H.34.b
Res Co H.29.c.8.7
Supt Bn. N.3.d.3.4
Right Bn. H.29.d.9.0]

[Second diagram:
Bn. Battle H.Q. N.1.c.d.18
Bn. H.Q. Fort de Vendeuil
Co. H.Q. O.19.a.5.3
Co. H.Q. O.25.d.0.7
Rouguenet F.M.
55 Bde N.31.69.2
Co. H.Q. N.34.d.7.8
Fort de Liez]

⊗ = VISUAL STATION (LUCAS LAMP)

A Divisional Visual Scheme is being drawn up.

(v) **Pigeons.**

Eight pigeons are allotted to the Division on every other day. Each Brigade receives four birds.

(vi) **Message Rockets.**

Troughs for releasing Message Rockets are to be installed and sited in all strong points in the Battle Zone, in order to provide communication between these strong points and battalion Battle H.Q.'s. It should be remembered that the range of these rockets is 2,400 yards, and that they are accurate and quite reliable, provided the trough is sited correctly in the first plac

A map of communications in the Divisional Area is being prepared and will be ready shortly.

[Signature]

Major R.E.,

2nd March, 1918.   O.C. Signals, 18th Division.

DIAGRAM OF WIRELESS
COMMUNICATIONS
18TH DIVISION
2-3-18

Left Bn:
I.19a 0.8
KAC ⊕ (171)

Left Bde
53 Bde
H33a 6.7
W/T DO.
P.B FL
(168) T△ A⋏

3,600x
1,100x
4,000x

(170) A⋏
Right Bn:
I.25a Central
KAB

3,600x

12,000x

5,100x
T△ A⋏ (167)

Right Bde
55 Bde
N31b 7.4
W/T DN
PB KAN

(169) A⋏
Ford Bn:
N18c 5.7
KAO.

6,200x

(166)
W△ 18TH DIV: HQ
S28a 3.5
LI.

KEY.

⊕ = Power Buzzer Stn.
A⋏ = "   "   " & Amplifier.
T△ = Trench Set Stn.
W△ = Wilson Set Stn.
∼∼∼∼ = Route between Wireless Stns.
─ ─ ─ =   "   "   P.B. & Amplifier Stns.
W/T DN = Wireless Call.
PB KAN = Power Buzzer & Amplifier Call.
(166) = Corps Key Number.

Power Buzzer-Amplifier KAN-KAO at present
practically inoperative. KAO now working to FL.

SECRET.

18/SYR/807.

B

General Staff,
    18th Division.

        I attach a map shewing communications (Route Diagram) in the new 18th Divisional area. These consist (with the exception of the buried cables from LIEZ to FORT de VENDEUIL and from BIBERCOURT to BENNAY) entirely of permanent line and ground cables.
    They are not only very circuitous but are also unreliable in the event of shelling or bombing by the enemy. I therefore recommend that a buried cable route be installed along the following lines:-

(i)   Point N.1.a.9.9 near CIBERCOURT to Point N.13 central near REMIGNY.
        N.B. I have arranged that the 14th Division Signals should start this section.

(ii)   Point N.13. central to Brigade H.Q., LIEZ - N.31.b.6.3.

(iii) Brigade H.Q., LIEZ - T.7.a.0.2 - Point S.24.a.0.4.

(iv) Point S.24.a.0.4 - Point S.22.c.9.2.
        N.B. The above scheme fits in with the Fifth Army Scheme. Line of proposed buried cable route is shewn in yellow on attached map.

Labour required for completing the above sections is as follows:-

(i)   Distance 2000 yards. (This will in all probability be half completed by 14th Division). Labour required 400 men for 2½ days.

(ii)   Distance 3200 yards. Labour required 400 men for 8 days.

(iii) Distance 4500 yards. Labour required 400 men for 11 days.

(iv) Distance 2000 yards. 400 men for 5 days.

    Total length of proposed buried cable route is 10,700 yards.

    Total labour required is 400 men for 30 days.

    Twentyeight pairs will be laid throughout the entire length of this buried cable route.

23-2-18.

(sd) J.C.WILLIS Major R.E.,
O.C. Signals, 18th Division.

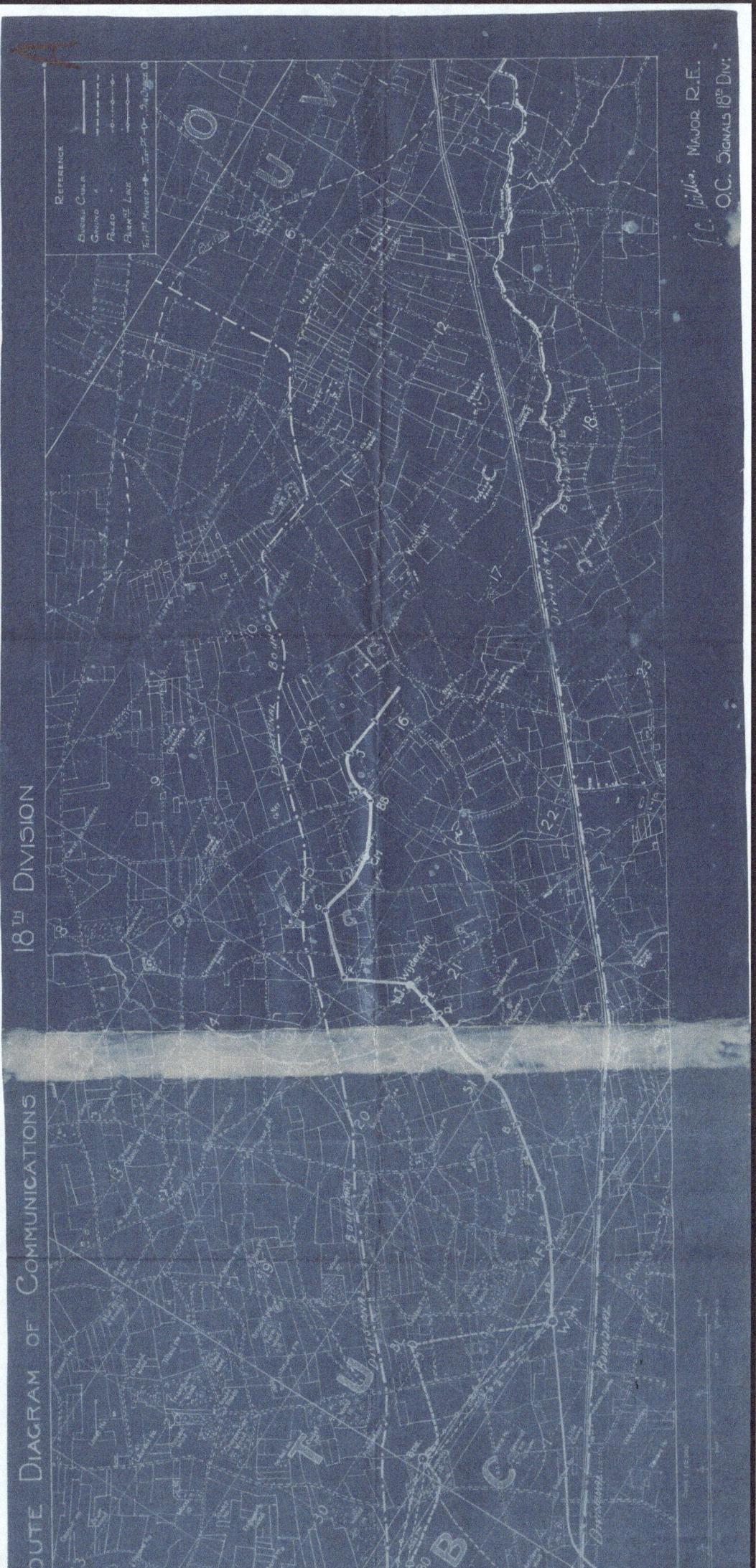

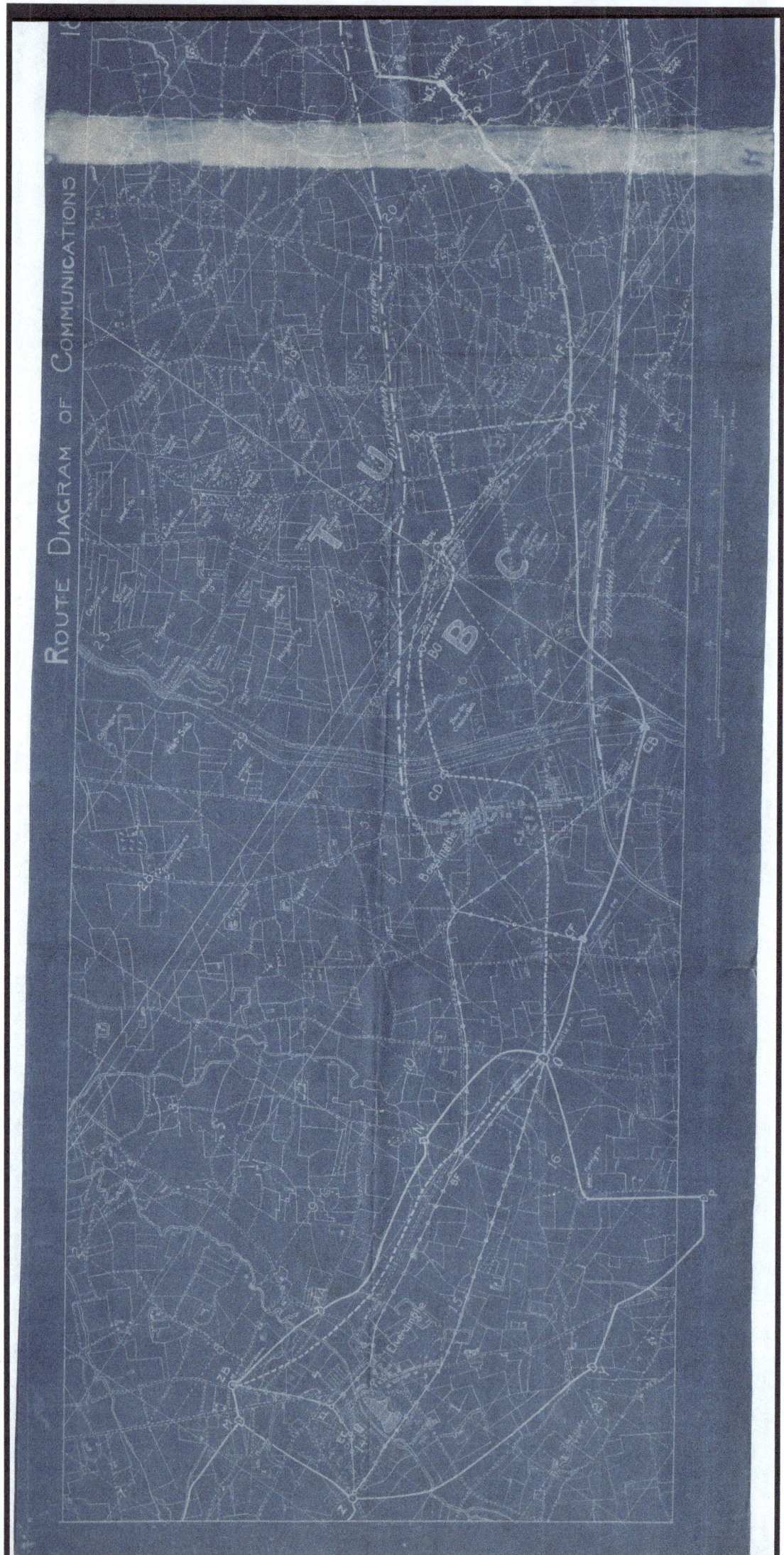

A

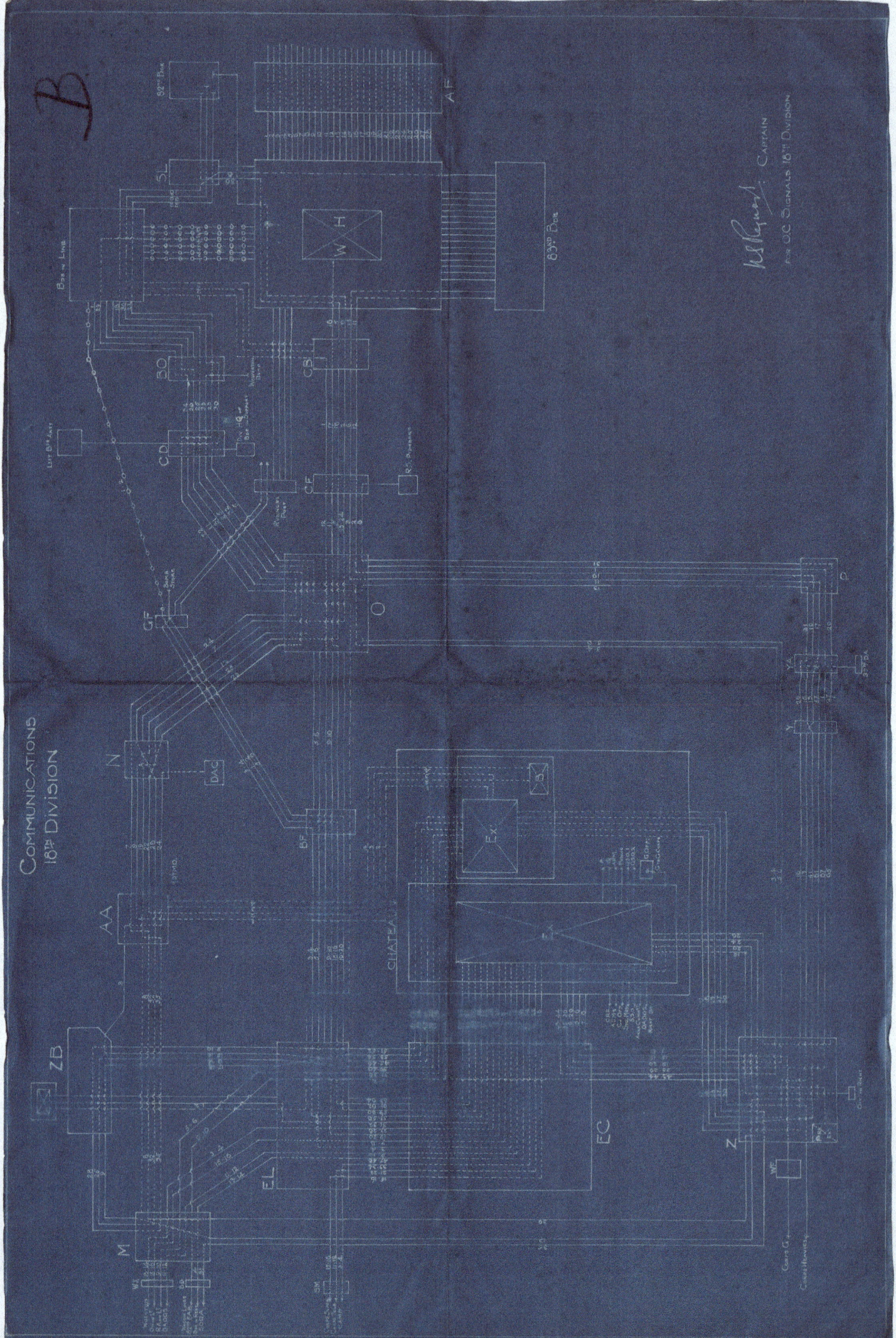

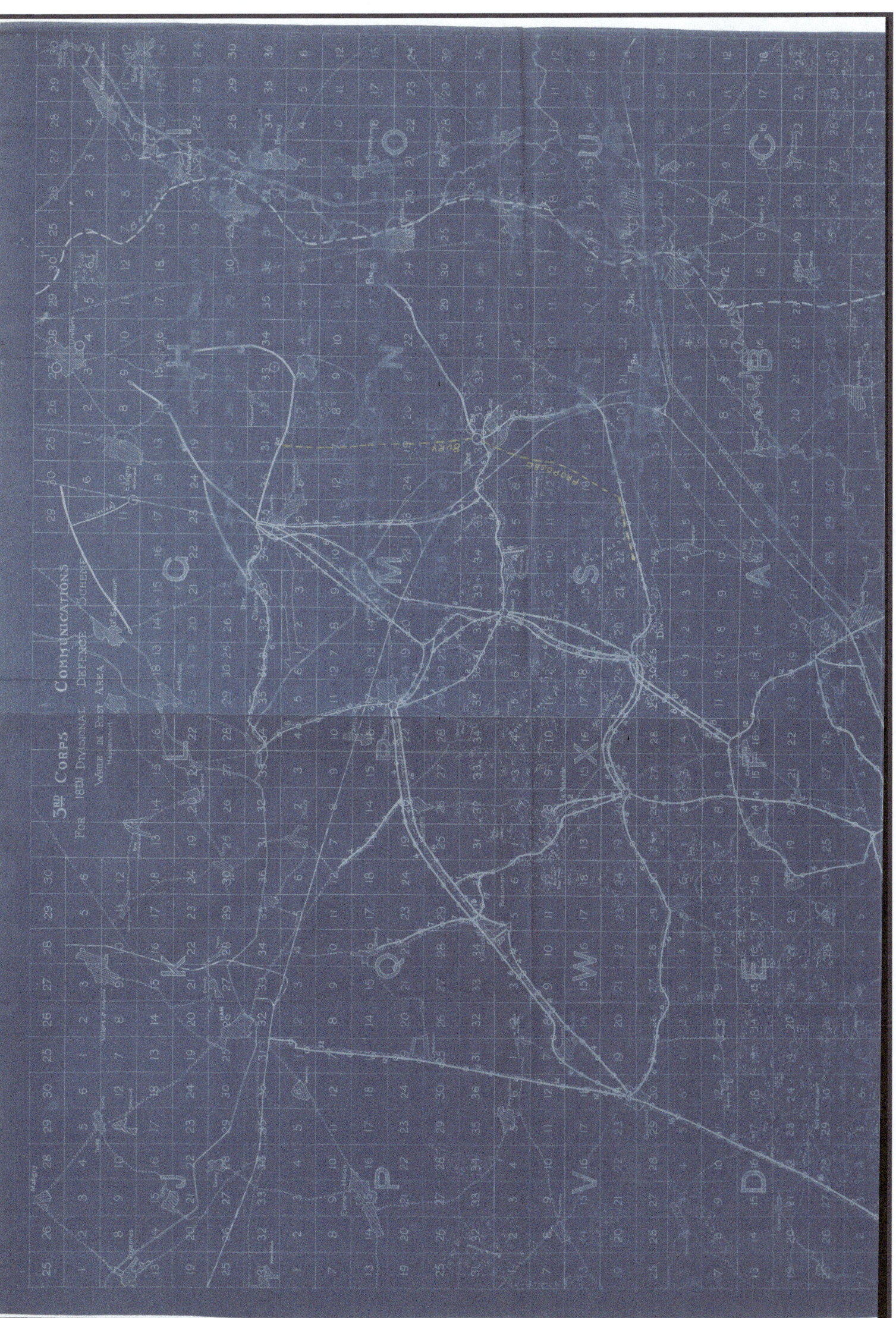

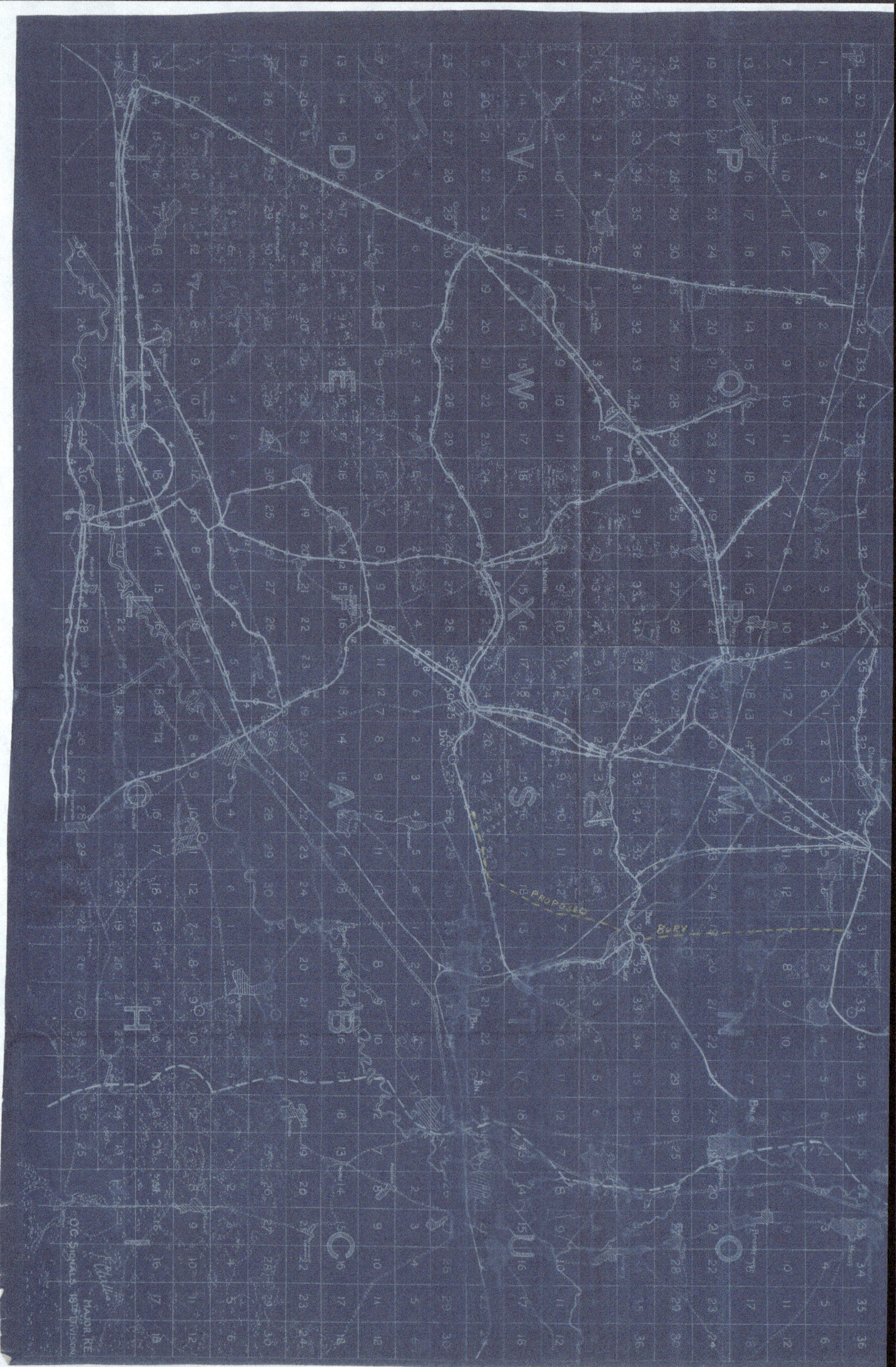

C

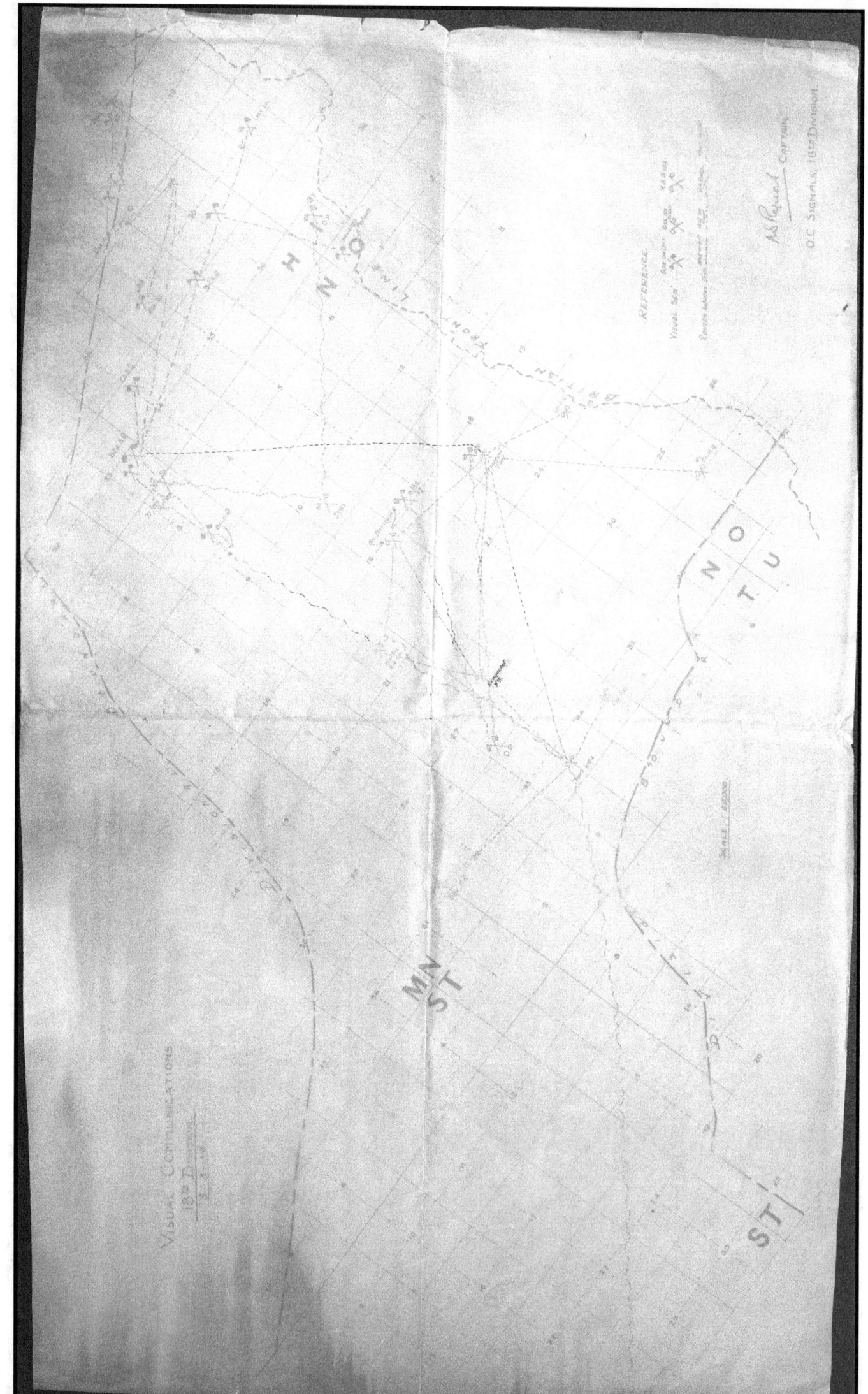

On His Majesty's Service.

War Diaries of
Admd 36th Dar
108th Fld Ambce
109"
110

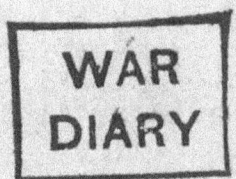

18th DIVISIONAL SIGNAL COMPANY, R.E.

MARCH

1918

Attached:-

Appendices A, B, C & D.

Army Form C. 2118.

WAR DIARY
or
INTELLIGENCE SUMMARY.

18th DIVL. SIGNAL CO., R.E.

(Erase heading not required.)

MAR 1918

Vol 29

Place	Date	Hour	Summary of Events and Information	Remarks and references to Appendices
ROUEZ	1st		Work on construction of lab pole route from HIEZ to REMIGNY continued	
	2nd		Hop pole route from HIEZ to REMIGNY completed and buried cable carrying visual to the route across the REMIGNY-TUSSY and REMIGNY-MONTESCOURT roads. Burial of Walker and Machine Gun Contact at REMIGNY connected up to Visual & Extgys at REMIGNY. "NE" Cable Section attached for duty and employed on work lines cable systems.	
	3rd		One pair pole & cable route inside France from ROUEZ to Divl Bomb store at Sth salient. Four pair French light pole route from MONTESCOURT to the MONTESCOURT – LY FONTAINE Road regulated and to pair pole through between same front. Work on buried cable system commenced. D no 3 over from infantry being draws for diggers.	
	4th		Work on bury continued between HIEZ and REMIGNY. Additions now made to the ariel-approach cable between ROUEZ and TUSSY.	App 24/6 "A" + "B"
	5th		Walk on bury between REMIGNY and HIEZ and between HIEZ and FORT HIEZ continued. Work commenced on wiring of new dugout office (Nissen Hut) at Div HQ dugouts.	

W Hampet Captain
for O.C. 18th DIVL. SIGNAL CO., R.E.

Army Form C. 2118.

WAR DIARY
or
INTELLIGENCE SUMMARY.
(Erase heading not required.)

18th DIVL. SIGNAL CO., R.E.

MAR 1918

Instructions regarding War Diaries and Intelligence Summaries are contained in F. S. Regs., Part II. and the Staff Manual respectively. Title pages will be prepared in manuscript.

Place	Date	Hour	Summary of Events and Information	Remarks and references to Appendices
ROUEZ	7th		Six foot cable trench dug from QUARRY at HIEZ to Railway Bridge at difficulty.	
	8th		Thirty pairs tested out and labelled in trench from HIEZ to Railway Bridge and from HIEZ to FORT HIEZ.	
	9th		Summer Time carries into force at 11.0 pm. Busy from HIEZ to FORT HIEZ completing.	
	11th		Two pair light pole route (G.I.) built from ROUEZ to the aerodrome at T.19.a along south side of road. One 2-pair army added to existing route from ROUEZ to BUISSY.	
	12/3		Trenches dug for reception of lead cables from Command poles at ROUEZ FARM and "G" office to H.Q. dug outs.	
	13th		Cables laid in trench between terminal poles and BD/R dug outs.	
	14th		Two pair light pole route from ROUEZ to aerodrome at T.19.a completed. All lines in two routes back to VILLEQUIER AUMONT and on the forward route to QUESSY terminated at terminal poles and bridged across to their own legs to H.Q. dug outs ready for move to new Signal Office.	
	15th		Made a dummy night of HILST to see rapid officer officers H.Q. dug outs, all telephone lines being led on to 35-line exchange installed in the dug outs.	
	16th		Test boxes placed on buy at aerodrome on T.19.a and at HIEZ all cabling being led	

W.Kirkwith Captain
For OC 18th DIVL. SIGNAL CO., R.E.

Army Form C. 2118.

WAR DIARY
or
INTELLIGENCE SUMMARY

18th DIVL. SIGNAL CO., R.E.

MAR 1918

(Erase heading not required.)

Place	Date	Hour	Summary of Events and Information	Remarks and references to Appendices
ROUEZ	16th (cont.)		on to Kennel etc. One lineman sent to Rouvroy for maintenance.	
	18th		Forward Divisional Exchange established at REMIGNY. Visual station established at the Butte to north branch to FORT LIEZ, the station being connected to Div. H.Q. by telephone.	
	20th		Work on buried continued. One pair D.I. twisted cable laid to H.Q. 8th Infantry Regiment and HAUTE TOMBELLE WOOD at M 34 to 88.	
	21st	4:0am	German offensive started. All forward communications to Left Range Sn. (53rd) at REMIGNY were destroyed and wireless was also out of action owing to the aerial being shattered by enemy shell fire. Communications to Right Bde. (55th) by Buzzer and telephone remained intact. 5:30am Breakdown party of 6 linemen sent forward by lorry to GIBERCOURT Test Point to restore wireless communication to Left Bde. This was accomplished by 10:30am but was subject to intermittent interruption during the morning and afternoon. 6:30pm An advanced office consisting of 1 ten line magneto exchange and 1 amunde board at GIBERCOURT Test Point. This office was subsequently moved back to "Is" Test Point W.F REMIGNY and staff was relieved by personnel of the advanced office previously	

W.Grant
for O.C. 18th DIVL. SIGNAL CO., R.E.

Army Form C. 2118.

WAR DIARY
or
INTELLIGENCE SUMMARY.
(Erase heading not required.)

18th DIVL. SIGNAL CO., R.E.

MAR 1918

Place	Date	Hour	Summary of Events and Information	Remarks and references to Appendices
	21st Contd.		opened at REMIGNY which had to be abandoned owing to heavy concentration of enemy shelling. Up to the time that 53rd Bde moved from its Battle H.Q. in the quarry N. of LY FONTAINE, telephonic communication up to the Test Point at GIBECOURT and rearwards were kept forward by S.R. from this point. Wireless communication was re-established about 6.0am and provided the only direct means of communication with this Bde. Telephonic communication with Right Bde (55th) remained uninterrupted during the whole of the day. Left Bde had moved by the evening to REMIGNY, and during the night "L" Test Point W. of REMIGNY and the village of FAILLOUEL became no man's land. 54th Bde which was in Corps Reserve at FAILLOUEL moved forward during daylight on 21st and established Bde H.Q. in old Corps H.A. position near the cross roads in FAILLOUEL. Direct telephonic communication with this H.Q. was already established on permanent route via VILLEQUIER AUMONT.	
UGNY-LE-GAY	22nd	Mid.t	Div. H.Q. moved from ROUEZ to UGNY-LE-GAY about midnight March 21/22nd and took over H.Q. vacated by III Corps. 53rd Bde H.Q. closed at LIEZ and opened up at old Div. H.Q. ROUEZ shortly after midnight. Contact Rees[?] via Signal	

for O.C. [signature] Captain
18th DIVL. SIGNAL CO., R.E.

Army Form C. 2118.

WAR DIARY
or
INTELLIGENCE SUMMARY
(Erase heading not required)

18th DIVL. SIGNAL CO., R.E.

MAR 1918

Place	Date	Hour	Summary of Events and Information	Remarks and references to Appendices
UGNY-le-GAY	22nd	Contd.	Officer relief moved by march route to UGNY-le-GAY at 3.0 am and Corps despatch officers were taken over at 8.0 am, formations then being situated as follows:- III Corps - NOYON; 18th Div. - UGNY-le-GAY; 53rd Bde. - FRIÈRES FAILLOUEL; 54th Bde - FAILLOUEL; 55th Bde. - ROUEZ. 53rd Bde. eventually moved to ROUEZ at 8.0 pm. Communications were as follows:- Telegraph and telephone superimposed to Corps on permanent route via MAREST DAMPCOURT. To 53rd Bde. by open wire on French route via VILLEQUIER AUMONT and FAILLOUEL with a cable lateral between 53rd and 55th Bdes. To 54th Bde. by open wire on French route through VILLEQUIER AUMONT with open wire lateral between 54th and 55th Bdes also through VILLEQUIER AUMONT. To 55th Bde by open wire on French route to VILLEQUIER AUMONT and thence by portable permanent route VILLEQUIER AUMONT to ROUEZ. 8:0 am One cable detachment under an officer laid one pair D3 cable from VILLEQUIER AUMONT to FAILLOUEL along road, a second cable detachment laid 1 pair D3 cable across country from UGNY-le-GAY to ROUEZ to provide an alternative route to 55th Bde. A third cable detachment was detailed to test through permanent route, laying cable when necessary, to provide direct communication from UGNY-le-GAY to CAILLOUEL, which was	

W.Raynal Captn.
p/ O.C. 18th DIVL. SIGNAL CO., R.E.

WAR DIARY
or
INTELLIGENCE SUMMARY
(Erase heading not required.)

MAR 1918   **18th DIVL. SIGNAL CO., R.E.**

Army Form C. 2118.

Place	Date	Hour	Summary of Events and Information	Remarks and references to Appendices
	22nd (cont)		intended to be next position of Divn. H.Q. nor the event of a further retirement being ordered. Cable detachment sent out at 10.0pm to lay a pair D.2 cable from ROUEZ to FRIERES FAILLOUEL for use of 53rd Bde who had established there early on morning of 22nd	
	23rd	9.0am	An advanced office consisting of 2 operators and 3 linesmen with a 10-line magneto exchange was established at VILLEQUIER AUMONT and a direct line to the 7th (Dismtd) Cavalry Brigade which was then under orders of 18th Division was taken on to this exchange. 11.30am 54th Bde. H.Q. moved back from FAILLOUEL along the main FAILLOUEL - VILLEQUIER AUMONT road and took up a position in the vicinity of LE FOUR CROIX; 53rd and 55th Bdes occupying a combined H.Q. at ROUEZ	
		4.0pm	53rd Bde moved back from ROUEZ to a position near CHAUNY - VILLEQUIER AUMONT road about 2 miles outside latter place. Communication still established by means of the cable pair laid during the morning from UGNY-LE-GAY to ROUEZ	
		5.30pm	54th Bde H.Q. established at VILLEQUIER AUMONT after which the advanced Divn. office was closed and personnel withdrawn to UGNY-LE-GAY. 6.00pm 55th Bde moved out of ROUEZ and joined up with 53rd Bde in their new position 9.0pm All Bdes by this time had moved back and were in positions between VGNY-LE-GAY and	

W.M. Rowel
Captain
for O.C. 18th DIVL. SIGNAL CO., R.E.

Army Form C. 2118.

WAR DIARY
or
INTELLIGENCE SUMMARY.
(Erase heading not required.)

18th DIVL. SIGNAL CO., R.E.

MAR 1918

Place	Date	Hour	Summary of Events and Information	Remarks and references to Appendices
CAILLOUEL	23rd cont.		and CAILLOUEL section Div H.Q. closed at UGNY-le-GAY and opened at CAILLOUEL at same time. Communications to Brigades during the night by DR with the exception of 54th who had some across the line from CAILLOUEL to UGNY-le-GAY in the vicinity of BETHANCOURT. Communication to III Corps by telephone and telegraph on interphones route via MAREST-DAMPCOURT, along the CHAUNY-NOYON route.	
BABOEUF	24th	9.0 am	Div H.Q. closed at CAILLOUEL and opened up at same time at BABOEUF. On advance exchange was kept on at CAILLOUEL and took on all 3 Brigades and 18th Div Arty which by this time were all located in CAILLOUEL. Cable detachment detailed to lay 1 pair D.8 cable from BABOEUF to CAILLOUEL via GRANDRU and CREPIGNY and 1 single D.5 line via MONDESCOURT and CREPIGNY as alternative route to the spare route between CAILLOUEL and BABOEUF via MAREST DAMPCOURT and the main CHAUNY-NOYON route. A visual station was established at the eastern end of BABOEUF village to work direct to CAILLOUEL if required. During the afternoon the advanced exchange at CAILLOUEL had been closed down and the spare route linking up BABOEUF and CAILLOUEL given up as impracticable owing to constant interruptions. All Bdes were then	

W Renard Captain
for O.C. 18th DIVL. SIGNAL CO., R.E.

WAR DIARY
or INTELLIGENCE SUMMARY.

(Erase heading not required.)

18th DIVL. SIGNAL CO., R.E.

Army Form C. 2118.

MAR 1918

Place	Date	Hour	Summary of Events and Information	Remarks and references to Appendices
	24th (cont)		"Kept" in on the 2 cable lines laid during the morning and taken on to a Buzzer exchange at BABOEUF. Two linesmen — 2 at GRANDRU and 2 at CAILLOUEL — were sent out to ascertain these 2 cable routes. Communication to III Corps as before via the main CHAUNY-NOYON route. During the afternoon 2 pair cables were laid into BABOEUF which hooked up at 7 p.m. Cross sheathed cable laid up canal and thence by cable to VARESNES. These 2 pairs subsequently provided communication to III Corps at NOYON and to Bdes at BABOEUF when Div H.Q. moved to VARESNES.	
VARESNES	25th March 8:00am		Div H.Q closed at BABOEUF and opened up at same hour at VARESNES. An advanced exchange was kept on at BABOEUF which gave communication to III Corps and to Bdes. 2:0 p.m. Owing to the proximity of the enemy the advanced office at BABOEUF was closed down and withdrawn. At the same time the CHAUNY-NOYON route which provided the sole means of communication to III Corps was destroyed by shell fire and consequently communication with Corps ceased. ~~Cable is being laid to establish it but~~ VARESNES to the Rly. Bridge & mount back on the borders of forest	

W.R. Ward
Captain
for O.C.
18th DIVL. SIGNAL CO., R.E.

Army Form C. 2118.

WAR DIARY
or
INTELLIGENCE SUMMARY

(Erase heading not required.)

18th DIVL. SIGNAL CO., R.E.

MAR 1918

8A.

Place	Date	Hour	Summary of Events and Information	Remarks and references to Appendices
	25th (contd.)	3.00pm	The 53rd and 55th Bde H.Qrs. which were situated in the vicinity of BABOEUF came in on the pair of cables which had been thrown along by the closing down of the advanced exchange at that place. 54th Bde. H.Q. at this time was not in communication owing to its position being unknown.	
		5-30pm	A pair of cables were laid from the canal to pick up the existing pair back to VARESNES and extend them to the cross roads at SALENCY on the NOYON–CHAUNY road. The 53rd and 55th Bdes also had moved back to this position (same as this Division 55th Bde were in communication with Division). By 9.0pm all Brigades had withdrawn and come into VARESNES.	
			line and re-established communication with Division. 55th Bde were withdrawn south of the Canal and were in the vicinity of VARESNES.	

W. Kinnnnl Capton
for O.C. 18th DIVL. SIGNAL CO., R.E.

Army Form C. 2118.

WAR DIARY
or
INTELLIGENCE SUMMARY.
(Erase heading not required.)

18th DIVL. SIGNAL CO., R.E.

Place	Date	Hour	Summary of Events and Information	Remarks and references to Appendices
CAISNES	26th		Company moved from PONT OISE to CUTS at 2·0am by marched route and after a four hour halt moved to CAISNES. Divl H.Q. closed at VARESNES at 10·0am and opened up at CAISNES at same time; all three brigades being established in that village. One pair cables laid to BIERANCOURT and connects to French exchange at that place. By this means communication was re-established with III Corps also at CLAIRE VOIX near COMPIEGNE. Divl H.Q. closed at CAISNES at 5·0pm and opened at same hour at AUDIGNICOURT, 18th Divl Arty taking over old Divl H.Q. at the former village. Cable detachments laid one pair cables from French exchange at NAMPCEL to AUDIGNICOURT. No 3 Detachment detailed to remain with 18th Divl Arty.	
	27/28/29th		Divl H.Q. at AUDIGNICOURT. No active operations. Headquarters 53rd Bde at CHEVILLECOURT, 54th Bde at ST. AUBIN, and 55th Bde at AUDIGNICOURT.	
	30th		During the early morning the Division, less 54th Bde, moved by bus to area S.W. of AMIENS. Divl H.Q. closed at AUDIGNICOURT at 10·0am and opened up at ST SAULFLIEU at 10·0pm. Office relief and stores moved by lorry to ST SAULFLIEU. Dismounted personnel of H.Q. remained at AUDIGNICOURT for	

W.F. Ryward Captain
for O.C.
18th DIVL. SIGNAL CO., R.E.

Army Form C. 2118.

WAR DIARY
or
INTELLIGENCE SUMMARY
(Erase heading not required.)

18th DIVL. SIGNAL CO., R.E.

MAR 1918

10/

Place	Date	Hour	Summary of Events and Information	Remarks and references to Appendices
	30th (cont)		orders to return via French lorries later during the day, and the company including 3 cable detachments complete and H.Q. transport prepared to move by march route to ST. SAUFLIEU.	
	31st		Div. H.Q. closed at ST SAUFLIEU at 10.45am and opened up at BOVES at same hour.	
			Average strength of company during month:- Officers 10 OR. 282 Horses 118	
			Battle Casualties:- Killed 2 Wounded 3 Missing 5.	
			Enclosures:-	
			"A" Work on Communications week ending 9th	
			"B" Proposed buried cable system	
			"C" System of Communications	
			"D" Notes on signal communications	

W.B.[?]
Captain
for O.C. 18th DIVL. SIGNAL CO., R.E.

APPENDICES

A, B, C & D.

WORK ON COMMUNICATIONS.
completed
during week ending March, 9th, 1918.

(a)   One arm added on French semi-permanent open wire route from Div. H.Q. to BUTTE in S.24.d. and 2 pairs wired.

(b)   Six pairs of cables laid in 3' 6" trench from sandpit at T.19.a.1.3 to railway bridge at M.36.central, and from this point 6 pairs cables laid in French cable ditch to Right Brigade H.Q.

(c)   Six foot trench dug from railway bridge at M.36.central to Right Brigade, 30 pairs laid and trench filled in from just east of canal to Right Brigade. The western end of the trench is dug 6' and left open for 30 pairs of cable which is not yet available.

(d)   Three foot six trench dug and 6 pairs laid from Right Brigade H.Q. to a point at H.31.c.8.6 where in joins up with the French bury from MONDESCOURT to Left Brigade.

(e)   A 2 pair hop pole route built and wired from Right Brigade H.Q. to N.7.a.0.2, joining up with a French cable and semi-permanent route running from this point to MONDESCOURT, and thence picking up 2 pairs in French bury   to Left. Brigade mentioned in para (d) This provides a good lateral between Right and Left Infantry and Artillery Brigades.

(f)   A 6' bury with 14 pairs completed between Right Brigade H.Q. and FORT LIEZ.

(g)   Six pairs laid out and roped between N.23.a.10.7 and Right Battalion H.Q. in Quarry juste north of REMIGNY - VENDEUIL Road. This requires a 6' trench for cables to be laid and filled in.

(h)   Burying of leads into dug-out from main routes at Div. H.Q. commenced and partly completed but held up on account of cable not being available.

   The above work has been carried out and completed during the past week.   All lines laid in 3' 6" trenches and those in 6' buries have been tested out and proved correct.
   A rough sketch illustrating work done is forwarded herewith.

10th March, 1918.   for / O.C. Signals, 18th Division.
                                                    Captain,

File   18/SYR/907   B

General Staff,

   18th Division.

      I attach a map Shewing communications (Route Diagram) in the new 18th Divisional Area. These consist (with the exception of the buried cables from LIEZ to FORT DE VENDEUIL and from GIBERCOURT to BENAY) entirely of permanent line and ground cables. They are not only very circuitous but are ~~are~~ also unreliable (in the event of shelling or bombing). I therefore recommend that a buried cable route be installed along the following line :-

(i)   Point N.1.a.9.9 near GIBERCOURT to Point N.13 central near REMIGNY.
        N.B. I have arranged that 14th Division Signals should start this section.

(ii) Point N.13 central to Brigade H.Q. LIEZ N.31.b.6.3.

(iii) Brigade H.Q. LIEZ - T.7.a.0.2. - Point S.24.a.0.4.

(iv) Point S.24.a.0.4. - Point S.22.c.9.2.

        N.B. The above scheme fits in with 5th Army Scheme. Line of proposed buried cable route is shewn in yellow on attached map.

Labour required for completing the above sections is as follows:-

(i)   Distance 2000 yards (This will in all probability be half completed by 14th Division). Labour required 400 men for $2\frac{1}{2}$ days.

(ii) Distance 3200 yards. Labour required 400 men for 8 days.

(iii) Distance 4500 yards. Labour required 400 men for 11 days.

(iv) Distance 2000 yards. 400 men for 5 days.

Total length of proposed buried cable route is 10,700 yards.

Total labour required is 400 men for 30 days.

Twenty-eight pairs will be laid throughout the entire length of the buried cable route.

J. Challis

Major, R.E.,
O.C. Signals, 18th Division.

23.2.18.

SECRET.

SYSTEM OF COMMUNICATIONS - 18th DIVISION.

The system of communications in the Divisional Area will be dealt with in detail under the following headings:-

  (i)   System of Lines, both Telegraph and Telephone.
  (ii) Wireless and Earth Induction.
  (iii) D.R.L.S., Mounted Orderlies and Runner Systems.
  (iv) Visual System.
  (v)   Pigeons.
  (vi) Message Rockets.

(i) System of Lines.

The system of lines will be described :-
  (a) As it exists at present.
  (b) As it will exist.

(a) There are two main routes of lines forward of Divisional Headquarters, ROUEZ Camp (S.27.a.1.2), the first to the Left Infantry and Artillery Brigade Headquarters, ADOLPHE QUARRY (N.33.d.central) via VILLEQUIER-AUMONT - FAILLOUEL - JUSSY (with alternative lines along the railway) to LIZEROLLES. At this point this route goes into a French buried cable route running just north of GIBERCOURT, to a Test Point 400 yards N. of LY-FONTAINE. This bury turns at this point and runs due N. to BENAY, but inter Divisional and Brigade lines are all taken off at Test Point N. of LY-FONTAINE, and run in to the Brigade H.Q's on ground cables.

The second main route forward of Divisional H.Q. runs to QUESSY passing just north of the BUTTE de VOUEL, and from QUESSY along the right side of the canal up to Right Infantry and Artillery Brigade H.Q's, LIEZ (T.31.b.7.3). There is a lateral line of cable between Left and Right Brigade H.Q's.

All the above lines, with the exception of the Brigade lateral, are open wires (Permanent Line) of French construction and of course in the event of shelling or bombing could not be relied upon.

Forward of Brigades, in the Left Brigade sector, all lines to battalions and batteries are ground lines and are unreliable. In the Right Brigade sector there is a French buried cable route of 12 pairs running from LIEZ to FORT de VENDEUIL. Lines to battalions and batteries are all put through on this route.

(b) The system of communications as it will exist when completed is as follows. Forward of Divisional Headquarters there will be 3 main routes to Brigades; the first 2 will be from ROUEZ to the sand pit 600 yards N.E. of the BUTTE de VOUEL along different routes. At this place there will be a mined Test Point, and lines will be put through to Brigade H.Q's,

2.

LIEZ on a 6 ft. 6 ins deep buried cable route now in course of construction. From this Test Point forward to Brigade H.Q. LIEZ there will be three alternative routes; the first buried cable, the second airline to LIEZ and the third French permanent line via QUESSY to LIEZ. From LIEZ forward to Left Brigade H.Q. there will be three alternative routes also. The first a 6 ft. 6 ins deep buried cable route now in course of construction, running from LIEZ (N.13.a.4.5) due west of RUMIGNY (N.31.c.central) and thence via French buried cable to Brigade H.Q., ADOLPHE QUARRY. The second a route of open wires (semi-permanent line) running parallel to the LIEZ - ESSIGNY Road and about 50 yards off it, to a point 500 yards east of MONTESCOURT, and thence along old German permanent line via GIBERCOURT and LY-FONTAINE to Brigade H.Q. The third a poled cable line from LIEZ to RUMIGNY Exchange (N.14.a.2.4) and thence via buried cable forward spur from RUMIGNY to point 500 yards south of LY-FONTAINE and on to Brigade H.Q. as a ground line.

The third main route forward of Divisional H.Q. to Brigades will be the same as that described in para (i), sup-para (a), i.e., ROUEZ via VILLEQUIER-AUMONT - FAILLOUEL - JUSSY - LIEZROLLES via French buried cable to Brigade H.Q. The line to Brigade in Reserve runs via VILLEQUIER-AUMONT to CAILLOUEL.

Forward of Brigade H.Q. in the Left sector there will be a "forward spur" 6 ft. 6 ins. deep from the French buried cable route starting from Test box 400 yards north of LY-FONTAINE, to battalion headquarters. In the Right sector there will be two buried routes forward of LIEZ, one to FORT de VENDEUIL (12 pairs completed), and the second to FORT de LIEZ (14 pairs, 6 ft. 6 ins. deep) now under construction.

In all cases the lines will be so arranged that each line will serve the Headquarters of a Unit in its present position and its Battle Zone position. All lines must be buried into all H.Q's of Division and Brigades in Line (Infantry and Artillery), and all Telephone Exchanges are to be in dug-outs.

(ii)   Wireless and Earth Induction System.

This is as shewn in attached diagram.

(iii)   D.R.L.S.

All despatches are carried forward of Divisional H.Q. to Brigades in Line by motor cyclist D.R. Route as follows:- ROUEZ - VOUEL - LIEZ - RUMIGNY - GIBERCOURT - LY-FONTAINE.

In cases of urgency a D.R. can do the journey between Divisional H.Q. and the furthest away Brigade (Left Brigade) in 35 minutes. Brigades will organise their own D.R.L.S. systems, the Left Brigade by runners and the Right Brigade by mounted orderly.

3.

(iv) **Visual**.

The visual systems of both Brigades in Line are at present in process of being altered. The approximate visual scheme is as follows:-

[Diagram of visual stations (Lucas Lamp) showing connections between:
- *53 Bde H33d 6.8*
- *ZEC H33d 8.8*
- *Coy at Coponne Fm H34b*
- *Left Bn*
- *Supt Coy H24b 8.8*
- *Res: Coy H29c 8.7*
- *Supt Bn N3a 2.4*
- *Right Bn H29d 0.0*
- *Bn Battle HQs N16a 7.8*
- *Bn: HQs Fort de Vendeuil*
- *Coy HQs O19a 5.9*
- *Coy HQs O25d 0.2*
- *Rouquenet Fm*
- *55 Bde N31b 9.2*
- *Coy: HQs N34d 7.8*
- *Fort de Liez*
- *Legend: ⚑⚑ = Visual Station (Lucas Lamp)]*

A Divisional Visual Scheme is being drawn up.

(v) **Pigeons**.

Eight pigeons are allotted to the Division on every other day. Each Brigade receives four birds.

(vi) **Message Rockets**.

Troughs for releasing Message Rockets are to be installed and sited in all strong points in the Battle Zone, in order to provide communication between these strong points and battalion Battle H.Q.'s. It should be remembered that the range of these rockets is 2,400 yards, and that they are accurate and quite reliable, provided the trough is sited correctly in the first place.

A map of communications in the Divisional Area is being prepared and will be ready shortly.

J. Curtis

Major R.E.,

2nd March, 1918.   O.C. Signals, 18th Division.

Diagram of Wireless
Communications
18th Division
2·3·18

Left Bde
138 Bde
KAC (171)

Left Bde
53 Bde
N3b 6·7
W/T OO
P B OL
(169)

Right Bde
I.25a Central
KAB (170)

Ford Bn
N18a 5·7
KAO (168)

Right Bde
55 Bde
N3cb 7·4
W/T ON
P B KAN
(167)

(166)
W 18th Div HQ
S28a 3 T
LI

KEY.

⊕ = Power Buzzer Stn.
⩎ = "   "   " & Amplifier.
T△ = Trench Set Stn.
W△ = Wilson Set Stn.
〰〰 = Route between Wireless Stns.
———— = "   "   P.B. & Amplifier Stns.
W/T. D.N. = Wireless Call.
P.B. KAN = Power Buzzer & Amplifier Call.
(125) Corps Key Number.

Power Buzzer-Amplifier KAN-KAO at present
practically inoperative. KAO now working to FL.

SECRET. 18/SYR/28.

NOTES ON VISUAL COMMUNICATION
in
18th DIVISIONAL AREA.

(Reference attached map of Visual Communications)

East of the canal there are two outstanding central Visual Stations, one at FORT LIEZ and the other at FORT VENDEUIL.

The Right Brigade is enabled to work to the Left Brigade either through FORT LIEZ and FORT VENDEUIL, which is in direct communication with the latter, or through FORT LIEZ to N.9.b.1.7 (south of LY FONTAINE), at which point a station is manned by personnel of Left Brigade and is connected to the latter by telephone. In the Right Brigade sector, Brigade H.Q. is working to the battalion in line at N.16.d.8.6, through FORT LIEZ and FORT VENDEUIL, or via FORT LIEZ and ROUQUENET FARM at which point there is a central visual station serving a Relay Post situated in the farm. Battalion in line of Right Brigade works to one company in the line through FORT VENDEUIL, the other company in the line is not in visual communication at present.

In the Left Brigade sector, Brigade H.Q. is in direct communication with right battalion and works to left battalion through one transmitting station. A station at N.30. central transmits for right battalion of Left Brigade to one company in the line and an isolated platoon in O.1.a. One station at N.30.b.2.8 provides indirect visual communication between left battalion of Left Brigade and Brigade H.Q., and the reserve company to H.Q. of former. The same battalion headquarters require requires one intermediate station at N.24.c.2.8 to work to the right and left companies.

A Divisional Visual Station will shortly be established at Point 104 in S.28.d. by which visual communication will be workable except under adverse atmospheric conditions, to both Brigades in Line through FORT LIEZ.

The attached map has been compiled from schemes submitted by Brigades and the psoitions of the stations are approximately correct.

[Not attached all]

8th March, 1918.

Captain,
for/ O.C. Signals, 18th Division.

18th DIVISIONAL SIGNAL COMPANY, R.E.

A P R I L

1 9 1 8

WAR DIARY or INTELLIGENCE SUMMARY

Army Form C. 2118.
18th DIVL. SIGNAL CO., R.E.
APR 1918

Place	Date	Hour	Summary of Events and Information	Remarks and references to Appendices
BOYES	1st		Advanced Exchange opened up at GENTELLES with lines to 53rd and 54th Infantry Brigades and GENTELLES and to 55th Inf. Bde. near VILLERS BRETONNEUX. This office also accepted telegrams and D.R.L.S. for all units in the neighbourhood of GENTELLES and was in telephone communication with Div. H.Q. Signal office, BOYES through 61st Div. Exchange.	
	2nd		One pair D3 cables laid from the Signal office BOYES to Advanced Exchange GENTELLES to give direct communication	
	3rd		One pair D8 cables laid from H.Q. Signal Office BOYES to Advanced Exchange GENTELLES to provide an alternative line in case of breakdown	
	4th		One pair D8 cables laid to 29th French Division (Right Div.) at FOUENCAMPS	
	5th		One pair D8 cables laid to 9th Australian Inf. Brigade (who were under orders of G.O.C. 18th Division) at BLANGY TRONVILLE	
	6th		During the day the centre end of BOYES wire was chafed intermittently and the greatest difficulty was experienced in keeping forward lines through	
	"		One pair D8 cables laid by 58th Division from their H.Q. at FORT MANOIR FARM to 18th Div. Exchange BOYES to provide communication to 175th Regt. 12	

OC 18th DIVL. SIGNAL CO., R.E.

WAR DIARY
INTELLIGENCE SUMMARY

Army Form C. 2118
18th DIVL SIGNAL CO., R.E.
APR 1918

Place	Date	Hour	Summary of Events and Information	Remarks and references to Appendices
	9th (contd)		Inf Bde of 58th Division in GENTELLES.	
	9th		The pair D.G. cables laid from Divr Exchange, BOVES to CAGNY to provide communication to 51st Inf Bde who had been withdrawn from line and has established their H.Q. at that place.	
			Line picked up on forward route from BOVES to BLANGY TRONVILLE, H.Q. of 5th Australian Division (Left Div)	
	10th		One pair of cables between BOVES and GENTELLES poles to avoid interruption from horse transport.	
	11th		Divisional H.Q. closed at BOVES at 3·30am. and opened up at ST. FUSCIEN at 9am. hour. Office relief sent forward by lorry at 11·am. remainder of wireless personnel by march route via DURY and SALEUX, clearing BOVES at 3·pm.	
ST FUSCIEN	13th		Advanced Exchange at GENTELLES closed down and lines stripped through as necessary. 53rd and 54th Brigades of 18th Division remained in line under orders of 58th Division. Communications from ST FUSCIEN were as follows:— 1 pair to IIIrd Corps at DURY, 1 pair to 58th Division at FORT MANOIR FARM and 1 pair to 54th Inf Bde at BOUTELLERIE. These lines were all picked up.	

J. Mollo
O.C. 18th DIVL. SIGNAL CO., R.E.

WAR DIARY
INTELLIGENCE SUMMARY

Army Form C. 2118

18th DIVL. SIGNAL CO., R.E.

APR 1918

Place	Date	Hour	Summary of Events and Information	Remarks and references to Appendices
	13th (cont'd)		Permanent routes from Corps Test Point at ST. FUSCIEN.	
	18th		Line brought in by French from 58th French Anti-aircraft Section at ST.DL.5-5.0	
	19th		AMIENS and taken on to 18th Div. Exchange.	
			No. 5 Section (M.G. Bn) parties from infantry suppliers from 12th Entrenching	
			Battalion and placed under training.	
	21st		18th Div. Artillery H.Q. established at CAGNY.	
			Infantry Exchange BOUTELLERIE.	
	23rd		Line allotted by Corps on 7-pair cable between ST FUSCIEN and CAGNY to	
			give direct communication to 18th Div. Arty.	
	25th		Cable Section less officer who is not at present available, sent to	
			M.G. Bn. and were given a skeleton establishment of cable and instruments.	
CAVILLON	26th		Div H.Q. closed at ST FUSCIEN at 11am and opened up at CAVILLON	
			at same hour. All communication through South Army Exchange at	
			FLIXECOURT. A Div. Report Centre was kept open at ST FUSCIEN to deal with	
	27th		work to and from 53rd and 54th Inf. Bdes.	
			R.C. at ST FUSCIEN closed down, the line to 53rd Bde being stopped	

O.C. 18th DIVL. SIGNAL CO. R.E.

Army Form C. 2118

WAR DIARY
INTELLIGENCE SUMMARY
18th DIVL. SIGNAL CO., R.E.

APR 1918

Place	Date	Hour	Summary of Events and Information	Remarks and references to Appendices
	28th		through to 5th Division. Sub-office opened at WARLUS to deal with work for 53rd and 54th Bdes who were moving into that area. Lines picked up on permanent route between CAVILLON and Fourth Army Schools at LE QUESNOY, and a line from the HQrs there to WARLUS was allotted by Fourth Army Signals. 55th Bde were at this time in the forward area (1612 BAIZIEUX) under orders of 5th Australian Div.	
	13th to 30th		During the period from 13th to 30th the Div was in Corps and Army Reserve and no active operations were undertaken. The opportunity was availed of to have a much needed check of all technical wagons and stores and to have all deficiencies made up as far as possible. All instruments were thoroughly overhauled and any necessary repairs effected. Several days were devoted by each Detachment to cable drill, particular attention being paid to poled and buried lines.	

T. [signature]

O.C. 18th DIVL. SIGNAL CO., R.E.

WAR DIARY or INTELLIGENCE SUMMARY

18th DIVL. SIGNAL CO., R.E.

APR 1918

Army Form C. 2118

(5.)

Place	Date	Hour	Summary of Events and Information	Remarks and references to Appendices
			Average Strength of content during month:-	
			Officers 9 OR. 273 Horses 117	
			Honours and Awards:-	
			<u>BAR TO MILITARY MEDAL</u>	
			172211 Sapper (A/2/Cpl) G.E. MORRIS. M.M.	
			103961 Sapper (A/L/Cpl) F.M. HARTLEY. M.M.	
			<u>MILITARY MEDAL</u>	
			54151 M/Cpl A.R. THWAITES 4739 Pioneer F. ANGELL	
			54141 do. A.E. BUDD 152677 do. G. WRIGHT	
			82553 Sapper A. BAMPFYLDE	
			Enclosures:- "A" Route Diagram of Communications at BOVES.	

[signature] Major R.E.
O.C. 18th DIVL. SIGNAL CO., R.E.

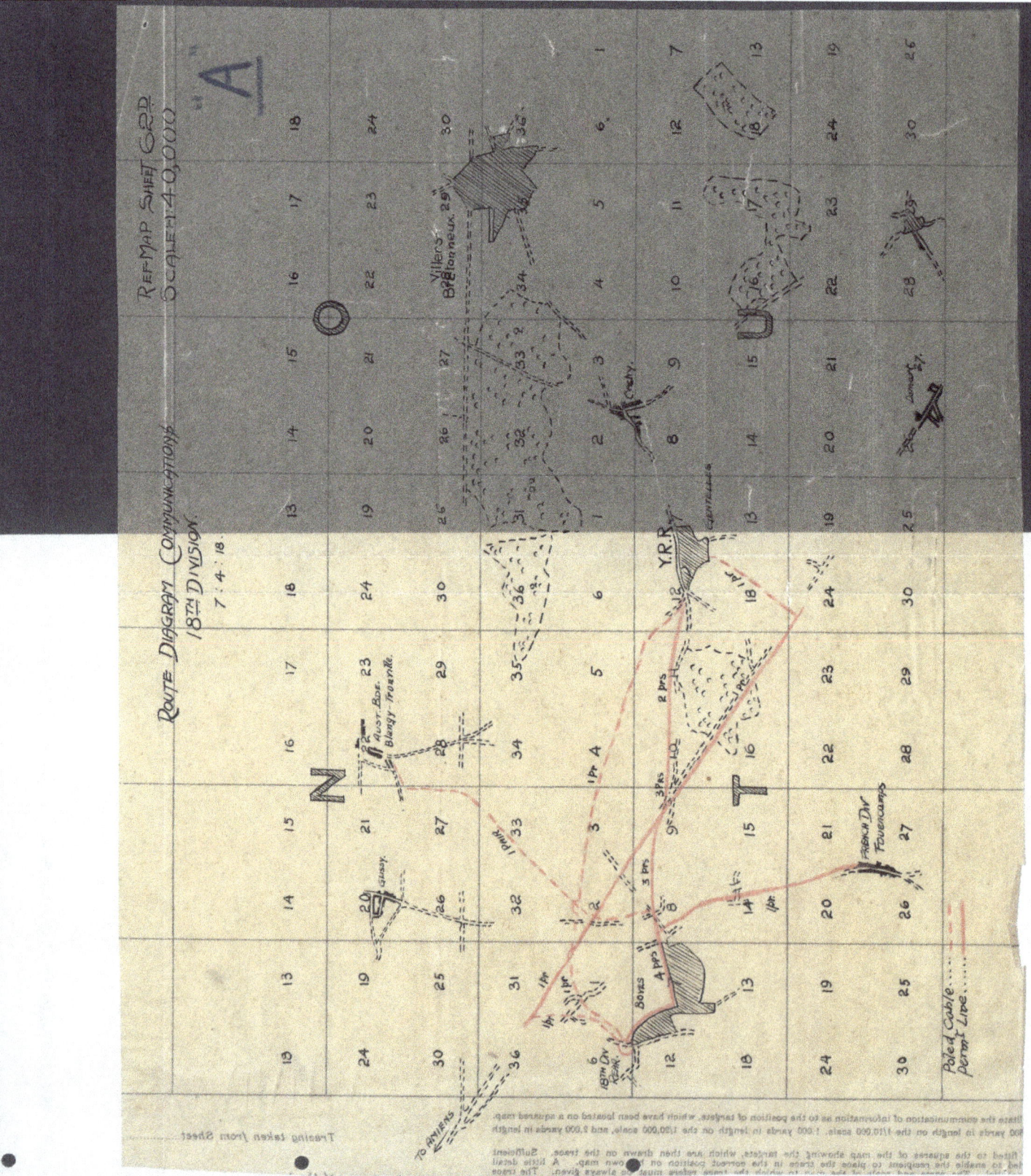

WAR DIARY
OR
INTELLIGENCE SUMMARY.

(Erase heading not required.)

Army Form C. 2118.

18th DIVL. SIGNAL CO., R.E.

MAY 1918

Place	Date	Hour	Summary of Events and Information	Remarks and references to Appendices
CAVILLON	May 1918 1st to 5th		From 26th April to 5th May the Division was in III Corps Reserve and were disposed in the CAVILLON training area. The time was principally devoted to first cable drill and the company was also practised in anti-gas drill.	
BAVELINCOURT	5th		Div. H.Q. closed at CAVILLON at 10.a.m. and opened at the same hour at BAVELINCOURT. Division took over Right sector of III Corps front from 58th Division whose Headquarters were at ESBART FARM. Communications were taken over after extensions being laid from ESBART FARM to BAVELINCOURT Chateau where recently Forward Exchange established at BAIZIEUX and the following lines laid; 1 pair D.8 from BAIZIEUX to ESBART FARM (O.S. 14.c.q 58 d.7); 1 pair D.8 cable from 54th Bde. H.Q. BAIZIEUX to ESBART FARM; 1 pair D.8 cable from Forward Exchange BAIZIEUX to H.Q. 55th Bde. at D.7.b.; 1 pair from cross roads at C.16.a.3.b (to pick up a pair on permanent line) to H.Q. 55th Bde.; 1 pair from forward Exchange to 17th Div. forward Exchange on BAIZIEUX and 1 pair from forward Exchange to H.Q. 54th Bde. All the above were ground cables but were	
	6th			

(1)

for O.C. 18th DIVL. SIGNAL CO., R.E.

Army Form C. 2118.

WAR DIARY
or
INTELLIGENCE SUMMARY.
(Erase heading not required.)

18th DIVL. SIGNAL CO., R.E.

MAY 1918

Place	Date	Hour	Summary of Events and Information	Remarks and references to Appendices
	9th		Subsequently tied. All communication in the area was either by overhead routes or poles or ground cables and a buried system to replace most of these routes and ensure greater reliability was commenced on 11th May.	
	10th		Commenced work on poling of cables laid on 8th. Poling of cables continued and one additional pair laid from terminal pole in permanent route. One pair of the existing 2 pairs to 53rd Bde extended to rear position of latter and one pair from this rear position to 55th Bde H/Q at C.18.a.0.2. One pair D.8 cables laid from Forward Exchange BAIZIEUX to rear position of 54th Bde Rear H/Q. at C.5.a.2.0.	
	11th		Started work on buried cable system as shown on attached map, a party of two infantry were allotted to digging and an average section of new trench completed daily i.e., trench dug to an average depth of 4 ft and 32 pair cables laid and trench filled in.	
	15th		Two 7 pair armoured cables laid along trench to 53rd Bde H/Q Cables	

for O.C. 18th DIVL. SIGNAL CO. R.E.

Army Form C. 2118.

WAR DIARY
or
INTELLIGENCE SUMMARY.
(Erase heading not required.)

MAY 1918

18th DIVL. SIGNAL CO., R.E.

(3)

Instructions regarding War Diaries and Intelligence Summaries are contained in F. S. Regs., Part II. and the Staff Manual respectively. Title pages will be prepared in manuscript.

Place	Date	Hour	Summary of Events and Information	Remarks and references to Appendices
	18th		Being stapled on to bottom of fire step. Two extra pair D.8 cable added to the top pole route from	
BAVELINCOURT			BAVELINCOURT to the dug out east of the copse on C.15.c. where they	
			picked up 2 pairs in loop.	
	19th		Two extra pair D.8 cable built on the top pole route running south of the wood in C.8 central to a point on the route nearest the dug out east of the copse on C.15.a. From this point a route carrying 3 pair was built to the dug out.	
	23rd		Repairing 3-pair poled cable route damaged by tank on night of 22/23rd near C.15 central.	
MOLLIENS-AU-BOIS	25th		Relieved by 47th Division. Bus.No. Clerk at BAVELINCOURT at 10.15am and closed at same hour at MOLLIENS-AU-BOIS. Necessary lines allotted by III Corps Company Sig. Signal Office personnel remained at BAVELINCOURT for work on loan. A small forward Exchange was kept open at BAVELINCOURT the forward office at BAIZIEUX being closed down.	
	26th 6.30pm		Between 26th and 31st work was continued on buried cable system.	

for O.C. 18th DIVL. SIGNAL CO., R.E.
Captain

WAR DIARY
or
INTELLIGENCE SUMMARY.

Army Form C. 2118.

18th DIVL. SIGNAL CO., R.E.

MAY 1918

(4.)

Place	Date	Hour	Summary of Events and Information	Remarks and references to Appendices

Average strength of Company during month:- Officers 12, O.R. 28x Horses 119

Awards during month:-

D.C.M.:-
45858 Sergt. F. Whitehead M.M.

Bar to M.M.
56757 C/2/Cpl. S.G. Martin M.M.

M.M.
45249 Sapper C.W.D. Appleby

Endeavours:- Handing over notes of 18th Divl Signals in BAVELINCOURT SECTOR, with "A" Line Diagram; "B" Route Diagram; "C" Wireless Diagram and "D" Visual Diagram

W. Purcell Captain
for O.C. 18th DIVL. SIGNAL CO. R.E.

HANDING OVER NOTES OF 18th DIVISIONAL SIGNALS IN THE BAVELINCOURT SECTOR.

The system of communications of the 18th Division will be dealt with in detail under the following headings:-

      (a) Telephone System.
      (b) Buried Cable System.
      (c) Wireless and Earth Induction.
      (d) Pigeons.
      (e) Visual.
      (f) D.R.L.S.

(a)   Telephone Exchanges are established at the following places:-

    18th Div. H.Q.   )   BAVELINCOURT.   C.7.a.1.0
    18th Div.Arty.H.Q.)

    Advanced Infantry &)   BAZIEUX.   C.12.b.0.7
    Artillery Exchange)

    N.B. 1 Cpl. i/c
         3 Exchange Operators. ∅
         3 Linemen.   ∅
         2 Ten Line Cordless Exchanges, with test strips and multicore.
         1 5 by 3 Buzzer Visual Exchange.
         2 Extension Telephones.
         2 D.III Telephones.
         3 Lineman's Tappers.
         1 Folding Table.
    ∅ One man supplied by R.A., H.Q. Detachment.

    Left Brigade H.Q.   D.4.c.3.5
    Right Brigade H.Q.   D.21.b.6.2
    Reserve Brigade H.Q.   BAZIEUX.   C.11.b.9.9
    M.G.Bn. H.Q.   BAZIEUX.   C.12.a.3.9
    82nd F.A.B., H.Q.   D.7.a.90.50
    83rd F.A.B., H.Q.   D.7.d.4.7
    96th A.F.A. Bde. H.Q.   C.11.b.9.5

    The above exchanges are connected up as shewn in the attached diagram. The lines shewn are either buried cable or poled cable, with the exception of 2 pairs from BEHENCOURT to cross roads at C.16.a.4.9, which are on permanent line.

(b)   <u>Buried Cable System</u>. - The buried cable route of 32 pairs has been completed between the points **V** and X (as shewn on attached diagram "B") and all joint boxes installed and joints made. Test points with terminal strips on frames have been installed at "B", "C" and "D" points, and a mined dug-out is in course of construction at "E" point, south of HENENCOURT. This will be ready now in a few days time. Work is in progress making slabs of concrete to protect joint boxes. Lines in the bury are in use as shewn in Appendix I.

(c)   <u>Wireless and Earth Induction</u>. - The scheme of Wireless and Earth Induction communications of 18th Division is as shewn in diagram "C".

(d)   <u>Pigeons</u>. - Eight pigeons are supplied daily by Fourth Army; 4 pigeons for each Brigade Front.

(e)   <u>Visual</u>. - Visual communications of 18th Division are as shewn in attached diagram, marked "D".

2.

(f) D.R.L.S. - Time Table is as follows:-

D.R's leave 18th Division for III Corps at:-

7.30a.m.
1.00p.m.
5.00p.m.
9.00p.m.

D.R's leave 18th Division for Brigades at:-

7.00a.m.
12.00noon.
7.00p.m.

Major R.E.,
O.C. Signals, 18th Division.

23rd May, 1918.

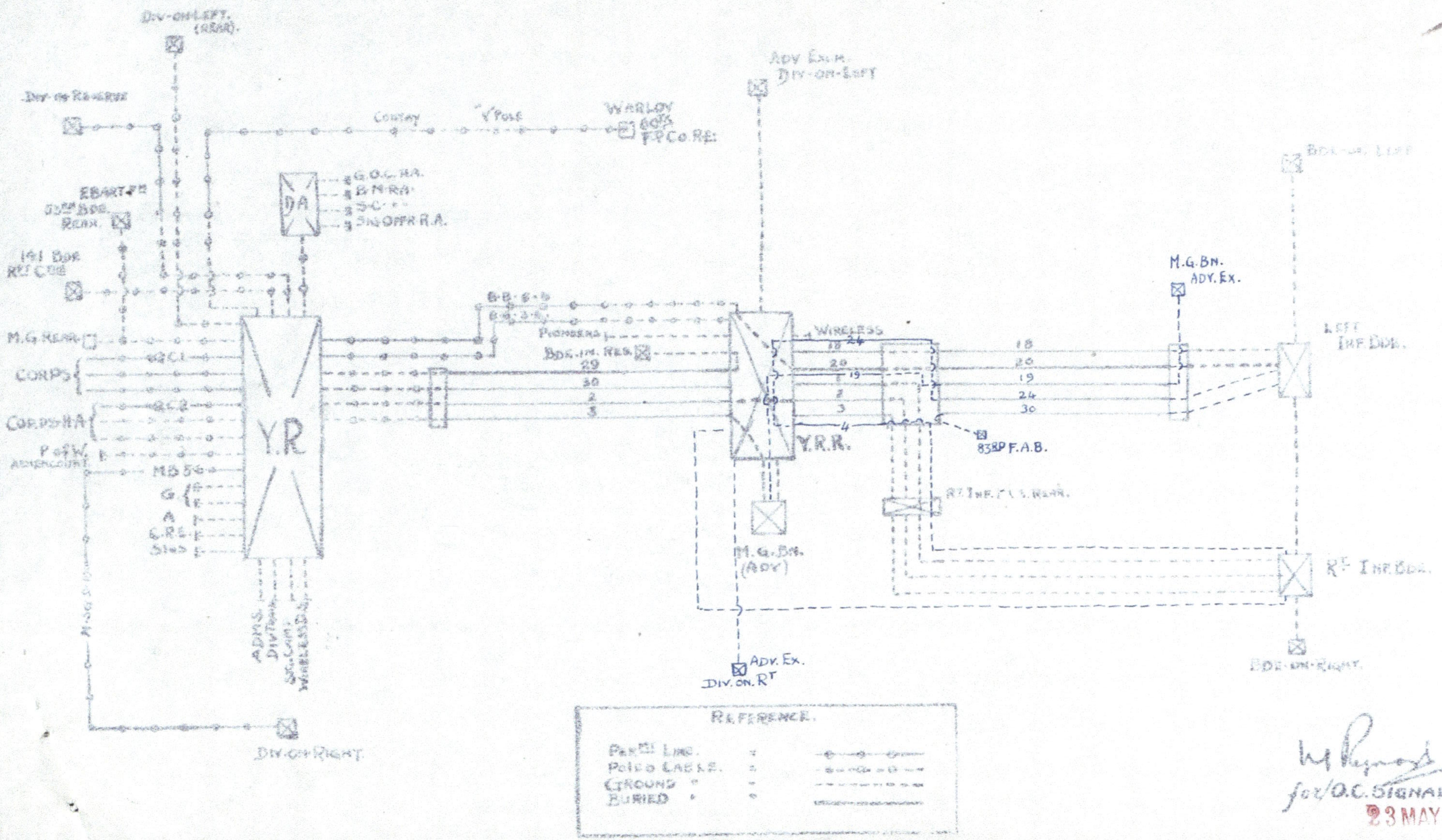

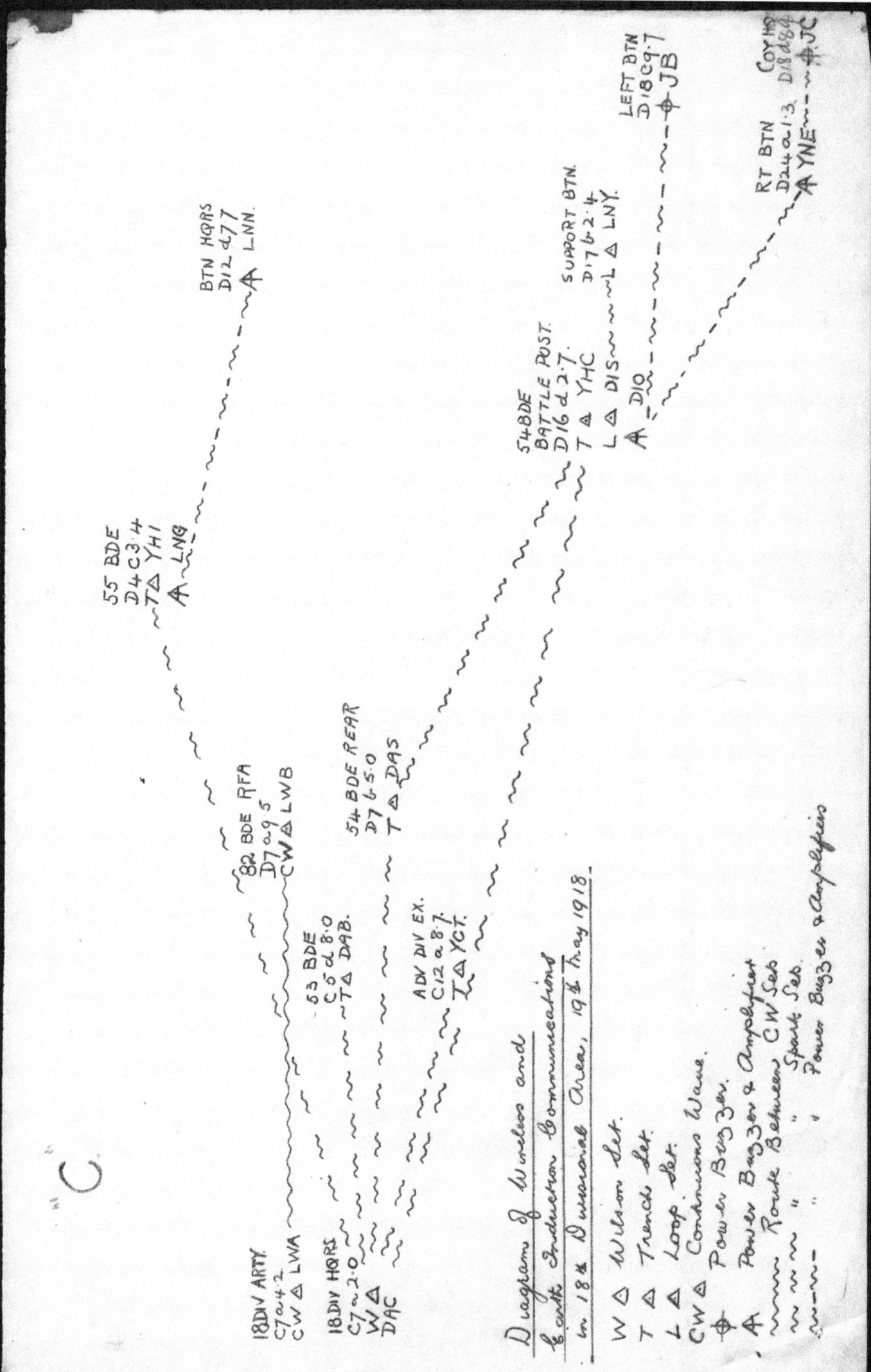

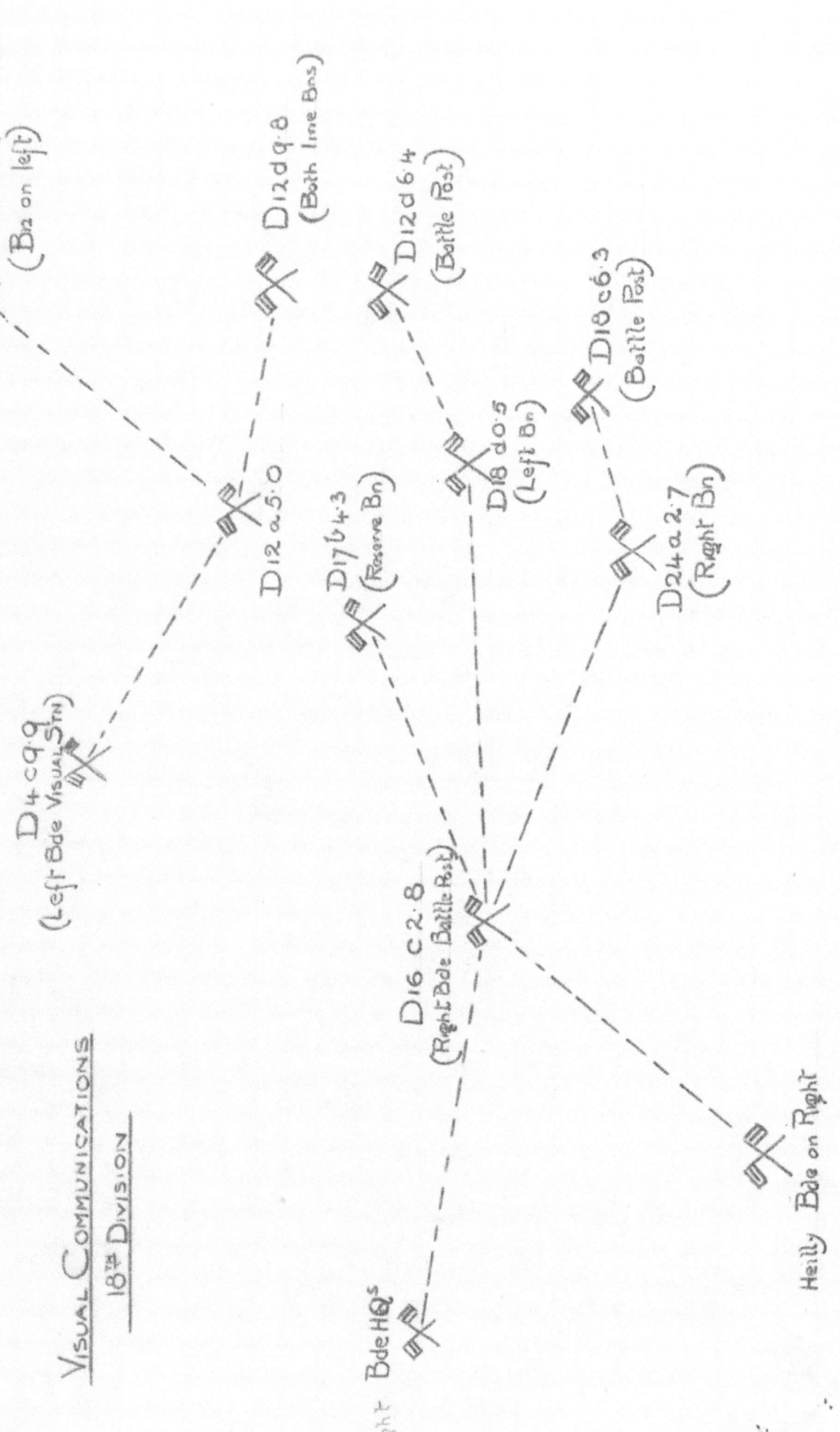

APPENDIX I.

ALLOTMENT OF LINES.

Route B - D. (BAIZIEUX)

Line No.			
2	YR	-	Right Brigade.
3	YR	-	M.G. Battalion.
11	18th D.A.	-	YRR
12	76th R.G.A.	-	YRR
13	18th D.A.	-	83rd Bde. R.F.A.
14	18th D.A.	-	
15	18th D.A.	-	
16	18th D.A.	-	82nd Bde. R.F.A.
21	47th Division.		
22	-do-		
23	58th Division.		
24	58th Division.		
25	-do-		
26	-do-		
29	YR	-	Support Brigade.
30	YR	-	YRR
32	142nd Bde.	-	YRR

Route D - Forward. (BAIZIEUX)

Line No.			
1	YRR	-	Right Brigade.
2	YRR	-	-do-
3	YRR	-	-do-
6	18th M.G.Bn.		
7	-do-		
8	-do-		
11	18th D.A.		
12	83rd Bde.R.F.A.	-	YRR
13	-do-	-	18th D.A.
14	-do-	-	YRR
15	82nd Bde.R.F.A.	-	YRR
16	-do-	-	18th D.A.
18	YRR	-	Left Brigade.
19	18th M.G.Bn.		
20	YRR	-	Left Brigade.
21	47th Div.		
22	-do-		
23	58th Div.		
24	-do-		
25	-do-		
26	-do-		
29	Left Bde.(for lateral)		
30	Left Bde.	-	83rd Bde. R.F.A.

WAR DIARY or INTELLIGENCE SUMMARY

Army Form C. 2118.

18th DIVL. SIGNAL CO., R.E.

JUN 1916

Vol. 31

Place	Date	Hour	Summary of Events and Information	Remarks and references to Appendices
U.21.d.37.	1st	10-0 am	58th Division relieves by 18th Division in Northern Sector of III Corps front. Divl. H.Q. established in dug-outs at U.21.d.37 and all lines in use by 58th Division diverted from 58 H.Q. of latter in CONTAY Chateau to new Divl. H.Q. Company less Signal Office personnel remaining at BAVELINCOURT	
CONTAY	2nd		Completing running of local lines to all H.Q. offices	
	3rd		Two pair cable route from Divl.H.Q. to "B" on bray poles and 2 drawer pair cable between CONTAY and BAIZIEUX teed up	
	4th		Nos. 1, 2 and 3 Detachments employed on teeing up drawer cables in Divisional area	
	5th		One pair D.8 cables laid from Divl.H.Q. Signal Office to H.Q. Reserve Brigade at U.29.a.86.	
	6th		Three pair cable route between Divl.H.Q. and "H" point on bray poles. Single cables leading from "V" pole to Signal Office replaced by suspended 7-strand brass-sheathed cables	
	7th		All field cable routes re-staped and regulated where necessary	

J. Olivine
Major
O.C. 18th DIVL. SIGNAL CO., R.E.

Army Form C. 2118.

WAR DIARY
or
INTELLIGENCE SUMMARY
(Erase heading not required.)

18th DIVL. SIGNAL CO., R.E.

JUN 1918

(2)

Place	Date	Hour	Summary of Events and Information	Remarks and references to Appendices
	10th		Work on extension of buried cable system from "K" point forward commenced and one 100 yard section completed.	
	11th		Buried cable route from "K" point completed as far forward as V.22.c.4.5 — limit of daylight working — 50 pair cables being put in from "K" point.	
	12th		Junction boxes installed on forward portion of buried.	
	13th		Infantry working party of approximately 600 men detailed for digging cable trench from V.22.c.4.5 forward to V.23.d.A.II. It was hoped that this party would complete a 6 foot trench, and that the cables would be laid and trench filled in during hours of darkness on night of 13/14th but owing to slow rate of digging by working party it was not possible to complete the section.	
	14th		Party of 100 infantry (Rhine Armour) details for cable burying on night of 14/15th. The work was successfully completed and 50 pair cables laid through to point at V.23.d.25	
	17th		Sections tested out and junction boxes installed on forward portion of buried.	

T. Mullin
O.C. 18th DIVL. SIGNAL CO., R.E.

Army Form C. 2118.

(3)

WAR DIARY
or
INTELLIGENCE SUMMARY.
(Erase heading not required.)

18th DIVL. SIGNAL CO. R.E.

JUN 1918

Place	Date	Hour	Summary of Events and Information	Remarks and references to Appendices
	18th		During week ending 22nd instant two cable detachments were employed daily on reeling up cables in the Divisional Area. Cable as follows was recovered:- D.V. single 1 mile; D.B - P/m miles; D.3 single 11½ miles; D.3 twisted 3½ miles; and D.1 and D.2 = 30 miles	
	19th		Buried cable coverings over defence lines revetted with sandbags	
	24th		Buried cable system completed from point reaches on 15th (V.23.d.2.5) to Left Brigade Advd SKS at V.23.d.1.1.	
	27th		Test of communications carried out between grooms and 7-9pm. During these hours telegraph and telephone circuits were not used. See Appendix "B"	
	29th		Telephone exchange and Test boards changed over from Signal office to mined dug-out and all lines extended into dug-out. One twin D.3 cable laid from "H" Point on Lorry to 185th D.I G.Par SKS at WARROI (U.21.d.21)	
			One pair D.8 cables laid from 185th Div Arty H.Q. (V.21.d.37) to N.G.14 Observation group at C.9.d.63 to give direct communication.	
			No action operations with the exception of raids were undertaken during the month and the work of the Signal Company was therefore	

O. C. 18th DIVL. SIGNAL CO., R.E.

Army Form C. 2118.

WAR DIARY
or
INTELLIGENCE SUMMARY
(Erase heading not required.)

18th DIVL. SIGNAL CO., R.E.

JUN 1918

(4.)

Place	Date	Hour	Summary of Events and Information	Remarks and references to Appendices
			Principally confined to the improving of existing communications and the completion of the buried cable system. Work done on latter by 18th Division is as shown on enclosed diagram marked "A"	
Average strength of Company during month :— Officers 12 ORs 352. Horses 116.				
Awards during month :-				
			MILITARY CROSS	
			Captain N.S. Regnart — 8th Hussars — 2nd in Command of Company T/Lieut T.F. Dillon — R.E. — No. 1 Section	
			MERITORIOUS SERVICE MEDAL	
			64795 Actg/Sergt. G. Smith — H.Q. 4-5858 Sergt. J. Whitehead N̲o̲.̲ 1 Section	
Enclosures :—			"A" Diagram of Buried Cable system "B" Report on Communication to date	

O.C. 18th DIVL. SIGNAL CO., R.E.

[signature]
Major R.E.

S E C R E T.

18th Division H.Q.G. 215.

18TH DIVISION LOCATION REPORT - 6 a.m. June 11th 1918.

11th Royal Fusiliers.   Front line W.21.b.4.9. - W.27.a.2.8.   H.Q. W.19.b.99.00.

2nd Bedford Regt.   V.23.b & d.

Otherwise no change.

L. G. Hubbert
for Major
Lieut.Colonel,
General Staff, 18th Division.

June 10th 1918.

All recipients of 18th Div. G.142 of 8.6.18.

18th Division G.638

SECRET

Signals,

1. A test of communications, during which the following means of communication only will be employed, will be held within the Division from 9 a.m. to 7 p.m. tomorrow 27th June :-

    D.R.L.S.
    VISUAL
    PIGEONS
    WIRELESS

2. During these periods telephones will not be used except

    (a) those required for the maintenance of Signal Lines.
    (b) from O.P's and wireless stations to batteries.

    Telephone circuits will not be disconnected.

3. Telephones may be taken into use by order of any commander of the rank of Lieutenant Colonel upwards to meet an enemy attack or other urgent tactical situation.

4. In the event of the tactical situation requiring the use of the telephone to be resumed, the fact will be notified by the commander concerned, through the usual channels, to Divisional Headquarters by PRIORITY telegram.

5. C.R.A., C.R.E., Brigades and Signals will forward a report on the results of the suspension to reach D.H.Q. by mid-day D.R. June 28th. This report will give any lessons learnt from the test and any points requiring further consideration.

6. This Divisional Test will be followed by a Corps Test, at a date and time to be notified later.

                        (Sd) P. ASHMEAD BARTLETT Captain
June 26th 1918.   for Lt. Col., General Staff, 18th Divn.

18/SYR/297

B

General Staff,
    18th Division.

Reference 18th Division G 638.

The telegraph and telephone circuits connecting Divisional Headquarters and the Brigades were not used yesterday between the hours of 9 a.m. and 7 p.m. Messages were disposed of by visual and D.R.L.S., 27 telegrams being sent by D.R.L.S. and 31 by visual; this represents a decrease of about 60 telegrams dealt with on the average day between the hours of 9 a.m. and 7 p.m. The visual station near Divisional Headquarters was established at U.21.d.8.5, the visual station for the 2 Brigades in Line at V.20.d.3.3, and the station for the Brigade in Reserve at U.29.a.6.3. The following are the numbers of telegrams dealt with between the Division and each Brigade :-

18th Division and 53rd Brigade	2
18th Division and 54th Brigade	24
18th Division and 55th Brigade	5

Helio and Lucas Lamp were used. All messages were transmitted correctly with one exception - a message to HEZI Q from 53rd Brigade (in which there was one mistake); but there was considerable delay on several of the messages. This is accounted for by the fact that several signallers were unaccustomed to using the helio. This is being rectified by classes, in which these men will receive careful instruction in the helio. These classes have been started today.

Wireless was not used at all.

I consider that these silent periods are a very valuable exercise for the Divisional Signal Company and I recommend that they be repeated once every week.

28th June 1918.

Major, R.E.,
O.C. Signals, 18th Division.

Army Form C. 2118.

WAR DIARY
or
INTELLIGENCE SUMMARY
(Erase heading not required.)

JUL 1918

Vol 32

Place	Date	Hour	Summary of Events and Information	Remarks and references to Appendices
Used 27	1st		10 S/parties of 32nd Divisional Signals reported for training with the Company	
CONTAY	2nd		Billets and made in MELBOURNE TRENCH and AUSTRALIA STREET beneath	
	3rd		In order to strengthen all joint boxes on buried Cable south from "K" to "X" Concrete slabs were to have forward in places in position.	
	4th		All derived cables in and around the Chateau and village of CONTAY measured.	
	5th		Wagons were thoroughly overhauled and all stores checked.	
			Visual practice and inspection for the "Silver Dog" on the 6th instant was carried out. Visual stations were established at the following points:— V20.d.3.4, V25.a.7.9, and U21.d.1.17. (Ref. Map "Senlis" Scale 1:20,000)	
	6th		Silent day. All telephone and telegraphic communications were suspended from 9 a.m. to 7 p.m. (within the Division) Urgent and Priority messages only, were allowed to be transmitted by Telegraphic communications. All other messages were disposed of either by Visual, D.R.L.S., Visual, or Pigeon.	
	7th to 9th		Work was carried out in the forward area of clearing all trenches mentioned below of disused cables. Western section of AUSTRALIA St, MELBOURNE TR. WATTLE St and the MAZE.	
	10th		Party under Lt. Biller M.C.R.E. sandbagged a buried crossing new defence line 500 yds E of VADENCOURT.	
			Visual classes from 9 a.m. to 12 noon.	

O.C. 18th Divl. Signal Co., R.E.

WAR DIARY
or
INTELLIGENCE SUMMARY

(Erase heading not required.)

JUL 1918 — 18th DIVL. SIGNAL CO., R.E.

Army Form C. 2118. (2)

Place	Date	Hour	Summary of Events and Information	Remarks and references to Appendices
	11th / 12th / 13th		Work was carried out in preparing for the move of the Co. to the CAVILLON TRAINING AREA	
			To CAVILLON TRAINING AREA. The 18th Division were relieved in the line by the 47th Div. and advanced	
			Advanced echelon for new area at 2.45 a.m. Marched NES. café at Coisy under Lt Col'n MASSE	
			HeadQrs at CONTAY at 10 a.m. and opened up at CAVILLON the same hour.	
CAVILLON	14th Sept		All cable on the previously used lines through were all dried earlier were picked up.	
			During the period, the work all telephones and "URGENT" were disposed of. On the request of the	
		4 p.m.	and 5 p.m. we make that all telegrams for use as necessary tomorrow.	
	7 Sept		Cable carts and all required through to make Visual stations were arranged at inspections	
			The weather inspected. Parts will making to the ground over till reaching channels despatch	
			Cable line from CAVILLON to PICQUIGNY was repaired and all DRs at the most unavailable by D.R.	
	25 Sept		Usual exercising of horses. Men to be kept for respecting under the supervision of Lieutenant FRANCE 11/C. Group R.E.	
	29 "		Party of horses proceeded to ST GRATIEN to form circuit thereon under all the work of the CA Brigade Divisional Exp.	
			to take up line	
	30/9/31		Signal Exh Instrument … found … from where we were sent to ST GRATIEN and a visit to the mess was	
			during the … were sunshine, that …	
			No action of note was carried out during the month, and the work of the signal company was	

W. Repeat.
O.C. 18th DIVL. SIGNAL CO., R.E.

WAR DIARY
or
INTELLIGENCE SUMMARY
(Erase heading not required.)

JUL 1918   **18th DIVL. SIGNAL CO., R.E.**

Army Form C. 2118.

Place	Date	Hour	Summary of Events and Information	Remarks and references to Appendices
			The Coy has principally been employed in the improving of existing communications. The availability of wire was small and other lines during the month could scarcely be called new.	
			Average strength of Company during month — Officers 12 OR 310. Horses 119	
			Area the during month — Nil	

W Renaud
O.C. 18th DIVL. SIGNAL CO., R.E.

18TH Division

Engineers.

18th DIVISIONAL SIGNAL COMPANY, R. E.

A U G U S T   1 9 1 8.

18/SYR/395.

"18th Division. "A".

Herewith War Diary for month of August 1918.

M Reynolds. Major,
18th Div. Signal Co. R.E.

10th Septr., 1918.

Army Form C. 2118.

WAR DIARY
or
INTELLIGENCE SUMMARY

(Erase heading not required.) 18th DIVL. SIGNAL CO., R.E.

Vol 33

AUG 1918

Place	Date	Hour	Summary of Events and Information	Remarks and references to Appendices
ST.GRATIEN	1st		Divisional Headquarters closed at CAVILLON at 10.0am and opened up at the Camp hut at ST GRATIEN. The Division relieved the 5th Australian Division in the left sector of the Australian Corps front. One complete office relay sent forward to ST.GRATIEN at 8.0am and a Forward Exchange was opened at FRANVILLERS. Company moved from CAVILLON to Camp just west of the PONT NOYELLES - FRECHENCOURT road at H.6.a.35.	
	2nd		Local lines laid at FRANVILLERS. The buried cable routes taken over in the rest area was in a very bad state of repair and it was found necessary to run out overland cables to all Brigades it being impossible to rely on the buried system for communication. Working parties were got out as quickly as possible to dig up, remake and test out all joints between the test points at HY - HY5 - HT.	
	3rd		Working parties sent out to overhaul buried cable routes between F5 and HY. Buried cables between F5 and HY tested out and cleared.	
	4th			
	5th		Six pair of D 8 cable laid out overland were poles between MT Test point and Tq.&.Sr (left &/Ada Div Hq). Necessary forward and stores sent forward to HEILLY	

M Ray. Major
OC. 18th DIVL. SIGNAL CO., R.E.

WAR DIARY
or
INTELLIGENCE SUMMARY

Army Form C. 2118.

18th DIVL. SIGNAL CO. R.E.

AUG 1918

Place	Date	Hour	Summary of Events and Information	Remarks and references to Appendices
	6th		to open up an Advd. Signal Office at that place, ready for work when required. Poling of 6 pairs between MT Test Point and J.9.b.81 completed. One pair D.8 cables laid from HY Test point to Div Bomb Store at J.13.b.59.	
	7th		Major J.C. Willis M.C.R.E. wounded. Advd Div Report Centre opened up at HEILLY in preparation for operations. He carried out an 8th instant. Two Signal Office relays with linesmen and motor cyclists sent forward to HEILLY. Major J.C. Willis M.C.R.E. dies of wounds.	
	8th		All Cable Detachments standing by from 6.0am at FS ready to keep up communications with Brigades if operations carried out by the Division successful.	
	11th		All stores, spare instruments and one Signal Office relief complete, together with linesmen and operators to work a Forward Exchange were sent forward to CONTAY preparatory to relief of 47th Division by 18th Division. Advd exchange established at "H" Test Point by main forward bury.	
CONTAY	12th		18th Division relieved 47th Division in Right Sector of III Corps front. Div H.Q. closed at ST GRATIEN at 10.0am and opened at CONTAY at same hour.	
	13th		No. 3 Cable Detachment attached to 25th Div Artillery for communications of	

W.Wynyard
O.C. 18th DIVL. SIGNAL CO. R.E.
Major

Instructions regarding War Diaries and Intelligence Summaries are contained in F. S. Regs., Part II. and the Staff Manual respectively. Title pages will be prepared in manuscript.

WAR DIARY
or
INTELLIGENCE SUMMARY.
(Erase heading not required.)

18th DIVL. SIGNAL CO., R.E.

AUG 1918

Army Form C. 2118.

Place	Date	Hour	Summary of Events and Information	Remarks and references to Appendices
	12th		82nd and 83rd Brigades of 18th Div Arty temporarily attached to 25th Div Arty. Two pair free cable routes between "Y" (U.21.a.9.2) and "B" (C.15.c.2.0) established. All pairs on loop between "E" and "O" Test Points in use by 18th Div and 18th Div. Arty tested out and regulated	
	15th		All cables running in valley between CONTAY and WARLOY tested out and above not in use marked for pulling up	
	16th		Advanced Div. Exchange established at HENENCOURT Chateau at 8.0 am	
	17th		One armoured loan laid from "X" Test Point via AUSTRALIA STREET to front line trench at N.27.d. Advd Exchange at "H" Test Point closed down and personnel and instruments sent forward to new Advd. Exchange at HENENCOURT Chateau	
	19th		One armoured twin laid from Right Bde Hq. (D.21.d.5.2) to new Advd Bde Hq at E.15.a.9.2. An alternative route was provided by looping via Bde D.2 cable from "O" Test Point to Advd Bde Hq. E.15.a.9.2	
	21st		Recovering cable in BAIZIEUX area	
	25th		Cable between "EA" Test Point and E.15 central poles	
	26th		Advd. Div. Report Centre closed at HENENCOURT Chateau at 1.0 am	

W. Raynard Major
O.C. 18th DIVL. SIGNAL CO. R.E.

Army Form C. 2118.

WAR DIARY
or
INTELLIGENCE SUMMARY

18th DIVL. SIGNAL CO., R.E.

AUG 1918

Place	Date	Hour	Summary of Events and Information	Remarks and references to Appendices
HENENCOURT	26th		Rear Div H.Q. closed at CONTAY at 10.0am and opened at HENENCOURT Chateau at same hour. Advd. Div. H.Q. closed at HENENCOURT Chateau and opened up at BECOURT Chateau at 5-0pm. D.8 Pair running from "EA" Test Point to E.15 central extended from "The SQUARE" to BECOURT Chateau and the O.3 line forward to VALLEY TRENCH extended along the BUSSENCOURT – ALBERT Road to BECOURT, thus providing two pairs forward to Advd Div H.Q.	
BECOURT	27th		Company moved from HENENCOURT Chateau to Camp at E.10.E.8.5. Lieut EXMALLON R.E. Killed in action	
	28th		Pair of D.8 cables laid from BECOURT to "The POODLES"	
	29th		Cables extended from "The POODLES" to proposed new Advd Div H.Q. S. of TRONES WOOD. Division did not move to this H.Q.	
S.27.a.2.6. (N.W. of MONTAUBAN)	31st		Advd Div H.Q. closed at BECOURT Chateau and reopened at (S.27.a.2.6.) N.W. of MONTAUBAN at 4.0pm. Rear Div H.Q. closed at HENENCOURT and opened at BECOURT at same hour.	

M Raynal Major
O.C. 18th DIVL SIGNAL CO. R.E.

Army Form C. 2118.

WAR DIARY
or
INTELLIGENCE SUMMARY.
(Erase heading not required.)

18th DIVL. SIGNAL CO., R.E.

AUG 1918

5.

Instructions regarding War Diaries and Intelligence Summaries are contained in F.S. Regs., Part II. and the Staff Manual respectively. Title pages will be prepared in manuscript.

Place	Date	Hour	Summary of Events and Information	Remarks and references to Appendices
			Average Strength of Company during month:-	
			12 Officers 310 O.R. 121 Horses	
			Honours and Awards during month:-	
			MILITARY CROSS:- Lieut. C.H. WEBB 8th Norfolk OC No 3 Section	
			Enclosures:- "A" Map shewing 5th Australian Divisional Inp.	
			"B" Notes on Communications during Operations 8th Aug to 5 Sept 1918	
			Captain (A/Major) N.S. REGNART M.C. 8th Hussars assumed command of company 7th Aug 1918.	
			N Regnart Major	
			OC 18th DIVL SIGNAL CO. R.E.	

NOTES ON COMMUNICATIONS DURING RECENT OPERATIONS.   B

1. Communications to Advanced Headquarters of Brigades.

Lines. Experience has shewn that in operations of this nature it is only possible to provide a very simple and limited system of lines. Forward communications consisted of a two pair cable route running down the centre line of the Divisional advance, which was extended as required, on each successive bound. The Headquarters of all Brigades were established along this route. It is not expected that in future operations of the same kind that a more liberal scale will be provided. From each position of Advd. Divisional Headquarters lateral communication direct was provided to flank divisions. Communication to the Rear Headquarters was established by using the rear portion of the two pair cable route thrown spare by the forward move of the Advanced office. In the same manner cable thrown spare by the forward move of the Rear office was reeled in and utilised for re-laying forward.

Congestion. Owing to the limited scale of forward communications described above, there is bound to be a certain amount of congestion owing to the heavy traffic due to active operations. This can only be decreased by a judicious use of the lines, both for telephone calls and number and length of telegrams. The number of "URGENT OPERATION PRIORITY" messages sent should be kept down to the minimum.

The position of Advd. Div. H.Q. affects the efficiency of Signal communications enormously. The further forward it is placed, the shorter will be the length of the forward communications, thereby increasing the speaking efficiency of field cable and decreasing the length of important lines to be maintained. It should be remembered that personnel has to be found not only for maintenance of lines already laid, but to extend the same at a very short notice. The number of linemen on maintenance duties decreases the number available for building new lines.

Wireless. Communication between the Wireless Directing Station at Advd. Div. H.Q. was preserved throughout with Trench Wireless Sets with each Brigade H.Q. On each move communication was rapidly established and maintained. Wireless was very little used, chiefly due to the fact that except for short periods telephone communication was maintained throughout, and secondly owing to the accepted disadvantage of enciphering and deciphering. This form of communication does not commend itself to the Staff.

Motor Cyclist D.R. Though no difficulty has been hitherto experienced in stationary warfare in delivering messages expeditiously, owing to the fact that despatch riding in this case is merely a matter of routine, when the war develops into one of movement, where Headquarters constantly change, the lack of initiative and training of D.R's in finding Headquarters in unknown country becomes apparent. An improvement in training is required in this respect.

Pigeons. This form of communication has not met with success and is due to the following:-
(a) Though the line has considerably advanced, Pigeon Lofts for obvious reasons have been obliged to remain stationary, thus entailing a long time for the birds to take in flight.
(b) A certain amount of delay has been experienced for the messages to be transmitted from the Loft to their destination, due to the block in telegraph circuits by other equally important messages.
(c) From the irregular releasing of birds and the meagre use made of pigeons for conveyance of important information, it is apparent that the value of the former as a method of communication is not fully realised by battalions. When Lofts are established further forward I consider that an

improvement.

improvement in respect of the time taken to get messages back will be experienced.

2. **Communication forward of Brigade Headquarters.**

   <u>Lines</u>. In most cases telephone communication was established between the Headquarters of the Advance Guard Brigade and battalion headquarters without unreasonable delay. I understand that on several occasions Staff Officers at Advd. Div. H.Q. utilised the forward lines to speak to Battalion Commanders, which in itself shews that the forward communication of brigades in this respect was satisfactory, though of course the time taken to establish them is the most important factor.

   <u>Visual</u>. This form of communication was used extensively by all brigades and provided practically the sole means (except by runners) forward of Battalion Headquarters. In moving warfare the value of visual between brigades and battalions and between the latter and the front line cannot be exaggerated. Lucas lamps have again proved their value as against other methods of visual communication. The state of the weather and the advantages afforded by the geographical nature of the country operated over, have greatly added to facility in establishing visual communication.

   <u>Earth Induction</u>. With the exception of one brigade, little or no use has been made of Power Buzzers and Amplifiers. It seems to be generally agreed that for moving warfare this form of communication is not suitable, due in the first place to the cumbersome nature of the gear required and secondly that the workable range of these instruments is not sufficiently great for the new conditions, thirdly that the increasing use of earth return telephone circuits practically make Power Buzzer and Amplifier working inoperative. It is also highly probable that the issue of these instruments will be discontinued in the near future, and their place taken entirely by Loop Sets.

   <u>Loop Sets</u>. Loop Set working forward of brigades was carried out to a certain extent by two brigades, but again their range is not sufficiently great. This, however, can be rectified by the use of sets made up of two "Rear" portions of the Loop circuit, instead of one "Rear" and one "Front" portion as exists at present. This improvement will be effected as early as possible. The value of Loop Sets is discounted by the fact that highly trained operators are required to work them, and it is the lack of the latter which has been the difficulty.

ARTILLERY COMMUNICATIONS - August 23rd to September 5th, 1918

The general distribution of Artillery on Divisional Front was four Brigades in action and one affiliated Heavy Brigade. Of these, one Brigade was detailed to be ready to limber up and move with one Brigade of Infantry as Advance Guard to pursue the enemy whenever possible.

As the four Field Artillery Brigades were worked in two groups of two Brigades each, the general scheme of communication was to push forward two parallel cable lines - one in each half of the Divisional Sector, avoiding villages. The Liaison Officer with the Infantry Brigade always had a line through the Infantry Exchange to his own Brigade and this was increased to a line to each covering Brigade whenever time and cable allowed. To assist this, Artillery Brigades always made Headquarters near Infantry Brigades. This meant that the liaison Brigade in each group could rarely be really close to its batteries, causing long lines to the latter which were difficult to maintain.

Visual was occasionally used to supplement the lines mentioned and owing to the exceptional nature of the country proved extremely useful for O.P. work when too far to lay lines for the short time the guns were in action in one place.

Continuous wave wireless was used throughout the battle, one set being allotted to the D.A., and each D.A. Brigade, while a fourth was lent to an attached Brigade according to its tactical position. Operators for this set were given sufficient training on the other sets in a week to enable them to carry on under supervision at the opening of the battle. The system worked well and kept continuous touch except for the short period when actually in transit from one position to the next.

Motor Cycle Despatch Riders - and Mounted Orderlies did good work. It was found expedient to send orderlies to move up with their headquarters and then return immediately to be ready to take evening operation orders usually issued after dark. Motor Cyclists were much hampered by any rain and at night by the broken nature of the less important roads which had to be traversed.

In the earlier stages with only one cable detachment and H.Q. very scattered it was found very difficult to maintain telephonic communication but later when the 18th Divisional Artillery came in to relieve an Army Brigade the two detachments could carry out the above scheme. Linemen were posted with Advanced Brigade for maintenance purposes, and a Forward Exchange established as soon as lines became inconveniently long. Insufficient men being available to supply each Brigade with Divisional Linemen, close touch had to be maintained with the Staff in order to try to anticipate moves. This was rendered difficult by the necessity of personal reconnaissance, control of detachments at work, and liaison with Brigades.

After the initial cable difficulties, units had sufficient cable for two sets of communication - one in use, and another in process of being reeled in or laid out. It was then only necessary to replace the wastage of ordinary wear and tear while advances were not rapid.

The delivery of small expendable stores and accumulators, and collection of returnable articles was a continual problem as no form of light conveyance was available. Frequent delays were caused by this and the inability of units to collect for themselves.

7-9-18.

Major,
O.C. Signals, 18th Division

Army Form C. 2118.

WAR DIARY
or
INTELLIGENCE SUMMARY

(Erase heading not required.) 18th DIVL SIGNAL Co. R.E.

SEP 1918

No. 35

Instructions regarding War Diaries and Intelligence Summaries are contained in F. S. Regs., Part II. and the Staff Manual respectively. Title pages will be prepared in manuscript.

Place	Date	Hour	Summary of Events and Information	Remarks and references to Appendices
DUGOUTS at	1-9-18		Sig Coys position BELLOY CHATEAU 5° E.270.2.8.	
E.270.2.8.	2-9-18		12 nn D.3 Cable team line from Bde HQ (B.27.c.9.5) to 54 Bde Dump (c.9.8)	
(N.W. of MONTAUBAN)	3-9-18		Div Am HQ closed at B.27.c.9.5 (N.W. of MONTAUBAN) at 5pm and opened at Bn.28.c.7.1 (BAZENTIN)	
NEW MAP SHEETS			Cables at BECORT closed all Sig working the same day. 2 Bn N° wire line from Div Bn HQ(BAZENTIN)	
BAZENTIN			to GOVERNMENT FARM (M.27.a. or 2° E. of BAILLES)	
BAZ	4			
5				
Bn 28	6		at 5.27.a.2.9. (N.W. of MONTAUBAN) at 2pm.	
(N.W of MONTAUBAN)				
	7			
	8			
	9			
	10			
	11			

O.C. 18th DIVL SIGNAL Co. R.E.

Army Form C. 2118.

WAR DIARY
OR
INTELLIGENCE SUMMARY
(Erase heading not required.)

18th DIVL. SIGNAL CO., R.E.

SEP 1918

Place	Date	Hour	Summary of Events and Information	Remarks and references to Appendices
	14th		Work commenced on the construction of two pr. D cable R.T's circuit consisting of 2 joint BB cables from forward	
			ador. Bn. H.Q. (D.D.A.&G.) forward to batteries H.Q. of Bdes in line.	
	15th		Buried cable RAD. constructed by VIII Corps pioneer coys. b (March 2, 1918) Reconn. 7 from [illegible] not detected the	
			following points: V.B. (F.17.a.a.a.) and QUARRY (E.18.c.9.5.). The [illegible] [illegible] [illegible] [illegible] [illegible] at Bde H.Q. [illegible]	
			and Bde. pairs not distinguished to cable trunks at Divisional End. The ends [illegible] [illegible] [illegible] [illegible]	
			[illegible] of attaching [illegible] to [illegible]	
HERAMONT (D.12.d.6.6.)	19th		Div. H.Q. closed at 9.07 A.M. [illegible] [illegible] [illegible] 11 P.M. [illegible] [illegible] HERAMONT (D.12.d.6.6.) [illegible] Div. H.Q. [illegible]	
			D.2.2.d.5.6. (S.W. of AIZECOURT LE BAS). Rear Bn. H.Q. at same time. NE.1 Subdivision [illegible] [illegible] Rear Divl. 1/2 [illegible]	
			now laid during the following:- AirQ Brand (A.12.d.4.6.) repd. Camp (D.22.d.2.8.) D.A.D.O.S. (D.22.d.6.8.) [illegible]	
			pair to BROOKWOOD (D.9.b.6.5) from Divl. and Bucharest (E.4.b.4.4) Point of All Cable laid from [illegible] to D.1.Q.	
			to Bn. in Reserve (13th H.Y. Bde.) at E.11.D.9.0. also a D/Line B/D between Bn. in Reserve [illegible] in [illegible] (E.5.b. [illegible])	
	18th		[illegible] [illegible] [illegible] [illegible] [illegible] [illegible] [illegible] [illegible] [illegible] [illegible] [illegible] [illegible] [illegible] [illegible]	
			4 EPEHY, KEMPIRE and BONNBOY. Burial [illegible] Sidings (E?.) Rd. between [illegible] [illegible] [illegible] [illegible] [illegible] [illegible] [illegible] [illegible]	
			(F.18.c.9.7.) and beyond the day 55th of Bde H.Q. [illegible] [illegible] [illegible] [illegible] [illegible] [illegible] [illegible] to F.12.b [illegible] [illegible] [illegible] [illegible]	
			54th Bde [illegible] [illegible] QUARRY. The [illegible] [illegible] Reserve Battalions [illegible] [illegible] [illegible] [illegible] [illegible]	
			1st D.S. Cable [illegible] 54th Bde (E.18.c.9.7.) 55th Y.S. to that [illegible] [illegible] [illegible] [illegible] [illegible] [illegible]	

W. Pimont Major.
O.C. 18th DIVL. SIGNAL CO., R.E.

A6945 Wt. W14422/M1160 350,000 12/16 D, D, & L. Forms/C.2118/14

WAR DIARY
or
INTELLIGENCE SUMMARY
(Erase heading not required.)

Army Form C. 2118.

18th DIVL. SIGNAL CO., R.E.

Place	Date	Hour	Summary of Events and Information	Remarks and references to Appendices
LIBRAMONT (Bois du.)	19th (Cont'd)		On completion of above 2 Brin DCGaLS Carlo with 1st Bn Quarry to 2nd Brigade and 155th Bn/Mxc H.Q. (relieving us)	
			Running Cable Pn G.F.R.G. 7/Quad (either from SE G.R.V. (End of Bucq.)	
			Tired O cables made known forming of Bde. and took 31 boxes to 1st Battn HR, Quarry Rendezvous Bn HQ Cb	
			2 Bind G.F. from W. to Quad Post 18 Pr fullies between F4 Cc5 & 4/Quad was shifted to officers D.R.C.	
			on present day	
			A party proceeded to Que 18 and Bde (Quad Post) at 6.00 hours and ran the Cable from here	
		21st	to YAK POST (First 2.3) preparatory to attack on 21st. Great difficulty experienced in keeping this Cable intact owing to	
			enemy M Gs and snipers.	
			Td Brigade Post was established at Lindy's Cong (R) - F4 Cne central	
		22nd	Lines to 5 units Cable ran about Wd to 2nd Corps wound D.W. about F4 B d hours	
			7th 8th & 9 Bde (55 Div) established with this 74 Bde Ch Ch on Q1 B d hour	
			Inom Quarry to Y/4 Bde	
		23rd	Lines to Bns Cable from from Bdes to Bns (as far as Rt (Bond and) to 55 Div established and by Carriers	
			Battn Cr/Battn Relays of Runners arranged, this working with each other and with aircraft from signal officers working with	
			each arr observation post was used.	
		24th	Bde Cable was stepped from forward from D.H.Q. no stages and resulted in and helping signal officers	

M Rupert Major
O.C. 18th DIVL. SIGNAL CO., R.E.

Army Form C. 2118.

WAR DIARY
or
INTELLIGENCE SUMMARY

(Erase heading not required.)

18th DIVL. SIGNAL CO., R.E. SEP 1918

Place	Date	Hour	Summary of Events and Information	Remarks and references to Appendices
HESSIGNY	25th		D.H.Q. closed at HERAMONT at 10.0 a.m. and opened at GAMBLES at noon same day. Route via... of N. Corps	
COMBLES			Pack leg 27th U.S. Division Signal Officer who had taken over of a.m. to 9 a.m. on 27th reported to present 12 a.m. Combles	
			moved from A.I.Z.E. COURT TE-BAS by march via E.	
	27th		This Company left H.Q. opened at 11 a.m. from FALFEMONT	
HERAMONT	29th		D.H.Q. closed at COMBLES at 4 p.m. and opened same hour with H.Q. at SERGEANT, following Day at 6 points of Divn.	
			between 27th U.S. Div. Communications troops are to relieve S.D. 1925 the men were to assume Div. Commns.	
			QUARRY to Amiens worked at F.BRAY (E.1.d.4) pick and 4th H.Q. of Edge on Roncoe (G.6.55) by Bdes.	
	29th		53/54 Bdes were moved from E.BRAY to TONSORLEM (31.b.12) 1st bde from 54th to 59 a/B/Bde. whilst switching of	
			4th C.H.Q. at S.J. at 4 p.m.	
	30th		53 Bdes laid main line from E.BRAY. Other H.Q. established line at MAY COPSE (E.8.6.4.). 11 Bde Div. mention last	
			from R.Y. 55 new H.Q. (MAY COPSE)	
Average Strength of Company during month:			12 Officers 315 OR 121 Horses	
Awards during month			No. 259625 Pvt. Hogg, A.S. and 242420 Cpl. Allen, L. MILITARY MEDAL	

W Raymond Major
O.C. 18th DIVL. SIGNAL CO., R.E.

Army Form C. 2118.

WAR DIARY
or
INTELLIGENCE SUMMARY
(Erase heading not required.)

18th DIVL SIGNAL CO., R.E.

Place	Date	Hour	Summary of Events and Information	Remarks and references to Appendices
LIERAMONT	1st		Relief by 50th Division started. 18th Division to move into rest area and established headquarters at BEAUCOURT. The company, less the patrol moved by march route from LIERAMONT to BEAUCOURT staying for the night at MONTAUBAN. Advance party consisting of one signal office relief, with known instruments etc sent forward by lorry with instructions to take over signal office and be prepared to open up communication at 10:00 hours 2nd.	
BEAUCOURT	2nd		Relieved in line by 50th Division. Our H.Q. closed at LIERAMONT at 10:00 hours and re-opened at BEAUCOURT at same hour. Divisional personnel reported by buses leaving LIERAMONT at 9800 hours. 53rd Brigade moved to ALLONVILLE, 54th to MOHLIENS AU BOIS and 55th to CONTAY. Direct lines were allotted by XIII Corps on existing routes.	
	3rd to 16th		During the period 3rd to 16th the Division was in rest at BEAUCOURT. All technical wagons were thoroughly overhauled and any necessary repairs effected. All stores were checked and any deficiencies indented for, and all instruments overhauled and repaired. Surplus stores were disposed of so far as possible. Classes were formed for the future of training.	

W. Renard Major
OC. 18th DIVL SIGNAL CO., R.E.

(2). Army Form C. 2118.

WAR DIARY
~~INTELLIGENCE SUMMARY~~
(Erase heading not required.) 18th DIVL. SIGNAL CO., R.E.

OCT 1918

Place	Date	Hour	Summary of Events and Information	Remarks and references to Appendices
			reinforcements, most of whom arrived from depôt kept with practically no knowledge of training. A few set Wireless Class was also formed on a basis of two per battalion and the majority of these men were sent back to their units with a useful knowledge of how set worked. About twenty miles of cable were recovered, repaired and made fit for re-use.	
			53rd Inf Bde moved from ABBEVILLE to ST GRATIEN on 5th instant and were allotted a sub-set line by Corps.	
	16th		Division ordered to move forward to relieve 66th Division in line south east of LE CATEAU. Company less H.Q. personnel sent forward by march route to BEUMONT, prepared new Div H.Q. Stopped for night at MAMETZ.	
RONSSOY WOOD	17th		Divisional H.Q. closed at BEAUCOURT at 1300 hours and reopened at RONSSOY WOOD at 1300 hours. Signal office closed at RONSSOY WOOD at 1300 hours. H.Q. 53rd Bde at VILLERS FAUCON. Personnel moved by tactical train from HEILLY to ROISEL. Direct line on permanent route - 54th Bde in vicinity of AIZECOURT-le-Bas - set on telephone communication - and 55th Bde at AIZECOURT - communication through 3rd Tank Bde.	

W Renwick Major
O.C. 18th DIVL. SIGNAL CO., R.E.

WAR DIARY or INTELLIGENCE SUMMARY

Army Form C. 2118.

18th DIVL. SIGNAL CO. R.E.

OCT 1918

Place	Date	Hour	Summary of Events and Information	Remarks and references to Appendices
SERAIN	18th		53rd Bde moved to MARETZ, 54th to SERAIN and 55th to BEAUREVOIR. Telephone communication with 53rd and 55th through 25th Division and direct line to 54th on permanent route.	
	19th		Div. H.Q. closed at RONSSOY WOOD at 1200 hours and opened at SERAIN at same hour. 53rd Bde moved to PREMONT, 54th to SERAIN, and 55th to ELINCOURT. Communication established with all three Brigades on lines allotted by XIII Corps. Company marched direct to REUMONT.	
REUMONT	20th		Div. H.Q. closed at SERAIN at 1600 hours and reopened at MARETZ (rear) and REUMONT (advd) at same hour. Relieved 66th Division on left sector of XIII Corps front. 53rd Bde moved to REUMONT during the morning but moved to vicinity of LE CATEAU later on the day. 54th Bde moved into line with the at LE CATEAU. 55th Bde remained at ELINCOURT. Communication with all three Brigades direct. On taking over from 66th the communication system was found to be very weak, and 2 pairs D.8. cables were laid from advd STR. to 54th Bde at K.33.6.33, with a 2-pair "See off" at Q.3.6. central going direct pair to 53rd and 54th area and a lateral between both.	

W Reynart Major
O C 18th DIVL. SIGNAL CO. R.E.

WAR DIARY
INTELLIGENCE SUMMARY

Army Form C. 2118.

18th DIVL. SIGNAL CO., R.E.

OCT 1918

Place	Date	Hour	Summary of Events and Information	Remarks and references to Appendices
	21st		55th Bde H.Q. moved to MAUROIS. One pair cables laid from Advd. Div. H.Q. to MAUROIS. 53rd Bde. moved into line - H.Q. at Q.4.c.9.5. (LECATEAU). Short lateral line laid between 53rd and 54th Bdes. Div. Bomb Store at P.26.d.70 connected up to Advd. Div. H.Q. Exchange	
	22nd		55th Bde moved from MAUROIS to form north H.Q. at K.33.A.9.L. 53rd Bde moved to K.35.c.5.4. and 54th to K.35.a.1.5. One pair D.8 cables laid from 53rd Bde H.Q. to (LE CATEAU) No. proposed new H.Q. at K.35.c.5.4. Two Tanks were allotted to Signals for operations on 23rd, one is to be used for forward cable laying and one for forward Wireless communication	
LE CATEAU 23rd (Q.4.c.9.5)			Division attacked in front of LE CATEAU. Div. H.R. closed at REUMONT and re-opened at LE CATEAU (Q.4.c.9.5) at same hour. Cable laying tank left laying up. Point K.26.d.75 at 0330 hours and proceeded via FEUILLE FARM crossing tank bridge at K.22.a.83 and arriving at K.34.a.70 at 0400 hours. A party consisting of 2 officers and 5 ORs with light cable cart left 53rd Bde H.Q. (K.35.c.5) at 0530 hours and laid 2 pairs D.8 cable along LE CATEAU - EVILLERS WOOD FARM road to the tank. These 2 pairs were picked up by the tank and extended forward	

O.C. 18th DIVL. SIGNAL CO. R.E.

WAR DIARY
or
INTELLIGENCE SUMMARY

Army Form C. 2118.

(5)

18th DIVL. SIGNAL CO., R.E.

OCT 1918

Place	Date	Hour	Summary of Events and Information	Remarks and references to Appendices

K.24.b.5.6 to h.18.c.4.3 where communication was opened up at 0725 hrs 53rd Bde to Advd Divr HQ at BEUMONT. Tactical messages were despatched from here by B.M 53rd Inf Bde. He informed the tank commander that he had central hub just been cleared of the enemy and that 55th Bde proposed to establish their H.Q. at h.18.c.8.3. The tank then proceeded to latter position where 55th Bde were but no communication immediately with Advd Div H.Q. The tank proceeded at about 1000 hours and laid 2 pairs D8 forward on L.9.C.26 to be FAYT FARM giving direct communication between 55th Bde and two of its battalions at FAYT FARM. At 1200 hours one of the Divisional pairs laid by the tank was split at K.20.b.1.1. and 2 pairs were laid to WHITE SPRING (K.18.c.9.0) where 5th Bde opened an Advanced Report Centre. These pairs gave 5th Inf Bde a direct line to Division and a lateral to 55th Bde. A squadron of 12th Lancers which were working with the Division were put on to 55th Bde exchange.

Two tanks fitted with CW wireless were detailed for work on the Divisional area both of which were to establish communication with a Directing Station at Divr HQ REUMONT. The Wireless Officer (Lieut. F.S. Speight)

M. Peverill
O C 18th DIVL. SIGNAL CO., R.E

Army Form C. 2118.

WAR DIARY
or
INTELLIGENCE SUMMARY

(Erase heading not required.) **18th DIVL. SIGNAL CO. R.E.**

Place	Date	Hour	Summary of Events and Information	Remarks and references to Appendices
			OCT 1918	
			was ordered to join No.1 Tank, which was specially allotted to the Division, at R.1.C.9.3. but on arrival at that point he found that the tank had not arrived. It was afterwards discovered that this tank had had a switch pit during the night. No. 2 Tank, with instructions to keep "A" Coy. 10th Tank Bn. Commander, who was operating with 55th Bn., in communication with Division and 2nd Tank Brigade, arrived at L.D.a.6.2 at 0745 hours and at once opened communication with Divn. HQ. Directing Station at REUMONT. Tactical messages were despatched from this point. Acting on orders received from 55th Bde. this tank proceeded to take control when it failed and stood up communication with A.S. at REUMONT which was maintained during 23rd and 24th.	
	24th		Advanced Divl. Exchange established at L.14.c.33. between FAYT FARM and 54th Bde at EPINETTE FARM. Details of lines laid between FAYT FARM and 54th Bde at L.14.c.33. Cable Main Divisional route piled as far as Advd. Divl. Exchange at L.14.c.33. was distributed as required by Brigades on 23rd and 24th from Signal Tank.	
	25th		One pair D.3. cables laid from LE FAYT FARM to 53rd Bde H.Q. in BOUSIES. One pair from 53rd Bde H.Q. to 53rd Bde N.Q. at cemetery BOUSIES and also enfair	

W.K. ? T. Myers
O.C. 18th DIVL. SIGNAL CO. R.E.

WAR DIARY
INTELLIGENCE SUMMARY

(Erase heading not required.) **18th DIVL. SIGNAL CO., R.E.**

OCT 1918

Army Form C. 2118.

Place	Date	Hour	Summary of Events and Information	Remarks and references to Appendices
	26th		from 54th Bde. round the outskirts of BOUSIES to H.Q. 55th Bde. at M. 4. C. 5.8.	
			One pair D.3 cables laid from Rear H.Q. of 54th Bde. at EVILLERS WOOD FARM to Advd. Divl. Exchange at L. 16. c. 3.3. Divl. 2-pair trunk cable route laid from	
	27th		eastern entrance to LE CATEAU on the LE CATEAU – LANDRECIES road to Advd. Divl. Exchange. D.3 cables between LE FAYT FARM and 55th Bde H.Q L.4.C.5.8 replaced by D.8 and the route diverted to avoid shelled areas as much as possible. Divisional 2-pair trunk cable route pled as far as LE FAYT FARM.	
	28th		One pair D.8 cables laid from H.Q. 53rd Bde at F.28 d.27 to 38th Divn. Advanced at F.16.a.3.1.	
	29th & 30th		During this period all detailed cable lines in back area were recovered, repaired and made fit for reissue.	

Awards during month:—

D.C.M. 360676 Sgt. L. Turngate. 2nd Bar to M.M. 56757 2nd Cpl. S.G. Marton. Bar to M.M. 52637 Pnr. Speight

MILITARY MEDAL – 259569 Pnr. Smith L. 504476 Sgt. McKilson. 478725 Spr. G.V. Lyles.
2824-31 Spr. W.K. Nall. 360677 Pnr. W. Prater. 253812 R/Spr. E.A. Wordster.

Average strength of Company during month:—

12 Offrs. 315 O.R. 121 Horses

Enclosures:— "A" Map showing cable routes
"B" Signal Instructions for operations on 23rd to 24th Oct 1918

W. Renard Major
O.C. 18th DIVL. SIGNAL CO., R.E.

SECRET.   "B"

SIGNAL INSTRUCTIONS for FORTHCOMING OPERATIONS.   23 OCT 1918
(IN Front of LE CATEAU)

The system of communications of the 18th Division will be dealt with in detail under the following headings:-

(a) Telephone System.
(b) Wireless. (Including Loop Set)
(c) D.R.L.S.
(d) VISUAL.
(e) Inter-communication with R.A.F.

(a) Telephone Exchanges are established at the following places:-

18th Div. Advd. H.Q.	-	REUMONT.
18th Div. Rear H.Q.	-	MARETZ.
18th Div. Arty. H.Q.	-	REUMONT.
53rd Inf. Bde. H.Q.	-	Q.4.c.9.5.
53rd Inf. Bde. Report Centre	-	K.35.d.2.0.
54th Inf. Bde. H.Q.	-	K.33.b.3.3.
54th Inf. Bde. Report Centre	-	K.29.b.6.7.
55th Inf. Bde. H.Q.	-	K.35.c.3.5.
18th Div. Arty. Forward Exchange	-	K.33.b.2.2.
82nd Brigade R.F.A.	-	K.33.b.2.2.
83rd Brigade R.F.A.	-	Q.4.b.6.5.
85th A.F.A. Brigade	-	Q.4.c.8.3.
250th Brigade R.F.A.	-	K.34.a.5.5.
251st Brigade R.F.A.	-	K.34.c.6.2.
18th M.G.Bn. Advd.	-	K.34.b.8.0.
18th M.G.Bn. Rear	-	REUMONT.

Lines. - From Advanced Divisional Headquarters, REUMONT, to each Brigade in the line there is one pair of D.8 cables on the ground, and a lateral of D.8 cable has been provided between the two Brigades. These two pairs are run together forming a two pair cable route. An alternative means of getting the Right Brigade is being provided via 25th Division and Advanced Corps Exchange.

As soon as possible after Zero hour it is intended to extend the two pair cable route from Right Brigade H.Q. in Q.4.c.9.5 (which will become the new Advanced Divisional Headquarters), along the light railway line to K.35.c.9.4, thence through EVILLERS WOOD FARM - X roads in L.19.d.4.3 - X roads in L.9.c.2.5 - and along the straight second class road to BOUSIES. It is intended that any subsequent position of Advanced Divisional Headquarters will be chosen along this line and those of Brigades as near as possible, entailing the provision of only short spurs being built to establish communications.

(b) **Wireless.** - A Wireless Tank, carrying Wireless Station complete with operators, to work direct with Wireless Directing Station at REUMONT has been provided for the purpose of receiving messages from runners and orderlies. Leaving a position close up to the forming up line at K.1.c.9.2 as soon as possible after Zero hour, it will proceed along the following route:-

JACQUES HILL - GARDE HILL - EVILLERS WOOD FARM - WHITE SPRING - thence up the valley to L.14.central - X roads at L.9.c.2.5 - and along the track to BOUSIES.

This tank will be distinguished by a large blue and white flag and will halt at each of the positions underlined above. All runners and signallers should be acquainted with the route to be followed by the tank, and hand in any messages for transmission to rear formations by Wireless. These messages will be received by the Wireless Directing Station at REUMONT, and those addressed to Brigades and other advanced units will be telegraphed "Priority".

Trench Wireless and Loop Set. - The Wireless and Loop Set communication of 18th Division are and will be as shewn in attached diagram. Each Advanced Brigade H.Q. in the line will work to a Directing Station at REUMONT. The scheme for Loop Set working will be a "Rear" Loop Set at each Battalion H.Q. in the line with

the

"Forward" portion carried by the attacking companies.

(c) D.R.L.S. - Times of D.R.L.S. as already advertised.

Mounted D.R's. - A proportion of mounted orderlies from the Northumberland Hussars is being allotted to each Brigade for communication purposes.

(d) Visual. - Each Brigade will arrange its own scheme of visual communication. The Left Brigade and 55th Brigade are establishing a visual station on the high ground in K.27.d., to work forward along the valley running up to L.14.central.

(e) Communication with R.A.F. - A message dropping centre will be established at dawn on Z day at Advanced Divisional Headquarters BEUMONT.

Dump. - Arrangements are being made to transport a quantity of light cable for use of Brigades and Battalions by Supply Tank. This Dump will be formed on the X roads at L.19.c.4.3, from which point Brigades can draw.

22nd October, 1918.

(Sd) N S REGNART Major,
O.C. Signals, 18th Division.

Army Form C. 2118.

WAR DIARY
INTELLIGENCE SUMMARY
(Erase heading not required.)

18th DIVL. SIGNAL CO. R.E.

Place	Date	Hour	Summary of Events and Information	Remarks and references to Appendices
LE CATEAU	1st		Forward area reconnoitred and routes marked out for lines to be laid prior to proposed active operations on 3rd inst. Nov.	
	2nd		Eight pairs D.8. cable laid from EPINETTE FARM (Proposed Advanced Divl H.Q.) to Cross Roads at L.9.b.2.6. These were carefully labelled at the cross roads with a view to being picked up and continued forward after the advance. No. 5 pair at Cross roads picked up and extended to 54th Inf. Bde Report Centre at F.26.c.9.1. One pair D.8 laid from EPINETTE FARM (L.3.C.5.) to proposed Advanced H.Q. 53rd Inf. Bde at BOUSSIES WOOD FARM (F.23.a.1.8). Lateral laid from BOUSSIES WOOD FARM (proposed Advanced H.Q. 53rd Bde) to Advanced H.Q. of Brigade on left (38th Bde) at A.1.b.5.3. N°'s 3.6 and 7 of pairs laid yesterday from EPINETTE FARM to Cross Roads at L.9.b.2.6. extended to F.29.b.2.8. where cable tank laid up for night ready to lay cables forward during offensive operations on 3rd.	
	4th		A Supply Tank was detailed to lay forward lines following up advancing troops but this broke down before reaching cable head. A cable detachment was ordered to fill up from tank and the detachment was then ordered to extend one pair cables to 53rd and 54th Brigades at PETIT PLANTY (A7 and) 53rd Inf Bde and	

A/O.C. 18th DIVL. SIGNAL Co. R.E.

Army Form C. 2118.

WAR DIARY
or
INTELLIGENCE SUMMARY.
(Erase heading not required.)

18th DIVL. SIGNAL CO., R.E.

NOV 1918

Place	Date	Hour	Summary of Events and Information	Remarks and references to Appendices
	5th		Relieved by 55th Bde and G.O.C. 55th Bde ordered the two pairs laid to PETIT PREUX to be extended to PREUX (A.15.c.7.0) his new Advd Brigade HQ after 3rd Objective had been gained. Subsequently the cable detachment was ordered to extend these two pairs along Route-la-PREUX to A.18 central. It was found impossible for the detachment to continue forward of A.18 central and the line was carried forward to Brigade HQ LE CROISILIN (B.10.c.8.8) by the Brigade Signal Section. Two pairs forming main forward communications of Division made safe from traffic and all D3 cable which it was found necessary to lay spotting replaced by D8. These two pairs were also extended to (B.11.G.9.0) and a forward spur was laid to Battalion HQ at LA ARMAGNOLE (B.7.c.11).	
	8th		55th Bde HQ closed at PREUX at 1000 hours and opened up at POMMEREUIL at same hour. Cables between Advd Divl HQ at EPINETTE FARM and PREUX thrown open by this move were relied up.	
	10th		Special Observer Force under Major General BETHELL formed by XIII Corps to keep in touch with enemy. One complete cable detachment under an officer and a Wireless detachment complete with wireless gear under the Divl Wireless Officer	

Bromonsley Captain
A/O.C. 18th DIVL. SIGNAL CO., R.E.

Army Form C. 2118.

WAR DIARY
or
INTELLIGENCE SUMMARY.

(Erase heading not required.)   18th DIVL. SIGNAL CO., R.E.

NOV 1918

Instructions regarding War Diaries and Intelligence Summaries are contained in F. S. Regs. Part II. and the Staff Manual respectively. Title pages will be prepared in manuscript.

Place	Date	Hour	Summary of Events and Information	Remarks and references to Appendices
	11th		ordered to be attached to this force.	
			Hostilities ceased 1100 hours.	
SERAIN	13th		Divl. H.Q. closed at LE CATEAU at 1100 hours and opened at SERAIN at same hour. 53rd Bde at PREMONT, 54th and 55th Brigades at ELINCOURT. Signal office by XIII Corps on existing routes.	
			The remainder of the month was devoted to salvage work and much valuable cable was recovered.	

Average strength of Company during month :- 12 Officers 317 O.R. 121 Horses

Honours and Awards:-

MILITARY MEDAL

64952 Spr S.A. Goss   10366 Spr. R. McCrindian   147738 Spr. P.W. Arrother
2115482 Cpl H.F. Knight   314421 2/Cpl E.G. White   258367 - Y.E. Murty
Bar to MILITARY MEDAL — 97873 Spr. A.C. Ansdan MM.

Enclosures:-
"A" Signal Instructions for operations MORMAL FOREST 1st-5th Nov 1918.
"B" Notes on communications in front of BOUSSIES and ROBERSART.
"C" Notes on Communications Oct 25th to Nov 7th 1918.

Signature   A/O.C. 18th DIVL. SIGNAL CO., R.E.

SECRET.

SIGNAL INSTRUCTIONS FOR FORTHCOMING OPERATIONS.

MORMAL FOREST. 4th & 5th Nov. 1918.

The system of communication of the 18th Division will be dealt with in detail under the following headings:-

    (a) Telephone System.
    (b) Wireless. (Including Loop Set)
    (c) D.R.L.S.
    (d) Inter-communication with R.A.F.

(a) Telephone Exchanges are established at the following places:-

18th Div. Advd. H.Q.	EPINETTE FARM.
18th Div. Arty. H.Q.	EPINETTE FARM.
18th Div. Rear H.Q.	LE GATEAU. (Q.4.c.9.5)
53rd Inf. Bde. H.Q.	L.4.a.9.9.
53rd Inf. Bde. Advd.H.Q.	HOUSSIER WOOD FARM.
54th Inf. Bde. H.Q.	F.23.c.0.9.
54th Inf. Bde. Report Centre	F.24.c.9.2. (Moving to ROBERSART).
55th Inf. Bde. H.Q.	L.4.c.6.8.
82nd Brigade R.F.A.	F.27.d.4.8.
83rd Brigade R.F.A.	F.27.d.4.8.
85th Army Field Arty. Bde.	F.28.c.6.5.
94th Army Field Arty. Bde.	?
76th Brigade R.G.A.(affiliated)	L.4.a.9.9.
50th Division Advd. H.Q.	LE FAYT FARM.
25th Division Advd.	?

    <u>Lines</u>. - A two pair cable route to form the forward communication of the Division will be built from EPINETTE FARM along the track running through the centre of HOUSSIES to the junction of the sunken and metalled roads at A.13.b.6.1, thence due east to the ENGLEFONTAINE - PREUX Road. From this point the cable route will follow the road in a S.E. direction through the X in PREUX to the X roads in A.21.d.8.7. From this point it will follow the ROUTE De PREUX.

    The above 2 pairs will be laid from a Supply Tank which will be distinguished by a blue and white flag.

    The route will be carried up to a point as near as possible to the present front line on Y day and continued by cable tank to start at about Zero + 2 hours.

    Direct lines will be provided by 12.00 hours on Y day between Advanced Divisional Headquarters and Report Centres of Brigades in Line. Advanced Divisional Headquarters will be connected up direct with Advanced Headquarters of Flank Divisions.

(b) <u>Wireless</u>. - The attached diagram shows the wireless communication at Zero hour and that which will come into force during Z day.

    A Wireless Tank, distinguished by a blue and white flag, working direct to a Directing Station at EPINETTE FARM will follow the same route as laid down for the cable tank. It will leave the forming up position - which will be notified later - at Zero + 1 hour and will be prepared to receive messages from runners and orderlies at the places marked by rings on the attached diagram, where it will halt to erect stations.

(c) <u>D.R.L.S.</u> - Motor cyclist D.R's will run between EPINETTE FARM and the Advanced Headquarters of Brigades as per scheduled timings.

(d) <u>Inter-communication with R.A.F.</u> - A message dropping report centre will be established at EPINETTE FARM at dawn on Z day.

<u>Cable Supply</u>. - The Supply Tank will carry a supply of D.5 and D.3 twisted cable from which forward units may draw on demand.

                                 (Sd) N.S. REGNART Major,
31st October, 1918.   A.D. Signals, 18th Division.

"B"

NOTES on COMMUNICATIONS during operations leading up to the capture
of
BOUSIES and ROBERSART.

1. Attention is drawn to the "Notes on Communications during recent Operations" written subsequent to the termination of the operations carried out by the Division between August, 23rd and Septr., 5th 1918.

2. Communication arrangements for the operations leading up to the capture of BOUSIES and ROBERSART were based on the same principles as emphasised in the previous operations, though a different means of laying out cable was employed.

3. Lines. - Up to Zero hour each brigade in the line was linked up with Advanced Divisional Headquarters by a separate pair of cables, with a lateral pair between brigades, forming a forward 2-pair cable route up to a point abreast of the positions of the Headquarters of the two advanced brigades.
   At Zero + 1 hour this two pair cable route was extended by a cable wagon to EVILLERS WOOD FARM (L.25.a.0.3). Meanwhile a tank, carrying a large supply of cable, had reached this point on the eastern side of the stream and carried on these pairs, following a route previously arranged by the General Staff on which all formations were to establish their Headquarters. The progress of the tank proved very satisfactory, chiefly due to the advantageous nature of the ground, and cable head was able to be preserved well forward and proved very valuable to Brigade Staff Officers in communicating progress of the attack from positions within a mile of the front line troops. When Headquarters of Brigades were established for the night the two pairs of cables provided the sole telephonic communication between Advanced Division and Advanced Brigades.

4. Wireless. - It was intended to use a tank carrying a wireless station and personnel to follow the same route as the cable tank, but this did not materialize owing to the tank having received a direct hit whilst moving up. Another wireless tank, however, belonging to the tank company operating on the 55th Brigade front, transmitted messages relating to the progress both of the infantry and tanks.
   Each brigade had, and used, trench wireless, working to Advd. Divisional Headquarters without interruption except for periods whilst on the move.

   Loop Sets. - Loop Sets were used by the 53rd and 54th Brigades in the initial attack, between battalion headquarters and assaulting companies. These proved of value in reporting objectives gained and transmitting short situation reports.

5. Visual. - The left brigade (54th) used visual to advantage. From the high ground west of MONTAY it is possible to see right up the valley towards L.14.central. A brigade station was established in the neighbourhood of K.28.a. and worked forward to stations operating for attacking troops in the neighbourhood of WHITE SPRING. Bad visibility, however, interfered in the early hours of Z day.

   With reference to the above notes it is desirable to point out that although tanks may prove extremely valuable in laying and moving up a large supply of cable, also for taking forward a wireless station, no great reliance should be placed on this method, as tanks are very liable to develop mechanical trouble, and a cable wagon should certainly be held in readiness to replace the tank if the latter becomes a casualty. In determining the hour at which the tank should be pushed on after Zero it should be timed so as not to be involved in any fighting, but at the same time soon enough to get the cable head sufficiently far forward to be of value to units in the earlier stages of the fight, who would otherwise possibly have no other means of communication.

9th November, 1918.   Major,
                                              O.C. Signals, 18th Division.

NOTES on COMMUNICATIONS during operations between

October 25th and November 7th, 1918.

1. Attention is drawn to the "Notes on Communications during recent Operations" written subsequent to the termination of the operations carried out by the Division between August 23rd and September 5th, and again those terminating November 9th.

2. Communications were based on the principles adopted in recent operations.

3. <u>Lines.</u> - Up to operations commencing on November 4th, two pairs of trunk wires were laid forward from Divisional Headquarters; one terminating at 55th Brigade H.Q. - L.4.c.5.9., and the other via L.4.c.5.9. to 54th Brigade H.Q. at L.3.b.8.9. Both these brigades had lines to 53rd Brigade thus giving Division communication with 53rd Brigade through either 54th or 55th Brigades. An Advanced Divisional Exchange was opened at L.14.c.2.2. which was in leak on one of the trunk lines, and in addition had a direct line to left flank division and the Corps ("TY" Exchange) at L.20.d.4.4.

On November 3rd an Advanced Divisional Office was opened at EPINETTE FARM - L.3.c.5.6. - Four pairs of cables were laid from here to the trunk cable lines at L.9.b.3.6, which were split, thus existing communications now passed through the office in EPINETTE FARM. In addition one pair of cables were laid from EPINETTE FARM to BOUSIES WOOD FARM, Advanced H.Q. 53rd Brigade, and continued on to ENGLEFONTAINE to A.1.b.6.2 which was to be Advanced Flank Brigade H.Q. and subsequently Advanced Flank Divisional H.Q. One pair to Right Flank Division, and two pairs were brought in for communication to Corps. Also one pair of cables were laid to Advanced 54th Brigade H.Q. - F.24.c.9.4 - and two pairs were laid via L.9.b.3.6 and road in N.E. direction through village of BOUSIES to F.25.d.5.3, from where the two pair trunk up the centre of the Divisional front was to be extended after Zero. For this it was again proposed to use a Supply Tank.

At Zero hour on November 4th Divisional Advanced H.Q. opened at EPINETTE FARM. Advanced Office at L.14.c.2.2. was closed down, one of the trunks being bridged through to Right Flank Division and the other to Rear Divisional H.Q. in LE CATEAU.

Shortly after Zero the tank was reported broken down in BOUSIES.

A Cable Wagon and R.E. limber which were standing by in case of need proceeded to cable head and at Zero plus 1½ hours continued the two trunk lines to new 53rd Brigade Advanced H.Q. at A.13.b.5.7, giving them direct communication with Division. At Zero plus 6 hours 55th Brigade H.Q. moved alongside 53rd Brigade at A.13.b.4.9 and the second pair was used for their direct line to Division. Two pairs of cables were continued on from this point via A.14.b.2.9 to A.21.a.7.8 where 55th Brigade H.Q. moved, one was used as direct line to Division and the other as lateral to 53rd Brigade at Zero plus 7 hours.

It was then decided to push on the cable head as far as the situation permitted and they were continued via A.21.d.4.8 and up Route de PREUX to Mon Fre de la Cabine - A.7.d.5.4 - the probable next move of 55th Brigade H.Q. As the detachment had no more cable they were ordered to return to Divisional H.Q.

On November 5th a Cable Detachment with R.E. limber proceeded to cable head and continued cable head to CROISIL INN - B.10.c.8.8 - where 55th Brigade moved. One pair was used for direct communication to Division and one pair to Advanced Divisional Exchange which opened at PREUX on the move of 55th Brigade. The two pair cable trunk was pushed forward to Rue de la Passe du Feu - B.11.b.9.0 - in case of a further advance of Brigade H.Q.

4. <u>Wireless.</u> - Each Brigade had and used trench wireless, working to Advanced Divisional H.Q. without interruption except for periods whilst on the move.

Loop Sets.

2.

5. <u>Loop Sets</u>. - These were only used in the initial stage of the attack.

6. <u>Visual</u>: - Visual was not used as the wooded nature of the ground was not suitable for visual.

It was proved that in very wet weather, to ensure anything like good speaking over long lines, it is necessary that cable should be raised from the ground and this is difficult to arrange for in a rapid advance. Wireless proved extremely useful and had the rapid advance continued would at times have been the only means of communication.

(Sd) (S.F Jackson)
Captain R.E.
16th November, 1918.   A/O.C. 18th Div. Signal Co. R.E.

18/SYR/

18th Division "A".

Herewith War Diary for month of December, 1918.

24th January, 1919.

W. Reynard. Major,
O.C. Signals, 18th Division.

Army Form C. 2118.

WAR DIARY
or
INTELLIGENCE SUMMARY.
(Erase heading not required)

18th DIVL SIGNAL CO. R.E.

DEC 1918

Place	Date	Hour	Summary of Events and Information	Remarks and references to Appendices
SERAIN	1st		Division complete was reviewed by Major General R. P. Lee & Bolumendy 18th Division.	
LIGNY-en-Cambresis	14		Divl HQ closed at SERAIN at 1430 hours and opened at LIGNY-en-Cambresis at same hour. Necessary lines were taken over on existing routes. Company moved by march route via Elincourt – Selvigny – Caullery. 18th Divl Arty remained at MAUROIS. 53rd Infy Bde – no move 54th Infy Bde – Selvigny 55th Infy Bde – no move	

W Reynard
MAJOR.
O.C. 18th Divisional Signal Co. R.E.

Army Form C. 2118: A

WAR DIARY
or
INTELLIGENCE SUMMARY.

DEC 1918   **18th DIVL. SIGNAL CO., R.E.**

(Erase heading not required.)

Place	Date	Hour	Summary of Events and Information	Remarks and references to Appendices
			During the month all technical stores were overhauled and checked and all material surplus to A.F. G/1098 returned to Signal Park or Ordnance.	
			Salvage operations were continued and 52 miles of cable of various descriptions were picked up and returned to Corps Signal Dumps.	
			Average Strength of Company during month — Offrs. 12 O.R. 303 Horses 120	
			Honours and Awards during month —	

Bar to M.M.
64705 2nd Cpl. T.R.W. Graham M.M.
268855 Pioneer A. Q. Scott M.M.
50476 Sapper H. G. Wilson M.M.

M.M.
71446 2nd Cpl. F.N. Prior   69243 Spr. A. Mabee
46435   Spr. A.E. Church   424696 " J.H. Thompson
53099   "   A. Moody   72088 2nd A.H. Parker
471750   "   G.H.N.E   471524 " W.J. Taylor
56956 Cpl. (A.) Beale   5645   " B.A. Cooper

W. Kerr / MAJOR,
O.C. 18th Divisional Signal Co. R.E.

Army Form C. 2118.

WAR DIARY
of
INTELLIGENCE SUMMARY
(Erase heading not required.)

of 18th Divisional Signal Co. R.E.

JAN 1919

Place	Date	Hour	Summary of Events and Information	Remarks and references to Appendices
LIGNY-sur-Cambresis			During the month cable operations were continued and 180 miles of various types of field cables were collected and handed on to XIII Corps Cable Dump at AUMTHY.	
			Thirty N.C.O's and men were demobilized between 1st and 30th and 18 horses were disposed of through XIII Corps Annual Collecting Camp BEAUVOIS.	
			Under orders from Division a store dump was formed at No. 3. C.C.S. (disused) CAUDRY and all surplus stores, no note no more not actually required for use were dumped there.	
	18th		On 18th January 55th Brigade H.Q. moved from ELINCOURT to ALIGNY. 18th M.G. Bn moved from PREMONT to ELINCOURT and took over communications thrown open by same. 55th Brigade Short cable line ran from Rear Hd. Qrs Signal Office to new 55th Bde H.Q in ALIGNY.	
	29th		On 29th January 55th Brigade H.Q. moved from PREMONT to CLARY. Line allotted in existing terminals to be.	

W Pepperd
MAJOR,
O.C. 18th Divisional Signal Co. R.E.

Army Form C. 2118.

(2)

WAR DIARY
of
INTELLIGENCE SUMMARY.
(Erase heading not required.)

O.C. 18th Divisional Signal Co. R.E.

JAN 1919

Instructions regarding War Diaries and Intelligence Summaries are contained in F. S. Regs., Part II. and the Staff Manual respectively. Title pages will be prepared in manuscript.

Place	Date	Hour	Summary of Events and Information	Remarks and references to Appendices
	January 1919		There is no incident of importance to record during the month. Games and concerts were organised on Friday in baracks and these were much appreciated by all ranks.	
			Average strength of Company during month:— 12 Officers 309 OR. 121 Horses.	
			Honours and Awards:— MERITORIOUS SERVICE MEDAL	
			211059 M/Sergeant N.S. Bowra	
			64626 Corporal H. Tyler	
			T/181260 Pioneer E. C. Brewer R.A.S.C. attached	

[signature] MAJOR,
O.C. 18th Divisional Signal Co. R.E.

www.ingramcontent.com/pod-product-compliance
Lightning Source LLC
Chambersburg PA
CBHW080921230426
43668CB00014B/2174